"Liz Wheeler is a terrific voice—and in this book, she offers modes and methods of argumentation every conservative will find valuable!"
—Ben Shapiro, host of *The Ben Shapiro Show* and editor in chief of The Daily Wire

"Outstanding work by Liz Wheeler in *Tipping Points* to empower and teach everyday Americans how to debunk the Left's talking points. Socialists have nothing left to say once their false narratives have been thoroughly exposed and debunked."
—Dana Loesch, nationally syndicated radio host and bestselling author of *Hands Off My Gun: Defeating the Plot to Disarm America* and *Flyover Nation: You Can't Run a Country You've Never Been To*

"Liberals thrive on emotion, not facts. But this book provides the information you need to guide them from their self-imposed fog and into the sunlight."
—Dan Bongino, author of *Life Inside the Bubble*, *Protecting the President*, *Spygate*, and *Exonerated* and host of *The Dan Bongino Show*

"Liz is a master at tackling leftist myths and misinformation with poised persistence. In *Tipping Points,* we get invaluable insight into exactly how she does it—allowing us to feel empowered and equipped to face what often feels likes a relentless onslaught of left-wing dogmatism. Practical and to the point, this book is the confidence boost young conservatives need to effectively engage with those with whom they disagree."
—Allie Stuckey, host of the *Relatable* podcast

"Liz is a person that doesn't hold back, or back down from her beliefs. I respect that in anyone, but especially from someone in such a visible status. She is a true example of what this country stands for, and she holds the values that we should be fighting to maintain every single day. To be truly unafraid to stand for what you know is right takes a special kind of person, and you can look no further than Liz Wheeler! We need more people like Liz in this country that know who they are and what they stand for! This book is yet another example of how she gets what is happening within our country and how to FIGHT back against the Left! She is awesome, the book is awesome, and you will LOVE everything about it!"

—Graham Allen, host of the *Dear America* podcast

"Liz Wheeler represents a rising young generation of conservatives who will no longer be cowed by a culture dominated by leftist activists, institutions, and corporations at odds with their deeply held beliefs. This book shows how to confront the Left with the fierce logic that has become a hallmark of Wheeler's approach to politics, and the reputation of someone who will never back down from a fight."

—Ben Domenech, publisher of The Federalist

Tipping Points

TIPPING POINTS

How to Topple the Left's House of Cards

LIZ WHEELER

REGNERY
PUBLISHING
A Division of Salem Media Group

Regnery® is a registered trademark of Salem Communications Holding Corporation

Cataloging-in-Publication data on file with the Library of Congress

ISBN 978-1-62157-925-0
ebook ISBN 978-1-62157-964-9

Published in the United States by
Regnery Publishing
A Division of Salem Media Group
300 New Jersey Ave NW
Washington, DC 20001
www.Regnery.com

Manufactured in the United States of America

10 9 8 7 6 5 4 3 2 1

Books are available in quantity for promotional or premium use. For information on discounts and terms, please visit our website: www.Regnery.com.

To my husband, Dan. You are the most wonderful man I know.

To my parents, Steve and Kathy. All of what I am is thanks to you.

*To my sisters, Maria, Amy, and Anne, and to my brother, Matt.
I'm proud to be part of this group of extraordinary people.*

*To Rose and Audrey. Everyone should be so lucky to have
such loyal friends.*

*To my Gram, and to my Gramps, who told me long ago,
"Everybody is entitled to their own stupid opinion." Gramps,
this is my opinion. I'll let you be the judge of the rest.*

CONTENTS

Introduction

There have been a lot of responses to Saul Alinsky's *Rules for Radicals*—most of them poorly done. This isn't one of those.

This is a new handbook for a new kind of fighting—a fight where we flip our opponent's argument on its head and then stomp on it. (If you're picturing a WWE GIF, you're right on the money).

We're not going to lie, cheat, or steal to win like our opponents do. We're not going to twist the truth, exploit minorities, and malign the characters of decent men and women like our opponents do. We don't have to. Because we're *right*.

We'll call it Newton's most overlooked principle. For every Democratic position, there is a hypocritical and obvious contradiction. (I swear, Sir Isaac wrote that himself! Then Sir Isaac asked me to write a comprehensive list of all the liberal lies and how to call them out. True story.)

Guess what happens when you arm yourself with the facts *and* the fighting tactics before you march into the ring? You trounce liberals.

For the past four years, I've been honored to spend every weeknight hosting an hour-long cable news opinion talk show on One America

News Network. (*Tipping Point with Liz Wheeler* at 9:00 p.m. EST. Don't forget to tune in! Wink, wink.)

From the get-go, I wanted my show to be different from other cable news opinion shows. I wanted my show to be more than an ideological echo chamber. Yes, I'm openly conservative. I proudly advocate for conservative principles, values, ideals, and government policies that fulfill those ideals. (More on why I'm conservative later.) But I wanted my show to *prove* to our viewers *why* conservative ideals are better than liberal nonsense.

How do you do that? Well, when the heart of the Left's platform is big government, identity politics, thought control, mind control, speech control, birth control, and a fundamental distain for individualism and family (which they betray in almost every one of their shallow talking points), it's not that hard.

This book shows how I do that every night on cable news and how you can, too.

We frequently introduce my monologue on my show by saying, "Our nation is at a Tipping Point. If we don't turn America towards liberty, then we risk losing the freedom that makes America exceptional."

In this book, we will begin Part 1 by laying out 5 Tipping Points. We will explore the Left's radical vision for our nation and the strategy the Left employs to codify their ideology into law. We will discuss the Left's attacks on religion, education, gender, and the family, as well as political correctness and identity politics. We will demonstrate how the Left's seemingly haphazard attacks on cultural norms are a meticulously planned tactical assault on the fundamental core of liberty in our nation.

Once you understand those crucial Tipping Points—once you're aware of the Left's goals and the tactics the Left uses to execute their strategy—then you'll be ready to learn how to fight back. In Part 2 of this book, we'll discuss how to tip the scales on every issue in favor of limited government and individual liberty. That includes 11 tactics for debating the Left, plus delving into the deeper question of *why* we believe what we believe as conservatives and how to articulate our beliefs.

In Part 3, we will detail how the Left has built their House of Cards. We will expose all the major talking points the Left utilizes in their political dialogue every day (and why these talking points are false) and we will analyze the five major historical lies the Left peddles in order to justify their current political agenda.

At the end of this book, I hope you will feel empowered to do battle and defeat the radical Left. I hope you will understand the Left's strategy and be able to identify the Left's assault points—the Tipping Points of our nation.

I hope you will recognize that my book is different from other conservative books. The point of my book isn't only to make the case for conservative principles, but to teach and train people—to deputize you—to do battle to defend conservative principles and defeat the Left's House of Cards.

PART 1

5 Tipping Points

Chapter 1

Professor Unidentified Blob Is Coming to Get You

L et the indoctrination begin.

What would our country look like if we adopted all the liberal nonsense they teach kids on college campuses? Like, really—what would it look like? You walk into a classroom, five, six years down the road, and up at the white board—which is not called a *white* board anymore because that's racist—up there at the board is a professor of some sort. A funny-looking dude.

The professor is gender-nonconforming and non-age-specific, and we don't know his race because it's offensive to ask, and we can't guess it based on his physical characteristics because that might not be how he—or, should I say, how *xe*—identifies. We can't hazard a guess, especially if we're white, because we white people are inherently racist. Again, who can tell how he identifies anyway? He might identify as a Mexican midget or a Siberian tiger for all we know. Because transspecies is a thing now.[1]

We actually don't know whether *xe* is a person at all, and we can't even say person anyway, can we? Because person is a sexist microaggression. You know, per-SON. Sons are male. That's a misogynist word.

So we have this gender-nonconforming individual who was born that way, but who is also free to change gender at any time because he-she-it-xe is gender-fluid.[2] His race defines him, but we can't know what it is.

This individual is teaching a physics class but can't do basic addition or subtraction because the hiring committee couldn't ask him about his qualifications. After all, saying that *"we're going to hire the most qualified candidate for the position"* is an ableist microaggression. And it doesn't matter anyway, right? Because everybody in the class will get the same grades anyway. Because that's true EQUALITY.

Unless you're a white man. If you're a white dude, you walk into class, you get a smack on the hand with a ruler because you were born male and the patriarchy is your fault—even though Professor Unidentified Blob said there is no such thing as gender. For men, there is. All our problems are your fault.

Halfway through the semester, this physics class isn't even a physics class anymore because we're prohibited from teaching science, grammar, or history. All those subjects further white supremacy.

At the end of the day, it doesn't matter anyway because radical leftist equality means everybody ends up in the same place with the same outcome. Oh, wait—that's old-fashioned liberal equality. It has evolved again. Now "equality" is redefined as a social pecking order to punish those whose immutable characteristics oppress others. So the only thing you'll be asked when you apply for a job is to mark down your privilege points.

Are you a straight, white, cisgender male? We don't have work for you, you patriarchal bastard.

Are you a transaged, gender-nonconforming, lesbian person of color? Congratulations. You've been oppressed. The job is yours.

■　■　■　■

This hyperbole is funny, right? (Thank you). It is and it isn't. Every example of radical leftist political correctness I used for illustration is real. UC Berkeley declared the statement *"the most qualified person should get the job"* to be a racist microaggression.[3] LGBTQI+ activists claim gender is fluid (it can change), but at the same time also say that you're "born this way."[4] California recently passed a law that allows the government to throw nurses in jail if they "misgender" their patients[5]— also known as referring to them by their biological sex—but there are no actual, legal standards you must meet to claim the opposite gender on your driver's license, passport, or Social Security card.[6]

Almost every week on my show, I challenge liberals who advocate for the radical progressive mindset where every person is defined as either the oppressor or the victim. It's critically important that we reject this social engineering because radical leftists don't just utilize this sort of rhetoric as a tool to push their agenda culturally. They want this extreme progressivism to be codified into law.

In order to make that happen, liberals disguise these policies of extreme identity politics as *compassionate*.

We're fighting for the little guy, they tell us. *It's time somebody stood up for the oppressed.*

Sounds peachy, right? Don't let them fool you. Radical leftists care only about power. They're using us—the voters—as their pawns. They're dividing us (divide and conquer!) by race, gender, socioeconomic status, religion, sexual orientation, skin color, and now gender identity as they slowly chip away at our freedoms as Americans. All the while, these liberals tell us that every punch, every black eye they inflict upon us, our culture, and our Constitution is for our own good. That's how the radical leftist progressives roll.

These embattled radicals will stoop to any low—including insulting the intelligence of the very people they claim to champion—to empower their own political agenda. It's a dangerous masquerade.

So, how do we beat liberals? How do we debunk and defeat the insane arguments we hear from the Left and the destructive policies they want to force down our throats?

It's easier than you think.

▪ ▪ ▪ ▪

I read a book once where the mastermind, a thief, hid his spoils—an envelope that contained a secret letter that would unlock the mysterious disappearance of "Uncle Jim"—by hanging the envelope in plain sight on the wall of his office. Seriously. The bad guy slipped the envelope into a picture frame, nailed it to the wall next to his desk, literally displaying it to the world, and nobody found it until, you know, the last chapter of the book. They tossed the house. Searched every nook and cranny. Half the book took place in that office. But the good guys didn't see the envelope hanging right in front of their faces because they didn't expect it to be...right in front of their faces. They expected it to be hidden. Camouflaged.

(My editors begged for a citation for this reference. Alas, I can't for the life of me remember the title of the book, though this scene sticks out as clear as day in my mind. If any reader knows the scene that I describe and title of that book...hit me up, and if you're the first, I'll send you a free copy of this book, signed).

The point is that this is what the radical Left does. They nail their envelope to the wall right in front of our noses, and we *still* try to convince ourselves to ignore the writing on the wall. In truth, the way the Left hides their true agenda is by the reckless and shameless audacity with which they push to control us under our very noses without hiding it.

So we can see what the Left wants America to look like if we simply look at what they're doing. Remember when a certain presidential candidate who was worshipped by the Left promised to "fundamentally transform America"?[7] Did you think he didn't mean it? Did you think he didn't go on to do everything in his power—and some things decidedly outside his power as chief executive—to make that fundamental change happen?

Let's hit the mute button on Democrats' rhetoric for a moment and look at what the Left is *doing* under our noses. Let's start in

California—our first Tipping Point—since nowhere is the agenda of the radical Left more blatantly visible.

In the Golden State, the Democrats lost their super-majority in the state assembly in late 2017 after several liberal lawmakers were outed for sexual harassment and other allegations of sexual misconduct.[8] (Ironic, huh? These champions of women!) But this slight hiccup didn't stop the California Democrats. They still have such a monopoly on the state government that they feel they have carte blanche to ram through their leftist agenda without any compromise (or disguise).

The abuse: In 2015, the California State Assembly and then the California State Senate passed a piece of legislation they called the "California Reproductive FACT Act," which required pro-life crisis pregnancy centers to post advertisements for state-funded, free abortions in the waiting rooms of their establishments.[9] In other words, the California government was compelling speech by private citizens. Under penalty of criminal prosecution, the proprietors of pro-life pregnancy centers were forced to choose between violating their consciences and violating the law. Outrageous is a tame word to describe the tyrannical behavior of the state forcing primarily religious pro-life groups to use their enterprise as an advertising platform to promote a procedure to which they are not only morally opposed, but to which their mission is dedicated to ending.

The lesson: California Democrats are totally fine with government *compelling* speech by private citizens. They don't think pro-lifers should be allowed to live their values. Instead, the Left believes pro-life people should be forced to advertise the radical leftist pro-abortion agenda.

In March of 2018, the Supreme Court heard oral arguments about this case, and on June 26, 2018, the court ruled that the California law likely violates the First Amendment right to free speech of the pro-life pregnancy centers.[10] The Supreme Court reversed a ruling from the Ninth Circuit Court of Appeals and sent the case back down to the lower court.

Justice Anthony Kennedy wrote a concurring opinion on this case (in addition to Justice Clarence Thomas's majority opinion) in which he lambasted the state of California. Kennedy called the law "a paradigmatic example of the serious threat presented when government seeks to impose its own message in the place of individual speech, thought, and expression."

Kennedy specifically chastised the leftist lawmakers who had voted in favor of this law, saying it "is not forward thinking to force individuals to be an instrument for fostering public adherence to an ideological point of view they find unacceptable."[11]

The Democratic attorney general of California, Xavier Becerra, called the Supreme Court's ruling "unfortunate."[12]

The abuse: In May of 2018, the California State Senate introduced a bill (SB-174) that would allow illegal immigrants to serve in state government.[13] So much for government of the people, by the people, for the people, right? This bill (which, as of the writing of this book, has not yet been sent to the governor's desk), would alter the current law that requires appointees to governmental boards to be both eighteen years of age and a citizen of the state. The new legislation drops the requirement to be a citizen of the state. In fact, the Left doesn't seem interested in the interests of American citizens at all. The author of the bill, state senator Ricardo Lara, says, "Undocumented Californians are our neighbors, co-workers, and parents, and as lawmakers we can't make good policy if their voices are left out of the discussion."[14]

Who is it that Democrats in Sacramento think they represent? (I'll tell them: The people who elected them—that's who they represent.) The entire idea of self-governance is decimated by this bill. Could any foreign national who breaches our borders, squats on our land, and sets up shop in the state of California become a lawmaker? Are we as citizens required to follow the laws made by illegal immigrants who broke our laws?

The lesson: The Democrats in California are more than "open borders" liberals (which is bad enough). California Democrats don't believe in Americans governing ourselves anymore. They believe in putting illegal immigrants ahead of the interests of American citizens. (More on *why* the Left champions illegal immigration later.)

Ultimately, the radical leftists in California don't believe in America as a nation anymore.

The abuse: In early 2018, a Democratic assemblywoman by the name of Susan Eggman introduced a bill targeting homeschooling families in California (AB-2926).[15] Under the provisions of this bill (and its companion bill, AB-2756),[16] government officials would be permitted to snoop on families who homeschool under the guise of "fire safety."

(Eggman's cronies claimed this bill would help prevent child abuse, too.[17] Wrong. This is a favorite tactic of the radial Left—to co-opt and exploit a tragedy and use people's feelings in order to shove through the liberal agenda. In this case, the Left was playing off the arrest of the Turpins, a couple in California who had egregiously abused their thirteen children whom they hid from the public by claiming to homeschool the kids.[18] In fact, the rate of child abuse inflicted on children who attend public school is higher than that of homeschooled children.[19])

The point is that the purpose of this anti-homeschooling bill was obvious. The Left didn't disguise the fact that they were trying to make it as difficult as possible (if not entirely impossible) for parents to choose to homeschool their kids. Home visits and inspections of the home? Talk about an invasion of privacy! Imagine the government showing up to your door unannounced (a provision allowed in the companion bill, AB-2756), snooping around your home, and ordering you to show credentials to prove you are a certified teacher. (Private school teachers in California aren't required to be certified, just to put this in context.[20] There is also no statistical proof that children taught by uncertified teachers fare worse academically than children taught by certified teachers.)[21] The purpose of the credentialing provision is simple: to eliminate as many parents as possible from being eligible to homeschool their children.

The lesson: California Democrats think they know better than parents. They want to prohibit parents from making decisions the parents deem best for their children. California Democrats want as many children as possible to be indoctrinated in their public schools (more later on how Democrats use public schools as a vehicle for Marxist ideology).

Fortunately, homeschooling families in California rebelled against this insane attack on parental rights and the unannounced "fire safety" check provision was stripped from AB-2756.[22] I wish I could report the same on the other bill.

As you can see, the attacks on freedom and liberty by Democrats in California are like a tsunami. Another day, another individual liberty fed to the snarling, burgeoning big government monster. *And Democrats don't hide their agenda.* Meanwhile, they have the nerve to tell us they're fighting for our rights. Are they? Do their actions increase our liberty and security or wreck it? You decide.

The abuse: In the spring of 2018, Democrats in the California State Senate nixed a bill in committee that would have prohibited early prison release for convicted sex offenders, cop killers, human traffickers, and rapists. SB-976 never even got out of committee.[23] We are not talking about releasing criminals who commit minor offenses that didn't hurt anybody. We're talking about crimes so heinous it's ludicrous to suggest that overcrowding in prisons supersedes the necessity to keep these violent offenders off the streets. According to the author of the bill, California Senate Republican leader Patricia Bates, these crimes include the following:

- Human trafficking involving a minor
- Battery with personal infliction of serious bodily injury
- Throwing acid or a flammable substance
- Assault with a deadly weapon on a peace officer or firefighter
- Rape where the victim is unconscious of the act, and
- Inflicting corporal injury on a child.[24]

Let that sink in. The Democrats in the state of California voted to allow these violent criminals to be released back onto our streets. Who are California Democrats representing, you may ask? Great question. Obviously not the law-abiding citizens of California who are now at risk of being the victims of these criminals that were freed before serving out their sentences.

The lesson: Democrats in California don't care about the rule of law. They don't care about the primary role of government: to keep people safe. California Democrats care more about what *they* think is best for our lives (and forcing us to do it) than about maintaining the rule of law.

See the envelope? It's staring at us right on the wall in front of our faces, taunting us as if to say, *Don't you believe what you're seeing?*

Of course, the Democrats constantly tell us that we're *not* seeing what we're seeing. They are masters of diversion, like a pickpocket magician. *Listen to me tell you I'm not stealing your wallet, while my hand slides into your pocket and takes the money right out of your pocket...see? I didn't take your wallet....*

We can see what the Democrats want for America if we stop listening to their diversionary words and letting their sleight of hand fool us, and instead start looking at their actions. They don't hide their agenda. And their agenda is not moderate. It's not common sense. It's not compassionate. It's radical.

We've just seen this for ourselves in California, haven't we?

The Democrats say they respect the rule of the law—but they don't. They undercut the criminal justice system and vote to kill a bill that keeps violent offenders off the street.

The Democrats say they are the party of "choice"—but they aren't. They infringe on parents' rights to choose to homeschool their kids. Since Democrats don't respect that choice, they try to make it as difficult as possible for parents to make that choice. (Another word for that is "tyranny.")

The Democrats say they are the party of tolerance—but nothing could be further from the truth. Not only do Democrats disdain anybody who disagrees with their agenda, but they are so *in*tolerant that they passed a law compelling pro-lifers to advertise free abortions.

The radical leftist agenda in action wears no mask.

The abuse: Just today, as I sit here writing, the California State Senate is gearing up to vote on a bill (SB-974) that would allow illegal immigrants to sign up for Medi-Cal.[25] (Medi-Cal is California's version of Medicaid, which was originally intended for children in poverty, disabled persons, and pregnant women. Contrary to these original intentions, even while poverty rates in our nation have gone down, the number of enrollees in Medicaid has skyrocketed.) Keep in mind: Medi-Cal is free, or close to free.[26] This bill being pushed by Democrats in California essentially gives illegal immigrants free health care. We're not talking free emergency health care. Nobody is opposed to providing emergency health care to people who need it, regardless of their immigration status. We're talking free, *comprehensive* health care. Think of the word comprehensive the way President Obama used it. Comprehensive. All-encompassing. Maternity coverage for men.[27] Substance abuse counseling for people who aren't addicted to drugs.[28] Comprehensive. *Everything.* Whether you want it or not.

Meanwhile, a growing number of doctors and medical providers in California won't accept Medi-Cal patients anymore because the reimbursement rate from the state is so pathetic.[29] Now, instead of fixing that problem so that *citizens* on Medi-Cal have better access to health care, liberals in California are dumping a whole new load of illegal immigrants into the program. And guess who pays for this? That's right—the taxpayer. By the way, nearly 40 percent of California residents pay no state income taxes to begin with,[30] so now taxpayers are not only subsidizing that 40 percent, but they're also paying for health care for people who are citizens of foreign countries.

The lesson: Democrats in California think they have a right to take your money and give it to somebody else. They think they have the authority to take a portion of your paycheck every week and give it to foreign nationals who broke our laws by jumping our borders. They think they have a right to force you to pay for gender-bending, puberty-suppressing hormones and genital mutilation surgery for the illegal alien next door who hopped the border fence.[31] And Democrats aren't hiding it.

The more radical the notion, the harder the Democrats work to codify it into law. Picture an evil scientist scribbling with a quill pen in his Big Book of Wicked Ideas. That's how I picture the Left. *Squeak, squeak*, goes the pen. The scientist cackles. *They'll never believe this even if I wave it under their very noses*, he chortles.

Sometimes the agenda is so radical and insane that it *is* hard to believe. Good thing we have proof.

The abuse: In October of 2017, then–California governor Jerry Brown (who is called "Moonbeam" for a reason) signed into law a piece of legislation that allows the government to throw nurses in jail if they "misgender" their geriatric patients.[32] (Funny side note: my Word document doesn't recognize the word "misgender." It's giving me the red, squiggly underline, telling me misgender is not a thing. Microsoft, for shame. How transphobic!) This law states that nurses are required to address their patients as *ze* and *zir* if so requested by their elderly patients—and there is no provision in this bill exempting Christian nursing homes, nor are there protections for Christian nurses who abide by the traditional Christian belief (and scientific reality) that there are only two biological genders. In other words, if any nurse caring for an elderly patient knows the patient wants to be referred to by an alternative, unscientific, invented pronoun and the nurse declines, the government has the power to throw the nurse in jail.

The lesson: California Democrats don't care about separation of church and state. They want to force everybody, regardless of their religious beliefs, to live according to their Church of Liberal Orthodoxy. And if you don't—they'll toss you in prison.

For a political party that decries incarceration of actual criminals, the Democrats certainly show a ferocious appetite to throw people—*conservative* people—in jail if they don't want to live their lives by the Left's anti-scientific pseudo-Marxism.

Like waitresses who offer customers plastic straws. (Oh yeah—that's a real thing.)

The abuse: This bill put forth by Democrats in the California State Assembly would ban servers at restaurants from offering customers plastic straws for their water.[33] In fact, the bill would make it a *crime* for waitresses to offer restaurant-goers plastic straws. If any waitress offered the straws before the customer requested the straw...under the provisions of this bill, the waitress could be thrown in county jail for six months. For offering somebody a straw.

Now, the assemblyman who proposed this bill promised that if the bill were to get past committee, he would tack on amendments to rescind the punishment for waitresses who violated the law.[34] To which I respond: *Yeah. RIGHT.*

The lesson: Democrats are nuts. The California Democratic supermajority cares more about the detrimental effects plastic straws allegedly have on climate change than the detrimental effects that going to jail for six months would have on a waitress who committed the heinous crime of thoughtfully offering a customer a straw before he asked.

Frighteningly, this radical leftist mindset is not limited to just plastic straws.

The abuse: California Democrats outlawed "single use" plastic bags too.[35] It's now illegal for grocery stores, liquor stores, or pharmacies in California to bag people's products for free in plastic bags. Instead, stores are required to charge people to purchase *recycled* plastic bags. *May I offer you a grossly overpriced, thicker plastic bag that's been previously used that you will surely still throw away after a single use? That will only cost you 10 cents a bag, with a side of judgment.*

And guess what happened after liberals implemented this environment-saving policy? The intended consequences: liberals bragged about a supposed 70 percent decrease in plastic bag litter. Great! The unintended consequences: at least partly because of scarcer access to plastic bags, San Diego suffered an outbreak of hepatitis because the burgeoning

homeless population had no plastic bags to contain their possessions...and their excrement.[36] Not so great!

The lesson: Would you look at that? What happened when government meddled in our lives and overregulated businesses? It hurt
people. Democrats telling us what to do under penalty of the law hurt
people, among whom are those who suffered from the hepatitis outbreak in San Diego after homeless people had no plastic bags into
which to defecate.

This assault on our liberty and freedom to choose how to live our
lives isn't "common sense." It's not "for the common welfare." It's radical and it's an infringement on our unalienable right to liberty and our
most fundamental rights.

The abuse: In 2016, the people of California voted into law a referen-
dum pushed by liberals and known to conservatives as "Gunmaggeddon"
(Proposition 63). As the name would suggest, the bill essentially spelled
death for gun rights in the Golden State, including absurd provisions such
as a permit to purchase ammunition.[37] (Gee, I bet that will deter murder-
ers!) Among the nonsensical regulations in this law are costly fees on
bullet sales and a complete prohibition on direct order ammunition sales.
In other words, what liberals might dub "commonsense bullet control."
In fact, the Gunmaggeddon prohibitions on ammunition are so burden-
some that Olympian Kim Rhode is suing the state of California for
ruining her business.[38]

Now Kim Rhode ought to be a liberal feminist's hero. Rhode is a
six-time Olympic medal winner and the first woman to win a medal in
six consecutive Olympic games (and the first Olympian, man or woman,
to win medals in Olympic Games on five different continents).[39]

Rhode is suing the state of California because in order to train to be
the badass she is, she orders practice ammunition online (or receives it
from sponsors who mail it to her) or she purchases it from a specialty
shop in Arizona and drives it to her practice range in California.

Once Gunmaggeddon hit the Golden State, both ways Rhode pro-
cured her ammunition became illegal, rendering Rhode without a way

to run her business. (Her business being her sport and herself as a world champion markswoman.)

(Ironic, isn't it? The "party for women" making it impossible for a badass lady to run her business, set world records, and continue breaking that glass ceiling. Remember when Democrats told us it was "patriarchal" to tell women what to do? Guess that doesn't apply here.)

The lesson: California liberals are trying to make it as difficult as possible for as many people as possible to exercise our Second Amendment right to keep and bear arms. Even though their words say "common sense," their actions show us their radical liberal agenda, as clear as that envelope nailed to the wall.

Meanwhile, while liberals in California criminalize waitresses who offer customers straws (I now automatically tip my server higher when they preemptively offer me a straw), criminalize nurses who "misgender" their patients, criminalize law enforcement officers who cooperate with federal immigration officials on the deportation of convicted criminal aliens (like MS-13 gang members), and try to criminalize an Olympian who is honing her sport, liberals in the state of California have *decriminalized* a hideous crime.

The abuse: Thanks to former governor Jerry Brown and his band of loony liberals, it is no longer a felony to intentionally transmit HIV to another person in the state of California.[40] Under the provisions of this law (SB-239), you can knowingly donate blood contaminated with HIV...and it's not a felony. You can knowingly transmit HIV during unprotected sex...and it's not a felony. Even if the other person is not aware of the risk of contracting HIV before or during intercourse. For intentionally (even maliciously) infecting somebody else with HIV and potentially transmitting a virus that could ruin their lives (if not cost them their lives entirely), liberals in California have reduced the penalty to a mere slap on the wrist. A misdemeanor. You know what else is a misdemeanor? Trying to sell margarine in Iowa but telling your customer it's real butter.[41] Hardly on the same level. But thanks to Democrats in California, the criminal charge is the same.

The lesson: California Democrats are trying to erase the consequences of sexual promiscuity. *Want another notch on your bedpost? High five! You won't suffer ANY repercussions.* (Of course, we know this is statistically false.) This is a particularly interesting (and critical) part of the Democrats' strategy to undermine traditional marriage and the nuclear family unit. They do this on purpose, and not out of tolerance for so-called alternative lifestyles. (In the next chapter, we will dive into *why* the Democrats have a bullseye on the back of traditional marriage.)

Democrats in California also have a greedy eye on your money. They can't fix the potholes in the roads in California...but, not to worry, they tell us, they can fix *climate change.*

The abuse: It's no secret that California Democrats believe in climate change—and I'm not talking about the normal fluctuations of global temperature, which have only been recorded via thermometer for the past 150 years anyway,[42] or the melting of ice caps due to warming in artic regions that's happened before in our history.[43] I'm talking about the United Nations' version of climate change: the give-us-your-money-or-all-the-polar-bears-will-die-by-the-end-of-the-week climate change. The *un*scientific kind. The California Energy Commission, an agency that falls under the purview of the California Natural Resources Agency (the same kind of government board, by the way, on which illegal immigrants are now allowed to serve, thanks to the new law we discussed earlier), approved a new regulation that requires all new homes to include solar panels.[44] The purpose, according to liberals, is to cut down on the carbon emissions that are destroying the world.

Now, this new building standard regulation goes into effect in the year 2020. The sole purpose is fighting the beast formerly known as global warming. (You know, until the temperature trends showed there is not significant warming happening globally. Then liberals changed the name to climate change).

Climate change scientists and their liberal cohorts in government can't tell us to what degree our carbon emissions impact the environment (we'll expound on this in Chapter 8), but regardless of the science of the thing—or, in this case, the lack thereof—they're totally fine with mandating that everybody who wants to build a new home must put solar panels into the construction plan. Guess how much this requirement will cost potential homeowners? This new government mandate from the California Democrats slams an additional ten thousand dollars onto the already outrageous cost of a single-family residence in the state.[45]

Commissioner David Hochschild said, "We cannot let Californians be in homes that are essentially the residential equivalent of gas guzzlers."[46]

Let. The government can't *let* citizens do it. Wrong.

The lesson: California Democrats are totally fine with forcing California citizens to pick up the check and pay the bill for their pet liberal policies. The Democrats in California don't care about science; they don't care about liberty. They just want to ram through their radical agenda, and so they'll codify into building regulations a legal requirement that compels you to pay for their favorite cause.

This same radical leftist agenda is pushed by Democrats as low as the local level in city government.

The abuse: The city of West Sacramento (shocker, where all the California state lobbyists and liberal lawmakers hobnob) just this year implemented a program using taxpayer money to snoop on citizens' social media posts.[47] You can't make this up. This is the same party that was outraged over the Bush-era surveillance programs (as well they should have been, perhaps). Now these same liberals are charging West Sacramento taxpayers twelve thousand dollars per year to license a software called ZenCity that scans people's social media accounts in an effort, according to the city council, to gauge people's moods.[48]

Talk about Big Brother creepy, right? (The angry emoji with the smoke coming out his ears that I just posted on Twitter is dedicated to the West Sacramento City Council. Gauge *that* feeling.)

Not to worry, the mayor of West Sacramento reassured the people of his city who were rightly shocked about this horrifying program.

Mayor Christopher Cabaldon assured people that this program isn't a violation of their privacy because it only scans posts that they haven't locked behind privacy settings. Wow, Mayor, thank you. That makes me feel so much better about government snooping on my social media.

Mayor Cabaldon went on to say, "It's not that ZenCity replaces other forms of civic engagement. It's just a way to listen more."[49]

How comforting.

The lesson: Democrats in California don't respect the privacy of law-abiding Americans. Democrats in California think it's entirely appropriate to snoop on citizens' daily lives—just because the citizens happen to leave their privacy settings less than fully secure. (Spoiler alert: it's not appropriate.) We don't even know if this software stores the names of people, or stores their demographic info (age, gender, zip code, and so forth). How does the government use the information collected? Is the name of the person attached to the feeling the government is gauging? Is the government going to target people based on these collected feelings to try to change those feelings?

Democrats in California don't understand (or don't care) that when government has the opportunity for abuse, it will happen. I can't think of one instance in modern history where the government kept a list of people based on their feelings (whether the feelings were religious, social, or political) that ended with anything other than a gross violation of the rights of the people listed. See, for example, the IRS keeping track of Tea Party groups under the Obama administration in order to deny conservative groups tax exempt status.[50] Or, a more egregious and tragic example, see Nazi Germany forcing Jewish businesspeople to display a Star of David in the windows of their shops to identify themselves as Jews.[51] You get the point.

■   ■   ■

The point is that all of these examples illustrate that liberal policies are striking at the heart of freedom and prosperity (and science) in our nation. Meanwhile, liberal talking heads divert our attention away from what liberals are *doing* and tell us: *You're not seeing what you're seeing. You are the paranoid one.*

But when we think for ourselves, we can see the truth for ourselves. The tricky, liberal snake oil salesmen don't seem so convincing when we're holding the 9,976-word "bullet control" bill in our own two hands.

We can see the juxtaposition with our own two eyes. (Apologies for the ableist microaggression!) Radical leftists tell us "commonsense" gun control won't infringe on our right to keep and bear arms. "Nobody wants to take away people's guns," said Democratic representative Jim Himes—as he advocated for Australia-style gun confiscation.[52] When we mute the Left's rhetoric, we can see for ourselves that the Left is, in fact, trying to take away our right to keep and bear arms.

Just ask Kim Rhode.

■   ■   ■   ■

So, what did we learn here? What do Democrats want America to look like? When liberal political correctness is not just a nasty cultural phenomenon, but is codified into law like our Democratic brethren want—where will that take us?

Keep in mind that the majority of the disastrous pieces of legislation we just discussed were all pushed in California in the space of *one year*. The rest came just a year or two prior to that. Imagine what a deep dive into the liberal stranglehold on California would look like. I don't have enough space in this one book to enumerate.

So circle back to where we began this chapter. Walk into that classroom five years down the road. Think of Professor Unidentified Blob. It's a crime now to question what he tells you in the classroom. You are legally prohibited from asking him his gender, his race, his qualifications, or whether he identifies as a hu-per-offspring (human minus man, person minus son replaced with offspring...obviously) or whether the esteemed educator identifies as an interplanetary goat hybrid.

You buy him a bag of goat feed, just in case, because it's your responsibly to "pay your fair share" for his food, since you are breathing. It's called *social justice*, okay?

Off campus, government is listening to you to gauge how you *feel*. You explain to the government that you feel violated because a vagrant hurled HIV contaminated blood on you, but a government official—an illegal immigrant—chides you and says the vagrant is only expressing his identity. You would defend yourself from the attack, but bullets are prohibited. You'd like to tell your children about what America used to be like, but parents are now forbidden from teaching their children at home after the government "safety" inspectors who were snooping in the homes of homeschooling families deemed it too dangerous for children to live next door to all the convicted sex offenders, cop killers, rapists of unconscious victims, and human traffickers who were freed from prison to roam our streets—thanks to the Democrats.

You think about going to work, but instead, you decide to visit the prison where your co-worker—your ex-coworker—is serving a six-month sentence for offering a customer a plastic straw with his water. While you're there, you stop by Cell Block B to wave to the nurse who yelled, "Quick, don't let *him* fall!" about a patient whose preferred pronoun this week is *xir*.

In the chapel of the church next to the jailhouse, as you walk out, the priest is sadly removing posters that proclaim, "Before I formed you in the womb, I knew you!" And next to the sign "Sacred Heart Pro-Life Crisis Pregnancy Center" the priest is using a nail gun to tack up a new poster that says, "The 10 Best Reasons to Have an Abortion and Where to Get One." You jump as the nail gun wheezes to life with a *thwack*, sending each nail biting into the old wooden walls of the church. The priest smiles sadly as you stare, and you almost trip over a giant pothole in the street that the government keeps promising to fix…as soon as they've got the climate changing the way they want it. They're running out of money again.

You sigh as you write another check. But at least you live in a home powered entirely by mandatory solar panels, right? That money you'll end up "saving" twenty years down the road—liberals promised!— would come in handy to help buy yourself something to eat today.

■   ■   ■   ■

This doom-and-gloom scenario is satirical, of course. But the truth of the matter is that the policies pushed by the radical Left aren't compassionate. They're not commonsense. They're not in the interest of the "general welfare" of the people.

Why the focus on California, you might be asking? The land of fruits and nuts. Hippie land. I don't live *there*.

I'll tell you why.

Much of the leftist big government insanity starts first in California politics. The California state capitol is the breeding ground—the petri dish wherein radical leftist orthodoxy festers.

Think of California as Patient Zero. The first person infected with the plague who infects ten more people who infect ten more people who infect ten more people, and so on until the pervasive illness (we'll call it "liberalism") is rampant, sweeping the nation, leaving strewn in its path victims formerly known as life, liberty, and the pursuit of happiness.

Make no mistake, what happens first in California is soon pushed into the furthest corners of our nation. Even to the small Midwestern towns that feel safe from the intrusion of an overbearing government. These policies are disseminated from California, many times by the radical leftist politicians who began their political careers...you guessed it...in California!

Speaker Nancy Pelosi—who called the one thousand dollar bonuses and Trump tax breaks for the middle class "crumbs,"[53] voted against the Partial Birth Abortion Ban,[54] voted against allowing the Ten Commandments to be displayed in public schools,[55] and who is under-credited for her significant role in convincing former president Barack Obama to pass the soul-crushing monstrosity that is Obamacare—is the former chair of the California Democratic Party[56] and the current Speaker of the House of Representatives.

When Kamala Harris was California attorney general, her team raided the apartment of investigative journalist David Daleiden after he exposed Planned Parenthood's heinous and illegal aborted-baby-body-parts chop shop.[57] Coincidentally, during her campaign for U.S. Senate, Harris had a tab on her website where people could donate to Planned Parenthood. I'm sure the relationship is not significant to Harris targeting Daleiden for exposing PP's criminal activity, instead of prosecuting PP for breaking the law. Right? Not only is Harris the former attorney general of California, but Harris also started as district attorney in San Francisco. Now Kamala Harris is in Washington, in the U.S. Senate, making laws for the rest of the country.

Then we have the far-left politicos who have found a safe haven in California after serving in the Obama administration, like former Obama secretary of Homeland Security Janet Napolitano, who is now in charge of the entire state-funded University of California school system. (More on the indoctrination on college campuses later in the book.)

And the California State Assembly hired Mr. Contempt-of-Congress himself, former Obama attorney general Eric Holder,[58] to help them craft a legal strategy to fight the Trump administration.[59] (Really, this is how our elected representatives are spending their time—and their constituents' money.)

I promise this is the last time in this book that I'll tell you to look for the envelope hanging inconspicuously on the wall. (But do it!)

The point is this: the Left does not hide their true agenda. We the people are simply too skeptical to believe them. We're quick to accept their words or their denials—and we forget to look at what they are *doing*. Their actions. The policies they push. The legislation they introduce. The regulations they mandate. The Left lie with their words, but if you look at their actions you can see for yourself what they want

America to look like: *California*. At this very moment as I sit here writing, California is a snapshot of the Orwellian dystopia our country is hurtling toward if we don't nip this radical leftist ideology in the bud.

Liberals will scoff at these accusations and accuse us conservatives of exaggerating and indulging in the "slippery slope" fallacy. But sit at the top of a snowy hill on a sled and see what happens. You slide down. Make no mistake—it's happening in our country.

Chapter 2

Just Tell Us How to Beat Liberals Already

Liberals don't peddle their extreme, progressive agenda haphazardly. They do it on purpose, with a purpose. If we don't understand the long fight for the culture, then winning a cable news debate or having Twitchy feature your brilliant and witty takedown of that idiotic Hollywood celebrity will feel exhilarating, but will be meaningless in the end.

The purpose of liberals' strategic attack is to morph culture into law. This is another critical Tipping Point.

When I say culture, think of what we're seeing on the giant social networks these days. For example, Facebook recently rolled out a "beta test" feature wherein users were asked about every post they saw as they scrolled through their timelines, "Does this post contain hate speech?"[1] Users were given an option to say no, but more important for Facebook's purpose—and algorithm—was the button that said, "Yes, this is hate speech." Facebook has claimed that it was an error for this test to be made public.[2] I call foul. This is a glimpse into the mind of the executive team at Facebook—a group of innovative geniuses and intellectuals who are intricately tied to the upper echelons of the liberal political elite.[3]

The purpose of that feature, beta test or not, is to teach the Artificial Intelligence algorithms at Facebook the definition of "hate speech," which FaceBook CEO Mark Zuckerberg could not define when he was asked during a Senate hearing.[4]

Lest we forget, there is no legal exception to the First Amendment for "hate speech."[5] In other words, as an American citizen, you have the right to say mean, nasty, offensive things if you want to. It's part of your right to free speech (even if the rest of us think you're a ding-dong).

Now Facebook, of course, is a private entity; they can pick and choose whom they want to allow to use their platform and they are likewise free to exclude anybody they want for any reason. But when you crowdsource a definition of "hate speech" for the purpose of identifying offensive posts, what result are you going to get? A bunch of offended snowflakes who band together to mark conservative content they don't like as "hateful" or "offensive" until traditional, commonplace, conservative political stances and age-old religious values are unacceptable culturally on the largest platform for human interaction on the Internet.

That's what I mean when I talk about culture.

Liberals began their coordinated, sustained assault on culture years ago in an effort to normalize the radical leftist ideology so that when they bridge the gap between culture and legal code, the American people will barely notice.

I like to think of it like the parable of the frog in a pot of boiling water. The story goes, if you toss a frog into a pot of boiling water, he'll jump out because it's hot and it hurts. He feels that extreme change in temperature and environment and his froggy warning bells go off, and he skedaddles before he dies. But if you drop a frog into a pot of tepid water, and *then* you turn on the heat and *slowly* heat the water to a boil, the frog will stay in the pot until he dies. He won't jump out. According to the legend, Mr. Froggy P. Soup won't recognize the gradual change in environment until it's too late. He's dead.

In other words, we the people are the frogs to the liberal Left. The pot is our country. The boiling water is law, and tepid water is culture.

When liberals gradually ramp up the heat and ease us into a culture of political correctness, before we know it, the laws are boiling up to our ears and it's too late to stop it.

We are at a Tipping Point in our country where the Left is attempting to morph cultural political correctness into the laws and statutes of our nation.

A perfect example of this is a story we covered on my show. The president of the NAACP, a man by the name of Derrick Johnson, is calling for mandatory implicit bias screening for all public officials.[6] What is implicit bias screening, you might ask? Great question. According to the radical Left, implicit biases are prejudices or bigotries people hold unconsciously that impact their actions toward other people. Think of white privilege. That's an example of an implicit bias, according to the Left. Or sexism, if you're a man. Now the NAACP is calling for mandatory tests, presumably to weed out anybody with "implicit biases" from serving in public positions.

Liberals might protest at any such supposition (hint: if liberals call you paranoid, you're probably right on the money).

But it does suggest the rational question: What does the liberal NAACP want to happen to people who get less than satisfactory results on "implicit bias screeners"? Why else would they want to mandate the screening if they aren't going to *use* it to disqualify people whose personal views or opinions or political stances or religious beliefs the NAACP doesn't like?

Remember, the president of the NAACP wants to make it *legally* mandatory for all public officials to undergo this testing. What could go wrong?

Well, I can think of a few things. For example, radical leftists claim that all white people have implicit bias against black people. So if the president of the NAACP gets his way and implicit bias screening becomes mandatory, would white people be disqualified from serving in public office? And what about men? Liberal feminists are famous for saying all males are inherently sexist.[7] So will all men be barred from serving in government roles because of that alleged implicit bias?

The day we covered this story on my show, I took the test NAACP president Derrick Johnson was talking about. The implicit bias test. Sounds like a fun experience, right? It was absurd.

The test itself was created at Harvard University,[8] and it's certainly not scientific. (I don't think they even claim it's scientific.) Now, I'm no scientist—although I can recite the entire periodic table of elements—but it doesn't take a nuclear physicist to see that the test measures...muscle memory. Here's how it works. First, they show you a screen and tell you that when you see a positive word—like happiness, flowers, or enthusiasm—you're supposed to hit the "I" key with your right hand. When you see a bad word—like unemployment, dismay, failure, misery, and so forth—you're supposed to hit the "E" key with your left hand.

Then they show you a close-up photograph of a white person's face and tell you when you see a white face, hit the right key. When you see a close-up of a black person's face, hit the left key. They run you through this routine for a while. Then, they combine the two (faces and words). They tell you, if you see a good word or a white person, hit the right key. Conversely, if you see a bad word or a black person, hit the left key. They make you do that repeatedly. You're supposed to identify the good and bad words and black and white faces as fast as you can. You are essentially creating muscle memory, so your answers are automatic.

But instead of admitting that they are deliberately training their test subjects to react to positive words and white faces with one response and to negative words and black faces with a different response, the test makers at Harvard act like the association that they have created is some kind of peek into the deepest recesses of their subjects' minds, revealing "implicit" prejudices and biases we don't know we have. (Cue the foreboding music.)

Finally, for the last exercise (the one that *really* determines how bad of a racist you are!), they switch it up. They tell you that if you see a white person's face or a *bad* word, hit the right key. If you see a black person's face or a *good* word, hit the left key. Are you ready to do this as fast as you can? Ready.... GO!

Essentially, the premise of this final exam is if you slip up and automatically put the good words and white faces together or the bad words and black faces together, you're a racist. Even though that's what the test had you practice for the entire previous fifteen minutes.

(What was my result, you might be asking? Well, if the result showed "bias" in favor of white people, liberals will tell me I'm a racist. If the result showed "bias" in favor of black people, liberals will tell me it's just white guilt. Funny how that works, right? A white person who tests with no negative biases towards black people doesn't fit the leftist narrative—we're an anomaly in the eyes of the Left—so they'll dismiss us as "the white person who claims they have black friends to prove they aren't racist." It's a lose-lose with liberals. So, I'll leave my result to your imagination.)

The point is, this test is not a scientific measure of anything—except the fact that you can inculcate muscle memory with practice. And author and journalist Heather Mac Donald explains what else is wrong with the test:

> Any social-psychological instrument must pass two tests to be considered accurate: reliability and validity. A psychological instrument is reliable if the same test subject, taking the test at different times, achieves roughly the same score each time. But IAT bias scores have a lower rate of consistency than is deemed acceptable for use in the real world—a subject could be rated with a high degree of implicit bias on one taking of the IAT and a low or moderate degree the next time around. A recent estimate puts the reliability of the race IAT at half of what is considered usable. No evidence exists, in other words, that the IAT reliably measures anything stable in the test-taker.[9]

In other words, the test is quack science, intended to prove a preconceived liberal political point and nothing else. Which brings us to the full quote from NAACP president Derrick Johnson, wherein he called for these unscientific implicit bias tests to be legally mandatory for all public officials, saying, "Everyone should get tested for implicit bias, and if you're a public official or receiving public dollars—it should be mandatory. It's just a matter of time before another black person is abused, arrested, or shot dead for flying, golfing, driving, walking, or drinking coffee 'while black.'"[10]

(Notice the part where Johnson said, "if you're receiving public dollars." Maybe we should give this test to Planned Parenthood leadership, then? They pocket five hundred million dollars in taxpayer money every year[11]...while the majority of their abortion clinics target minority women,[12] they accept donations earmarked specifically to kill black babies,[13] and they carry on the legacy of their founder, Margaret Sanger—the woman who spoke to the KKK, plotted with the founder of the "Negro Project" in an effort to reduce the number of black babies being born, and categorized "undesirable" people as "human weeds."[14] Isn't *that* implicit bias? But I digress.)

The point is that Johnson said it himself! His entire premise of "implicit bias" is built on a false, liberal narrative that black people are indiscriminately killed by police because of their skin color. That narrative is false. Black people aren't illegally shot by police for doing everyday activities. Black people aren't shot for "driving while black." Police don't systemically target black men because they are black and shoot them for no reason. That's a hideous and dangerous lie.

And it's been proven to be a lie with actual scientific data.

Harvard professor Roland Fryer, a young black economics professor, said the most surprising result of his academic career[15] was the conclusion from his comprehensive study of police reports from police departments all across America in which he found not only that police are not targeting black men disproportionately with lethal force, but that police officers are actually more likely to shoot a white person than a black person.[16]

"Hands up, don't shoot" is a lie, too. Even former FBI director James Comey, in his book *A Higher Loyalty*, debunked the "hands up, don't shoot" narrative as false, saying that the FBI had evidence that Michael Brown was assaulting Officer Darren Wilson at the time Brown was shot. Keep in mind that "hands up, don't shoot" is the foundation on which the whole Black Lives Matter movement was built. Therefore, the riots in Ferguson that were the beginning of the Black Lives Matter movement were based on a lie. The mobs of angry people burning businesses, assaulting cops, was all based on a lie. A lie propagated by people like NAACP president Derrick Johnson, who wants to make this lie part of our laws.

The point is that this "implicit bias" test that a prominent liberal leader wants to make mandatory for all public officials is *not* scientific, but is a load of hogwash, and that should scare us. Even putting emotion aside for a moment (and the terrifying reality that liberals believe this nonsense), Johnson's call to make his politically correct orthodoxy law also illustrates what we talked about earlier in the chapter: liberals have primed our tepid culture to the boiling point. They are ready to morph their pyramid of privilege points and cultural political correctness into law, and they expect us to simply fall asleep in the pot while they do it.

Boil, froggy, boil!

We've seen this happen in other countries when political officials codify their social engineering schemes into statutes in an effort to control the behavior of their citizens and solidify their own political power.

In China, the ruling Communist Party recently implemented what they call a "social credit score" (like your credit score for credit cards, car loans, and mortgages) wherein every citizen is rated based on their opinions and behavior.[17] Rated. By the government.

If you are a "good citizen," then you are allowed to fly on commercial Chinese airlines, you are allowed to buy property, and you are allowed to send your kid to a private school. If you are a bad citizen (according to this government-issued "social credit score"), then you are branded as an "untrustworthy person" and are banned from exercising your right to participate in any of these activities.

But who and what determines who is a "good" citizen and who is a "bad" citizen?

The government, of course. The Chinese Communist Party invents the standards for this social credit score and enforces them.

And what is the ideal Chinese citizen, according to the Chinese Communist Party?

According to the standards set forth by the Chinese Communist Party, if you cross the street at the cross walk, good point on you. If you jaywalk, bad point. If you participate in community service projects, that raises your score. If you smoke in non-smoking areas, you get downgraded. If you buy Chinese-made products, good point to you. If you post negative or critical thoughts online about the Chinese government, they take a point away.

It's chilling, isn't it? Almost as chilling as the comprehensive sets of surveillance cameras that the Chinese government have erected in order to catch their citizens in any of these actions and "better" compute their social credit scores...in order to better control, coerce, and create a communist minion of a citizen. A citizen they can exclude from society if that person refuses to toe their ideological line.

There rings our alarm bell.

Suddenly, this communist social credit score bears eerie similarity to a government-mandated implicit bias test, doesn't it?

Both are tools used by government for social engineering to force citizens to behave how *they* want us to behave. And of course, we're not just talking about following the laws of our nation that prohibit us from violating anybody else's fundamental right to life, liberty, or property. We're talking about the government forcing people to toe the liberal ideological line or be punished socially and legally for not doing that.

■   ■   ■   ■

Remember, as I said at the outset of this chapter, liberals don't wage this culture-to-law attack haphazardly. Their strategy is almost impressive (if you appreciate diabolical schemes). The radical Left are no petty grifters from the carnivals of olde—they are hardened radicals and they're in this game for the long con.

They know what they're doing. They know why they're doing it. And they know how their actions, their politically correct culture, and their political policies that turn culture into laws will lead to the progressive, Marxist America the Left envisions.

To "fundamentally transform America," they must first destruct the America that is.[18]

We can see the Left doing this right before our eyes.

Think of it this way. Imagine an angry horde of termites gnawing and burrowing into the structural beams of a house, slowly but surely destabilizing the integrity of the beam until the weight-bearing frame on which the whole house relies is nothing but a porous skeleton of what it used to be—unfit to hold the weight it was originally intended to bear. Weak. Crumbling. Useless. *Unlivable.*

That's what the Left is doing to our culture. The Left are the termites in this analogy. They are destroying the foundation that undergirds our society by targeting religious institutions, the education system, and most critically, the family.

But why would they want to do this, you might ask? America is the most successful, civilized, prosperous, humane, inclusive, free nation the world has ever known. Why would liberals try to destroy that? Great question. The short answer is this:

Half of liberals don't realize what they're doing. We'll call them the "bleeding-heart" type. They think their socialist policies are compassionate. They think they are knights in shining armor fighting the moral battle against bigotry (by calling conservatives Nazis). These bleeding-heart liberals are your neighbors, your Aunt Carol, your roommate at college, the guy in the cubicle next to you who won't shut up about Bernie Sanders and redistributing wealth—as he plays on his iPhone. They simply don't *know* what they're doing. We'll talk more about them in a bit.

The other half of liberals are the true radicals. They are the radical leftists who know *exactly* what they're doing. They are the Rahm Emanuels of the world— President Obama's chief of staff who sent emails to Obama's secretary of education Arne Duncan two days after the shooting at Sandy Hook Elementary School in Newtown, Connecticut, which left twenty children and six teachers dead, discussing how to squeeze the most political points out of the tragedy...in order to push their own gun control agenda. "Tap people's emotion," Rahm Emanuel said. "Go for a vote asap," he told Duncan, "before it fades."[19]

Talk about despicable. These radical leftists are the architects behind the Termite Strategy. The weaker the private institutions on which people rely, the more people will by necessity turn to government for...everything. Support. Guidance. Money. Family. God. You name it. Once the traditional institutions are crumbling at the joist and no longer able to support society, government can step in. And who benefits from a bloated, controlling government? Not the people, that's for sure. Liberal bureaucrats benefit from big government, that's who. The Termites. That's the short answer.

We can see this answer in play when we look at *how* the radical Left attacks our cultural cornerstones: religion, education, and the family.

Let's start with religion first, lest our gullible liberal friends scoff at the idea of the existential war on Christianity being waged by the radical Left.

Chapter 3

Go for Their Achilles Heel

In the spring of 2018 as I sit here writing, George Washington University is hosting a seminar aimed at combating what they call "Christian privilege."[1] The goal of the seminar is to teach students and faculty that Christians—especially white Christians—"receive unmerited perks from institutions and systems all across our country."

The professor leading this seminar (who ironically is an associate director of "inclusive" initiatives at the school) is teaching students that Christians enjoy an easier, privileged life with built-in advantages...just because they're Christian.

Now first of all, notice that when the Left attaches the word "privilege" to various characteristics—such as "white privilege," "male privilege," "Christian privilege," and so forth—they are reducing people who share a characteristic such as race or gender or sexual orientation to that characteristic. Isn't that the essence of stereotyping and racism? They're also labeling people with those characteristics as oppressors. And you know what the Left likes to do to so-called oppressors? Take them down.

Funny how that works, isn't it? Label Christians as privileged oppressors, put that target on their back, take them down. First point, check.

Second point, check…thank goodness that the third and final check is only *in progress*. In fact, radical leftists still deny they are waging a War on Christianity at all. They scoff at the accusation that they are targeting Christian religious beliefs and people who practice the faith. But we can see it for ourselves. The War on Christianity is at a Tipping Point.

In early 2018, a bill was introduced in the California State Assembly that could have banned the sale of books that teach traditional Christian doctrine on sexual morality, same-sex attraction, same-sex marriage, gender identity, and transgenderism. If the bill, AB-2943, had passed into law, it would become a crime in California to sell "goods or services to any consumer" that advertise, offer to engage in, or do engage in "sexual orientation change efforts with an individual."[2] The Left calls sexual orientation change efforts "SOCE" and claims the sole intention of the bill is to ban the "fraudulent" practice of "conversion therapy."

Well, what's wrong with that, you might be saying? Are they talking about pray-the-gay-away camps? A lot of conservatives think gay conversion therapy is hogwash, too. Chad Felix Greene, a prominent gay conservative, says, "I don't think conversion therapy is effective, like hypnosis for fat loss isn't effective." But Greene says banning it isn't the answer because "banning it essentially denies people the choice to pursue their own self-improvement goals."[3]

He's right. So the bill would be anti-liberty even if the legislation were only about sexual orientation change efforts, as the author of the bill, Assemblyman Evan Low, would have us believe.[4]

But that claim is not even *kind of* true. This bill isn't just about "sexual orientation change efforts" in the way that the average person would interpret that phrase.

In fact, the Left were very careful in the language of the bill to define what *they* mean by "sexual orientation change efforts"—and to include in that definition "any practices that seek to change an individual's sexual orientation. This includes efforts to change behaviors or gender expressions, or to eliminate or reduce sexual or romantic attractions or feelings toward individuals of the same sex."[5]

To change behaviors. Or gender expressions. Or reduce romantic feelings.

Herein lies the attack on Christianity and traditional Christian teaching on sexual behavior. And gender expression. And romantic feelings. Chilling, isn't it?

In fact, this bill claimed its first victim while it was still in the State Senate. A Christian organization called Summit Ministries canceled its scheduled conference in Los Angeles after the California State Assembly passed this bill because the group worried that its seminars on living chastely with same-sex attraction would draw the ire of law enforcement if Governor Jerry Brown signed this bill into law.[6] It's not an unfounded fear, given the language of the bill.

But it gets worse. Under the language of this bill—which you just read above—the prohibition of the sale of any goods or services that seek to change the sexual orientation of an individual—defined in the bill as anything that seeks to change even behaviors or feelings—could apply to any books that teach traditional Christian doctrine on homosexuality. Even the Bible itself.

After all, the Bible is very clear about same-sex sexual behavior. If the sale of any goods and services aimed at changing *behaviors* regarding same-sex sexual activity was banned—that certainly could be applied to the Bible, if the Bible were sold or used with an aim to influence same-sex sexual behaviors or feelings.

It doesn't matter that Assemblyman Evan Low's supporters claimed that the bill doesn't apply to the sale of books or religious teachings.[7] His words don't change the letter of the law. There is no exception in the bill's language exempting religious texts from the enforcement of this statute. Whether or not the California state government would have abused the power they were afforded in this bill to target the sale of material that teaches traditional Christian doctrine on homosexuality cannot be known. What's frightening is that if the bill had passed, they would have had the power to do so. And the target is on the back of Christian teachings.

Tell me *that* isn't a War on Christianity.

Assemblyman Low eventually pulled this bill from committee because of the backlash started by yours truly. We exposed this bill on my show, *Tipping Point*, and over twenty million people subsequently viewed the video on Facebook. Believers across the state pushed back against this potentially devastating government overreach, and to his credit, Low acquiesced and withdrew his bill, citing our outcry. Although he did promise to try to push this bill again in the future when the political climate was friendlier to his effort. It won't be—if I have anything to say about it.

Jump across the country to New York. Cynthia and Robert Gifford own a farm in upstate New York—a popular venue for rustic wedding receptions. In 2012, the Giffords declined to host a lesbian wedding on their farm, citing their belief that marriage is between one man and one woman.[8] They said it would violate their religious beliefs to facilitate a gay wedding. The lesbian couple sued them, and the New York Supreme Court sided with the lesbian couple, forcing the Giffords to pay a fine of thirteen thousand dollars.

The judge told the Giffords that they weren't allowed to live by the tenets of their faith while doing business. In her ruling, Judge Karen Peters wrote, "The Giffords are free to adhere to and profess their religious beliefs that same-sex couples should not marry, but they must permit same-sex couples to marry on the premises if they choose to allow opposite-sex couples to do so."[9]

In other words, either the Christian Giffords violate their religious beliefs, or they violate the law, or they close down their business. So much for religious freedom. You don't see Muslim business owners targeted for their views on homosexuality. Funny how it's just Christians who are targeted.

(And no, the Giffords are not discriminating against gay people. Gay people have the same right to marry a person from the opposite sex as straight people do.)

In a clever twist to the finale of this story, the Giffords found a way to proceed with their business and abide by the tyrannical dictates of the Left that otherwise would force them to violate their Christian beliefs. The following is now posted on the Giffords's website:

> At Liberty Ridge Farm, our deeply held religious belief is that marriage is the union of one man and one woman, and the Farm is operated with the purpose of strengthening and promoting marriage. In furtherance of this purpose and to honor and promote our moral and religious beliefs, we donate a portion of our business proceeds to organizations that promote strong marriages such as the Family Research Council. The patronage of all potential clients for all services offered is welcome regardless of race, creed, color, national origin, sexual orientation, military status, sex, disability, or marital status. All couples legally permitted to marry in the state of New York are welcome to hold their wedding at Liberty Ridge Farm. We serve everyone equally.[10]

Then we have Jack Phillips in Colorado, the baker and owner of Masterpiece Cakeshop. In 2012, Jack declined to create a custom wedding cake for a gay wedding, citing his Christian religious belief that marriage is between one man and one woman.[11] Of course, the gay couple sued him, claiming discrimination. Phillips defended himself by saying that the creation of a custom wedding cake was his free expression and he was free to choose not to use his free expression to express something that violated his faith (hence the term: free expression). But liberals ignored that logic and claimed that Phillips was homophobic and insincere in his faith and was discriminating against gay people.

Not so.

The claim of homophobia and discrimination is easily debunked. Phillips has also declined to bake Halloween cakes in the past because he believes that Halloween is a demonic celebration that violates his Christian beliefs. Counter to the claims of homophobia, Phillips said he would also decline to bake a cake disparaging of any person, including LGBTQ people.[12] As for the spurious claim made by the Colorado Civil Rights Commission that Phillips is insincere in his faith[13]—who died and left liberals to judge that? Why would a man insincere in his faith spend two years defending his right to practice his faith at the enormous cost that he's suffered?

The point is that this whole incident was clearly not a case of Phillips using his Christian faith as an excuse to discriminate against the gay couple. In fact, Phillips offered to sell the gay couple anything that was pre-baked in his store.[14] He said he'd bake them a custom cake for a birthday or other special event. He didn't discriminate against *them*. He simply declined to use his creativity to participate in a ceremony that violated his Christian religious beliefs.

But the Left didn't care about that. They don't respect Phillips's right to practice his faith the way he sees fit. They don't want traditional Christian doctrine to be acceptable in the public sphere.

In June of 2018, the Supreme Court ruled that Jack Phillips did not have to bake the cake for the gay wedding. In a 7–2 ruling, the Court found that the Colorado Civil Rights Commission had violated Phillips's First Amendment rights and treated him with religious animus. In fact, the court ruled that there *was* somebody who had suffered from discrimination during this ordeal—Phillips and his Christian beliefs. But that didn't stop the Left from their continued claims that Phillips had targeted these men because the men were gay.

These are just three examples of hundreds across our nation where the Left purposely and specifically targets men and women of faith *because* of their Christian faith. You can look anywhere and see it.

Christian nurses and doctors in our country fear discrimination and even being barred from practicing medicine if they refuse to perform abortions (since abortion violates their Christian values). And the radical leftists in Congress have refused to vote in favor of conscience protection for these Christians—a provision that would allow Christians to decline to participate in abortions without the risk of retaliation.[15] But the radical Left in Congress said, "Nope!" They would rather Christian doctors and nurses be unable to practice medicine than allow them to practice their faith.

The Left targeted nuns, too. After Obamacare was signed into law in 2010, Catholic nuns were forced to pay for abortifacient birth control in violation of their religious beliefs, thanks to the leftist Obama administration.[16] Why else would the Left force celibate Catholic nuns to pay for birth control, except to set a precedent of the government prohibiting Christians from practicing their religion in the workplace?

Not just the workplace, but elementary school, too. In California, an elementary school student who shared Bible verses with his friends in the cafeteria at lunch was targeted for doing so by the school district.[17] The school district sent a sheriff to the seven-year-old's house in order to make him stop. Remember, other public schools have allowed students to hang Che Guevara posters in their classrooms[18] while banning students from wearing t-shirts displaying the American flag[19] and have forced non-Muslim students to write the Shahada—the Muslim declaration of faith in Allah and Mohammad as his prophet.[20]

Suspending a child for sharing Bible verses his mom hid in his lunch with his friends is not about "keeping religion out of public school." This is about the Left trying to ostracize Christian beliefs from our society.

This intolerance for Christianity has grown into a full-blown assault not only against Christians practicing their faith, but against any opinions informed by Christian tradition, teaching, or doctrine, as well.

A college kid in Pennsylvania was kicked out of class for defending the Christian belief and scientific fact that there are only two genders.[21]

In Ohio, a judge stripped custody of a seventeen-year-old girl from her Christian parents because the teenager suffers from gender dysphoria and says she's transgender.[22] She wants to undergo hormone therapy and surgically transition to a man. Her parents said no, not until you're eighteen years old. So the judge gave custody of the girl to other people who will facilitate the little girl surgically changing herself to a man.

Never mind the fact that there is no medical evidence to support the progressive idea that gender mutilation surgery cures gender dysphoria.[23] Never mind the scientific data that *does* show that minor children with gender dysphoria grow out of it upward of 80–95 percent of the time if no gender-bending hormones are given to the child.[24] Never mind that the girl was seventeen years old, about to turn eighteen, and at that time could have made the decision for herself without her parents' approval. Never mind what a dangerous precedent it sets to use a child's threat of suicide as a reason to take her away from her parents and allow her to undergo life-changing surgery. Never mind the fact that the parents of this child are Christians and have a right to raise their child as they see fittest and healthiest and in accordance with their religious beliefs—the court blatantly disregarded this and ruled that the parents were unfit to be parents based on their scientifically and religiously informed parental choices.

And then, of course, we have the never-ending barrage of mockery hurled at Vice President Mike Pence by the Left for his fidelity to his wife, Karen. (Something one would *think* would be a universally admired and desired quality in a husband.)

But the Christian belief in the sanctity of marriage and the dignity and value of life from conception to natural death is ridiculed by the Left on a daily basis as misogynistic and oppressive.

Every corner of the public sphere and every aspect of our lives—elementary school, college, the convent, hospitals, medical clinics, bookstores, youth conferences, the therapist's office...even the privacy of people's homes like the Giffords's in New York and private businesses like Jack Phillips's in Colorado, and perhaps most shockingly of all, the rights of parents to raise their children according to their Christian faith tradition—are now battlegrounds on which the radical Left targets Christian beliefs and faith traditions in an attempt to eradicate Christianity from our culture completely.

This is not haphazard bullying by the Left. It's not merely ignorant intolerance either. It's a tightly controlled, far-reaching tactical assault aimed at the Judeo-Christian values on which this country was founded and without which our Founding Fathers believed our constitutional republic would not endure.[25]

George Washington, after all, proclaimed in his first inaugural address on April 30, 1789, that "the propitious smiles of Heaven can never be expected on a nation that disregards the eternal rules of order and right, which Heaven itself has ordained...."

Imagine what our nation will look like when the termites finally eat their fill.

■　■　■　■

And then we have the second pillar of our culture targeted by the radical Left: education. A critical cultural Tipping Point.

On the campus of the University of Michigan during the 2017–18 school year, students were told by the school to tattle on each other to administrators if they heard any of their fellow students use "microaggressions" or if they heard anything that hurt their feelings. What type of microaggression might hurt students' feelings? Well, students at Colby College reported the innocuous phrase "on the other hand." Why? Because, according to the Left, saying "on the other hand" is an ableist microaggression.[26] Duh! You might offend those who don't have hands, you big jerk!

Really. This happened. The University of Michigan, as I write, is facing a lawsuit filed by several students who claim that the university violated their First Amendment right to free speech by implementing so-called Bias Response Teams in an effort to stifle the students' free speech.

Yes, Bias Response Teams, or BRTs as their creepy purveyors call them, are just as Orwellian as they sound. BRTs are teams of administrators and campus police officers whose job is to detect "bias incidents" on campus and punish the students who commit these egregious offenses.

Well, kind of egregious. Not really. Not egregious at all, actually.

In fact, the Bias Response Team at the University of Michigan *had no concrete answer* when they are asked what constitutes a bias incident.[27] Doesn't that give you a nice chill up your spine?

(Oh wait, we can't say "chill up the spine," can we? In case we offend people who don't have spines. Or something.)

The point is that this liberal institution of higher learning—a public university funded by taxpayer money that comes straight out of our paychecks every week—is punishing students who didn't break the law…because the radical Left has convinced sensitive, progressive snowflakes to be offended by something other students said.

What better place than school to force the Left's radical philosophy into the minds of impressionable children who don't know any better? Impressionable children who have no leverage or position of power to challenge what school administrators force them to learn?

This is not a new tactic invented by the American Left. Radicals all around the world use school as a tool of state-sponsored indoctrination. As I write, just this week the Palestinian school system was exposed with a video showing preschoolers in Gaza staging a mock execution of an Israeli soldier, holding up a sign over the fake dead body that read, "Israel has fallen."[28] (And the liberal media wonder why Israel is constantly forced to defend herself from attacks by Palestinian terrorists?)

In another world, this is called brainwashing. But not when it suits the leftist agenda. *Attack the cultural cornerstones. Weaken the foundations of society until the only answer is reliance on a controlling government.*

The radical Left uses public schools as a medium for brainwashing of all kinds.

Ninth graders at a public school in Virginia were shown a graphic video on sexual techniques and encouraged to try them.[29] I apologize for the graphic description, and please feel free to skip to the end of this paragraph if you want to protect your sensibilities, but this video by "sex expert" Laci Green detailed how to give a blow job and enjoy doing it, how to perform anal sex on another man, and how girls can pleasure men...using men's balls. (You can see why parents of these ninth graders called some of these sexual practices "deviant.")

Let me repeat: not only were these graphic sexual practices discussed with fourteen-year-old children in the classroom, but the students also were *encouraged to try them.*

Were parents shown this video beforehand? Were parents warned by the school that their freshmen in high school would be shown such nasty, graphic content that promoted behaviors most parents do not want their children taking part in? Nope. In fact, the school defends their association with the group that supplied this video, only saying that airing the video in class was a "mistake in judgment."

(I don't know about you, but I don't typically mistakenly broadcast material to children teaching them how to sexually pleasure each other.)

In West Virginia, middle school students were forced to write the Shahada as part of a calligraphy assignment.[30] The Shahada is the Muslim profession of faith that says, "There is no God but Allah and Mohammad is the messenger of Allah."[31] Students were told that if they didn't complete this assignment, they would face detention.

The school defended this assignment and said it was part of a World Religions course and the students weren't required to write the Shahada if they didn't want to. But why would teachers threaten detention for an *optional* assignment? Maybe these teachers need to go back to third grade and study the definition of "optional." Or maybe the radical Left has co-opted public school curriculum to the point where blatant propaganda is taught to students...as long as the propaganda furthers the progressive agenda.

Funny, during the module on Christianity in this World Religions course, the students were not told to write a profession of faith in Jesus Christ.

There are hundreds of examples just like this happening every year in our public schools. Some incidents are reported, but sadly many are ignored by the liberal media. Many parents aren't even aware that this is happening in their children's classrooms.

And this is *elementary school*. If you think the indoctrination in primary school is blatant (where the leftist curriculum undermines traditional, mainstream morality and tells students to practice deviant sexual acts on each other, or attacks Christianity under the guise of a World Religions class by forcing kids to write the Islamic Shahada), wait until you see what's happening on college campuses all across the country. The Left doesn't even *pretend* the brainwashing on college campuses is "exposure to different beliefs." At colleges, the Left actively promotes communism.

At Bellarmine University in Kentucky, a student application to form a chapter of Young Americans for Freedom (a chapter of the Young America's Foundation, or YAF) was rejected by the school administration because the school said it was exclusionary to say, "Liberty is better than communism."[32]

Bellarmine University's director of Student Activities and Orientation, Jessica Lynch, told the students, "I do not support the idea that a person's beliefs/values are better or 'right' compared to another's. That is what I find concerning about Young Americans for Freedom."

To be clear: the Young America's Foundation believes conservative ideas of limited government and individual freedom are superior to Marxism, Stalinism, and Communism. *The horror.* How controversial, right?

Lynch says YAF's comments "in regards to others' beliefs being wrong, corrupt or immoral" are the problem. (You know, belief in communism....) She says, "I do not think this creates a space for all students to feel welcomed."

As opposed to under communism, of course. Where all people are welcome. Including the one hundred million innocent people who were killed under Communist regimes in the twentieth century.

These days on college campuses, even freedom is a microaggression. The terrifying proposition that all students might not believe the exact same thing...is a trigger. Houston, we have a problem!

Scary, right? The radical Left is past the point of trying to disguise what they're doing on college campuses. They don't pretend universities are a place to be exposed to all viewpoints. They simply refuse to tolerate anybody's beliefs if those beliefs differ from the radical leftist agenda.

Why do you think teachers' unions keep such a choke hold on public education? Why do you think liberals fight against charter schools and homeschools and discourage parental involvement in curriculum formation? Why do you think colleges require freshmen to live on campus rather than encouraging kids to live with their parents and commute to community colleges during the first two years? Why do you think Common Core is chock-full of revisionist history and "lessons" about how white men and the patriarchy are to blame for all of the nation's problems?

Because without the iron grip on public schools, the Left would lose their feeding tube, their primary tool to forcibly indoctrinate young people to parrot the radical leftist agenda.

Without the public school system from preschool through college polluting the heads of children with leftist nonsense, children might have to rely on their parents and their families for their social formation.

And so the Left takes aim at the family, too—perhaps the gravest Tipping Point of all for our nation.

■   ■   ■   ■

Boys are boys and girls are girls. They're different from each other.

This statement is a routine recitation of basic biology—an elementary, scientific fact. It's also common sense. (Or, in the words of Phil Robertson from *Duck Dynasty*, "Strip naked in front of a mirror and take a look and you ought to know. If you need a medical textbook, take that with you. Look in the medical textbook. Look back in the mirror. Look at yourself and say, 'I'm a man.'")[33]

But this same statement got a college student at Indiana University of Pennsylvania kicked out of class and told not to return for the remainder of the semester. The student was punished—and deprived of his opportunity to get the credits he needed to graduate at the end of the same semester—because he had the audacity to participate in a discussion in class about gender and pointed out the truth that, scientifically, there are only two genders.

For this high crime, the professor expelled him from class. That's how the radical Left rolls.

This is a crucial part of how the Left attacks the traditional family. It's not complicated. There's a very simple and dangerous reason that radical leftists are intent on destroying the scientific fact that there are two genders:

If we erase the idea of biological gender, then by nature (no pun intended) that erases traditional gender roles in society.

If we erase gender roles and traditional gender norms in our culture, that erases traditional relationships.

If we dissolve traditional relationships between men and women, that breaks down marriage.

If we attack marriage, that destroys the family structure.

As we summarized at the close of Chapter 2, if we lose the family unit, people will be forced to resort to relying on government instead of relying on their family unit for...everything. Emotional support. Education. Financial assistance. Morals. God. Friends. Everything from A to Z.

And what happens when people are wholly dependent on government? *1984* happens. Plus, the liberal politicians who forced this cultural suicide on us in the first place—now in a position of absolute power and control over every aspect of our lives—grow very, very rich.

In other words, when New York city proposes a new law to add a third gender option to birth certificates—male, female, and X—it's not about inclusivity.[34] (And it's not, as a liberal comically claimed on my show, about the hermaphrodites who don't know what to mark on their birth certificates.)

It's a tactic that reminds me of a book I read in high school called *Red Hugh, Prince of Donegal*. I don't remember all the details of the plot, but in one scene after Hugh is captured by the bad guys, his captors slit his

Achilles tendons in order to prevent Hugh from escaping the fortress and running away (again). A horrible, brutal, inhumane, and entirely effective way to keep Hugh in prison. Incapacitate him. Literally cut off his ability to walk. Or stand. Or support his own weight. Render him wholly dependent on his captors.

That's what the radical Left does when they dismember gender. They decimate the two necessities for marriage—man and woman—making the traditional family unit obsolete.

It's an absurd proposition for government to declare that anybody can legally identity as any gender they want simply based on how they *feel*. In New York City, gender "X" on the birth certificate requires no proof, no doctor's note, no diagnosis, nothing whatsoever as proof.[35] The only determination is how the person *identifies*.

So where does this end?

Men who identify as women. Women who identify as men. Transgender individuals who say their birth gender is not who they are. They say they are trapped inside the wrong body. The radical Left embraced this.

Then the radical Left tried to give us transracial. Rachel Dolezal, the white woman who told everyone she was black while serving as president of a chapter of the NAACP in Washington state,[36] says she wasn't *pretending* to be black. Dolezal says she *is* black—even though both her parents are Caucasian. Because she identifies as black. She was born white, she says, but she feels black. So she is black. She's transracial, she says.

Then, we got transabled. Physically healthy people who feel they should have been born disabled. A man in Canada cut off his arm because he felt like an amputee.[37] A woman in North Carolina poured drain cleaner in her eyes because she felt blind.[38]

And this is only the beginning.

Transgender. Transracial. Transabled. The "you are what you feel" movement is feeding off itself.

A grown man posted an ad on Craigslist soliciting a nanny because he identifies as a baby and wants a nanny to take care of him.

They call it transaged.

There are clubs online for people who identify as dogs instead of people. They eat their food out of bowls on the floor and defecate under bushes in the backyard.

They call it transspecies.

And why shouldn't we accept this absurdity as reality? We've already given the thumbs up to men who say they are "real women" because they feel like women, even though they are biologically men. We've launched into celebrity a white person who says she's black because she feels black, even though she's Caucasian. Adult men wear diapers and identify as babies; meanwhile, the radical Left is well on their way to embracing the practice of healthy people mutilating themselves because they feel disabled.

If "you are what you feel," then what is reality?

How can we tell a teenager he can't purchase alcohol if he "identifies" as over tewnty-one years old?

How are we going to react when a thirty-eight-year-old man signs up for kindergarten and shows up in a frilly pink tutu because he identifies as a five-year-old girl?

What if a child wants to spend his day at doggy day care instead of elementary school because the child feels like a canine?

If a grown man can legally choose to be female on his birth certificate in New York just because he says he's a girl, how can we tell a child he must attend school? Or tell a teenager he must obey his parents? Or throw him out of the bar when he tries order a beer before he's old enough to shave?

As a society, we can't have it both ways.

And herein lies the reason the radical Left is advocating for this absurdity.

If children have a right to parents providing for them, and a man identifies as a child because he feels he is a child trapped in an adult body…if we are playing by disordered rules where delusion and emotion trump objective truth, aren't we violating the transaged man's rights by refusing him the love and care and financial support every child deserves?

Bingo.

Guess who will be providing that care and financial support? The government. Guess who will be funding the government? You and me.

The radical leftists know that when they push the boundaries of identity politics past the point of no return, there will be nothing left but cultural absurdity. They know fact from fiction. They're not stupid. They're strategic.

■   ■   ■   ■

It's worth noting that marriage is the best anti-poverty program— better than anything the government could ever sponsor. Married couples are less likely to live in poverty than couples who simply cohabitate or reproduce outside of marriage. Women, especially women with children, are significantly less likely to live in poverty if they are married than if they are single. Children are 82 percent less likely to live in poverty if their parents are married than if their parents are unmarried.[39]

I'm sure the radical Left is aware of that statistic as well, which is why they promote such massive government welfare programs under the guise of fighting poverty. You'd think it would be a much more effective, healthy strategy simply to encourage marriage, right? If we can spend taxpayer money trying to influence behavior—from anti-smoking ads to the "Got Milk?" campaign—why not promote behavior that studies show is the best protection against poverty?

Because that would defy the Left's agenda of destroying the family and making Americans dependent on the government for everything.

Instead, the Left assaults marriage by assaulting gender in order to achieve the same goal we introduced in Chapter 2: to render more citizens dependent on a big, controlling government. To do that, they deny any differences between men and women, and therefore reject the very essence of human nature. You know who tries to erase human nature? Communists.

In the past three chapters, we have laid out 5 Tipping Points for our nation: the Left's flagrant use of California as the Patient Zero state where they germinate and cultivate radical Leftist ideology in order to disseminate it across the nation, the Left's strategic effort to morph politically correct culture into law, and the Left's three-pronged assault on Christianity, on education, and on the family. We can see for ourselves the strategy the Left employs to fundamentally change America.

Now it's time to learn how to disrupt their strategy, defeat the radical Leftist agenda, and tip the scales in favor of limited government and individual liberty.

Part 2

How to Tip the Scales

Chapter 4

11 Tactics for Debating Liberals

If we look at what they're doing, the Left doesn't disguise their true agenda. We've established that fact. We can see it in the state of California, where thanks to the radical Left's choke hold on the state government, the state is now lovingly known to conservatives who live in the Golden State as the "People's Republic of California."

The Left is trying to morph culture into law. We've established that, too. They're indoctrinating our students with anti-Christian, anti-Western, unscientific, Marxist propaganda in school, and they're tearing down the traditional family by assaulting gender in the name of "human rights." (The Left literally calls the transgender moment the "next civil rights frontier.")[1]

The Left believes that every person is either an oppressor or a victim. They believe that oppressors—such as men—should be punished, and victims—such as gender-queer, transabled robots—should lord over oppressors.

The Left believes that government knows better than the individual. They use their War on Christianity, their assault on marriage, and their death grip on public schools to undercut the foundations upon which our society stands.

Until, of course, we the people are forced to turn to Big Daddy Government. *He'll give you everything you ever wanted, pumpkin! All you have to do is do whatever he says....*

So how do we defeat the radical Left? They will deny until the cows come home everything I have written above. But we know they are lying in their denial because we can look at what they're *doing* as proof of their agenda and their vision for our country. That agenda: thought control, mind control, speech control, behavior control.

So how do we expose the truth? How do we hijack the dishonest rhetoric and fear-mongering talking points of the radical Left and expose the agenda they're promoting? How do we debate liberals and beat them?

Below are eleven practical tactics for debating leftists, whether you're involved in politics, whether you serve in government, whether it's your hobby on social media, or whether your annoying Aunt Maureen won't stop nagging you about your conservative politics... you can and should dive into the debate—and win!

■   ■   ■   ■

#1: Be aggressive. Be polite, but don't be afraid to put liberals on the spot regarding their agenda. Make an allegation to put them on defense. Do it immediately. Keep in mind, an allegation is not an accusation. An accusation starts with finger pointing and ends with, "You did this!" That's inflammatory. An allegation is a simple statement of truth about their agenda.

First, lay it out very clearly. Take climate change, for example. Say that Democrats just want our money. They want to give away U.S. sovereignty to the United Nations. Democrats put crippling regulations and penalties in place as a tool to collect money in order to redistribute the wealth.

The liberal will inevitably answer that you don't want to cut back on carbon emissions because you want to nuke the environment: Don't you conservatives care about the earth at all?

Don't go on defense. Make another allegation.

Liberals can't even tell us to what degree our carbon emissions impact the changing climate! If liberals can't tell us exactly to what degree our actions (our carbon footprint) impact the climate, how is that science? Why should we give our hard-earned money to a liberal redistribution-of-wealth scheme that's not based on science?

You're already ahead. You've put him on defense. You (unlike him) did not accuse him personally of anything horrible. Instead, you were polite. You levied an allegation that exposed his agenda and the faulty argument behind it.

■　■　■　■

#2: Pretend you're a shrink. Let them talk until they run out of B.S. Once they've dumped all their talking points (without an interruption), they'll be running on empty.

We'll use abortion as an illustration. Meet Christine. Christine is an intersectional feminist. (According to her dating profile.) Christine is fictional. When Christine is confronted about her refusal to condemn Planned Parenthood—the largest abortion provider in our nation—for their cover-up of child sex abuse and rape,[2] the conversation quickly zeros in on abortion itself. After all, the radical Left is so afraid of any challenge to the legality of abortion that they're willing to defend Planned Parenthood's heinous pattern of covering up the rape of young teenage girls instead of reporting those rapes to police.

Christine begins by claiming my righteous indignation about the refusal of the Democrats—claiming to be the party that champions women—to call out PP for their coverups is a giant effort to undermine abortion "rights" in our country. (Yeah, she's right. Also: to protect little girls from RAPISTS.)

Now, I could cut off Christine mid-sentence with her first accusation. I could interrupt her to call out her B.S. (and there's plenty of it just in that one comment). Or I can picture in my mind the index card of talking points she carries in her mind. She probably has eight talking points cued up ready to launch at me:

Abortion is a woman's choice! It's her body. You don't get to tell a woman what to do with her own body.

This is about equal rights for women. If women don't have full bodily autonomy, they aren't equal to men.

This is a private, painful decision between a woman and her doctor. If you don't think government should butt into people's lives like you say as a limited-government conservative, why do you want to butt into this personal decision between a woman and her doctor?

Without abortion, we're regressing hundreds of years in the advancement of women's rights. I'm not going to force women to keep pregnancies they don't want or can't support. That's forced childbearing. I won't take us back to The Handmaid's Tale—*even if old, white, Republican men want to.*

Abortion is always tragic (this admission you won't get from the die-hards, but you will from liberals trying to appeal to emotion and find "common ground"), *but without safe and legal abortion, women will resort to back alley abortions with coat hangers, and more* women will *die. Abortion is a necessity for safety for women.*

If you're pro-life, why don't you care about children after they're born? Why do you want to cut Medicaid and food stamps? How can you claim to be pro-life when you don't support taking care of kids after the womb?

So, when you say abortion is murder, that means we'd have to punish women for abortion. Do you want to put women in jail for murder for having an abortion?

If you don't support a woman's right to legal abortion, you're a misogynist. You hate women.

If I interrupt Christine, she will use each of her talking points as a response to anything I say (whether or not the talking point is relevant), which could waste my arguments. But if I don't interrupt Christine, if I let her keep talking, she will burn through all her points all at once. At that point, once Christine has verbally donned her white bonnet and red dress and accused me of dragging her around by a chain of fertility (a patently unbelievable accusation), I can cut right to the point.

Does abortion end a human life?

She will probably say, *There is no scientific consensus on when life begins*—which is false. The preeminent biology textbooks define the beginning of human life as the moment of conception.[3] (We will expound on this more in Chapter 6, so hold tight.) Plus, when else does life begin during pregnancy besides at the moment of conception? There is no other specific, defining moment at which a non-baby turns into a baby during pregnancy…except conception.

And now the debate is on your terms. You can debate when life begins. Debate whether abortion ends a human life. Debate whether ending a human life is right or wrong. You will win every time. (Because you're right.) But that debate will only happen if Christine bloviates through her entire index card of talking points first. If you allow her to talk until she runs out of B.S.

■   ■   ■   ■

#3: Laugh. When liberals are serious, go ahead and laugh—but in the good-natured way. Nothing highlights absurdity better than genuine laughter.

In June of 2018, Twitter CEO Jack Dorsey found himself in hot water. He had tweeted a promotion of a new app he invented, and the tweet highlighted how much money he had saved on his purchase of Chick-fil-A because he used this app.[4]

In response to Dorsey's innocuous tweet, CNN's Soledad O'Brien tweeted at Dorsey, saying, "This is an interesting company to boost during Pride Month, Jack."[5]

(Chick-fil-A's founding family are Christians who support traditional marriage and have donated money to the Family Research Council.)

Dorsey replied, "You're right. Completely forgot about their background."

The liberal Twitter mob came after Dorsey, calling him tone deaf and insensitive despite his coerced apology because he didn't delete the tweet. They gave him the works, culminating in an article from the liberals at the Huffington Post titled, "If you really love LGBTQ people, you just can't keep eating Chick-fil-A."[6]

The proper response to this in a debate—after your liberal counterpart solemnly monologues about the discrimination against gay people in our country—is to laugh and ask, *Are chicken sandwiches bigots?*

See, Chick-fil-A doesn't discriminate against gay people. Gay people can eat there. Gay people can work there.

Then laugh again and ask your liberal sparring partner, *Is it appropriate to eat these bigoted chicken sandwiches during months that aren't pride month?*

Though you're laughing (which highlights the absurdity of pretending that attacking a Twitter honcho for eating a chicken sandwich and bullying him to apologize is the next front in the Civil Rights Movement), your questions get to the meat of the issue. (I do not apologize for the pun.) Yes, liberals believe we shouldn't eat at Chick-fil-A *any* month of the year—because the owners of Chick-fil-A are Christians.

The Left doesn't want equality for gay people—which Chick-fil-A does nothing to violate. The Left wants everybody to have to celebrate and promote gay marriage or else be disallowed from doing business in the public sphere and ostracized from society.

Laughter will disarm any serious defense of the radical Left's attack on Chick-fil-A and their ridiculous accusation that all people who eat chicken sandwiches are bigots.

■　■　■　■

#4: Ask micro-questions. Nothing invalidates an argument more than if the person making the argument does not know the basic facts and figures about the topic. You'd be surprised what liberals don't know. Trap them on the details.

Let's do Obamacare. Premiums are skyrocketing under Obamacare. Deductibles are unaffordable. The average premium increase hit 116 percent in Arizona in 2017.[7] In 2019, projections for some states are up to 30 percent increase in premiums.[8]

Even if more people do have insurance—because they were forced to purchase it or face a penalty under Obamacare—they are still having to pay for medical expenses out of their own pockets because of the insane deductibles. And that's on top of paying the outrageous premiums.

Yet Democrats claim Obamacare is a success. They say, *Well sure, it needs improvement, but let's not forget that twenty million Americans gained coverage because of the Affordable Care Act.*

That's a whopping misrepresentation of the truth.

Before we break down those numbers, hit this liberal talking point with a micro-question. Remember, the most important thing you can do with these debating tools is reframe the debate on your own terms. Once you're on your own terms, it's much easier to beat the liberal and win the argument—since you're right.

Ask the liberal, *Obamacare was supposed to provide universal coverage in our nation. How many Americans right now still don't have insurance?*

The answer to that question is nearly twenty-eight MILLION Americans.[9]

The liberal will not know that answer.

He'll stutter and try to pivot. So hit him with another micro-question.

How many Americans have been forced off of their health care plans because of Obamacare?

The answer to that is thirty million Americans have been dropped,[10] phased out, or forced to purchase a different plan because of Obamacare's rules and regulations. In other words, thirty million Americans lost the coverage they had—the coverage they chose as the best fit for themselves and their family—because of Obamacare.

The liberal won't know the answer to that one either. Now you've invalidated his credibility, because who wants to listen to an expert who doesn't know any details of the topic he's talking about? Plus, you showed that *twenty MILLION people gained insurance because of Obamacare* is a phony talking point.

The true number of people who have gained coverage because of Obamacare is approximately fourteen million—six million fewer than the liberal claim. Of that fourteen million, 11.8 million have been funneled to Medicaid (and for the most part, we're talking healthy adults with no disability and no children, which makes it more difficult for disabled Americans, children, and pregnant women in poverty to get the care they need via Medicaid on account of the burgeoning lines).[11] Elementary math tells us that fourteen million minus 11.8 million equals 2.2 million. So basically, it's not twenty million who have gained insurance coverage under Obamacare; it's closer to two million. (And that's without even subtracting the thirty million who lost their plans.)

■　■　■　■

#5: Don't fall into the liberal trap. Even if they bait you, be willing to let some things go. Liberals love the data dump. They make their large point…pivot…make a smaller point…pivot…don't stop for breath…make an irrelevant, tangential point intended to bait you. Nine times out of ten, it's okay to let the smaller points go. Tackle their big point—that's what they're trying to protect.

Senator Bernie Sanders utilizes this data dump tactic all the time. He's the master of this tactic, actually. That, and Sanders reframes questions he doesn't want to answer. More on that later.

During the 2016 primary elections, Senator Sanders was asked by CNN's Anderson Cooper during a Democratic primary debate how any kind of socialist could win an election in the United States.[12]

"First, we're going to explain what democratic socialism is," Sanders said (reframing the question). He then proceeded to...pivot. He slammed the top tenth of 1 percent (his favorite punching bag) for owning as much wealth as the bottom 90 percent.

Then he pivoted again. He called the American free market capitalist economy a "rigged economy." He claimed it's immoral that 57 percent of all income in the U.S. goes to the top 1 percent.

Once more, the man who owns three homes pivoted. He expressed outrage that other countries around the world "provide healthcare as a right" and the U.S. government doesn't. He shared his outrage that other countries mandate paid maternity leave. Then Sanders said we should look to countries like Denmark, Sweden, and Norway to "learn from what they have accomplished for their working people."

Finally, when Cooper pressed Sanders and asked him if the Republican attack ad didn't write itself because Sanders had admitted he wasn't a capitalist, supported Nicaragua's Sandinistas, and had honeymooned in the Soviet Union, Senator Sanders...pivoted again, accusing Republicans of winning only when there is low voter turnout.

Did Sanders answer the question? Of course he didn't. He was asked how a socialist could win in the United States. His response was entirely an attempt to bait Republicans on smaller (sometimes tangential) points like voter turnout.

So, in the heat of the moment in a debate, which point is it most tempting to answer? The attacks against ourselves, obviously. *Capitalism is not about greed! We're not hoarding the wealth!*

Don't.

Don't fall into the trap even though they baited you. Let the smaller points go (for now). Tackle their big point.

Where has socialism ever worked, in the history of world?

Where has socialism not ended with millions of people brutally murdered by their government?

The most modern example of socialism in our world is Venezuela. In Venezuela, there is no toilet paper on the shelves. Children are being evacuated from maternity hospitals because of tear gas.[13] If you speak out against the government, you can be shot and killed.[14] Seventy-four percent of Venezuelans have lost an average of twenty pounds in the past year because of food shortages. Families are standing in line for hours for a loaf of bread.[15] Venezuela used to be one of the most prosperous nations in South America—until they went socialist.[16] *Why would you want to bring socialism here to the U.S.?*

Think of the liberal pivot like a soldier providing cover for his comrades. He shoots in every which way to protect what he doesn't want attacked. That's what liberals do with the pivot. All you have to do in order to defeat it is listen for the main thesis, and don't let the smaller points distract you.

■ ■ ■ ■

#6: Know what you would say if you were a liberal. This takes critical thought and humility. If you were a liberal, what weakness would make you pounce on the conservative argument? Identify it.

Seventeen people were killed in the shooting at Marjory Stoneman Douglas High School in Parkland, Florida, on Valentine's Day in 2018—fourteen students and three teachers and administrators.[17] The attacker, a former student with a hidden record of violent behavior and mental health problems, opened fire on the school with an AR-15 rifle after pulling the fire alarm. The alarm caused students and teachers to file out of their classrooms straight into the shooter's line of fire.

Three months later in May 2018 in Texas, a student at Santa Fe High School opened fire and killed ten people—eight students and two teachers. Thirteen others were wounded.[18]

Now, rewind twenty years and journey across the ocean to the land down under.

In Australia in April of 1996, a maniac embarked on a rampage in the area of Port Arthur, Tasmania, killing thirty-five people and injuring twenty-three others.[19] The attacker murdered people in half a dozen locations and establishments before he was apprehended by police. He committed the murders at close range with an AR-15 rifle.

In the wake of the Port Arthur massacre—which was the deadliest mass shooting in Australian history—the Australian government passed strict gun control legislation. The new laws required citizens to surrender their firearms to the government or face a severe penalty. They called it a buy-back program, but it was mandatory. Gun confiscation. In the time since these gun confiscation laws passed in Australia in 1996, there have been no other comparable mass shootings in Australia.

If I were a liberal, that's what I would say.

I would mock conservatives and Second Amendment supporters because it looks from the outside like gun control and mandatory gun confiscation by the government worked to prevent such massacres in Australia, but conservatives claim gun control won't stop such shootings here in the United States. If I were a liberal trying to push gun control, I would hammer the Australia point.

Now, the reason to identify what you would say if you were a liberal is not simply to sound humble or to practice critical thought. And it's not to throw in the towel and admit that the liberal talking point is accurate or correct. (More below on why this is a false narrative and why the gun buyback in Australia actually didn't save lives, despite the subsequent lack of mass shootings.)

The point is that if you know what you would say if you were a liberal, chances are that's what a liberal will say. If you anticipate liberal arguments, you can head them off at the pass. Like so:

Listen, you're probably going to point to Australia like liberals always do and say gun control worked in Australia; they haven't had any mass shootings there since they did gun control! But as I always tell liberals, well, sure, but Australia's violent crime rate went up.[20] It was more dangerous in Australia after the gun confiscation than it was before gun control! That's not exactly something to emulate.

The point is that just because you've picked the point you would hammer home if you were a liberal doesn't mean that point is without flaws. Australia's gun ban certainly isn't.

We see the violent crime rate skyrocketing in London, too. London did gun control, and what happened? Their knife crime skyrocketed! The murder rate in London is higher than in New York City![21] And the murders are with knives. Guns aren't the problem.

Plus, Australia had three million firearms before confiscation.[22] America has three hundred million.[23] Not exactly a comparable task—for the government to forcibly collect three hundred million firearms. Plus, the number of firearms in Australia now is equal to or higher than it was before confiscation,[24] so I don't know if we can say it worked.

■　■　■　■

#7: Make yourself answer the Left's toughest point. Politicians are the worst at letting the fear of the "worst" point dictate their debating. Stop being afraid to answer the tough questions. Don't hope for the easy points. Pick out the point you *don't* want to answer and answer it preemptively.

This one builds on the previous tactic (#6). Once you know what you would say if you were a liberal, you can neutralize the point by answering it preemptively.

Let's take a social issue like abortion.

Now you might be wondering how I can say I support equality for women while also opposing abortion? Don't I support a woman's right to make choices about her own body? Well, of course I do, but science tells us abortion isn't just about one body. It's about two bodies. The woman's body and the baby's body.

Or an economic issue like tariffs.

Now you might be thinking, conservatives have always said tariffs are destructive to the economy. In fact, we saw what happened under President Bush when he levied tariffs on steel. He rolled back the tariffs after it cost two hundred thousand people their jobs![25] We saw what happened when President Obama levied tariffs on tires from China. The price of tires for consumers in the U.S. skyrocketed.[26] So why are some conservatives choosing not to condemn the tariffs President Trump is levying against China? Here's why.

Typically, a tariff is just a tax on the American people by another name. But it can be argued that the tariffs against China are different. The Chinese have stolen billions of dollars' worth of our technology over the past decades.[27] They are trying to become industry leaders in the high-tech realm with stuff they stole from us. We have to put a stop to that. It's not just a matter of trade; it's a matter of national security.

■   ■   ■   ■

#8: Call out liberals for their silly talking points. Disarm them by explaining exactly what tactics they're using in the debate.

Enter Brad. Brad is fictional amalgamation of the radical leftist mindset. Brad cheered in 2006 when then-senator Hillary Clinton and then-senator Barack Obama voted in favor of funding a wall along our southern border.[28] Brad said it's not fair for illegal immigrants to come to our nation by jumping our border illegally when legal immigrants who follow our laws are stuck waiting in line. On that score, Brad was right.

That was 2005. Now in 2018, Brad says any type of border structure is xenophobic. Brad is incensed by the idea of border security and is particularly triggered by any mention of a border wall. We know how angry Brad is because he tweeted, "No border wall! Only a monster denies safe passage to families searching for a better life. Undocumented immigrants are Americans, too. But a monster is who we have as president, who thinks all Mexicans are rapists #NOBorderWall." Brad tweeted this to his five hundred Twitter followers as he was waiting to exit his gated community. There was a hold-up because the mechanism that opens the gate at the gatehouse shorted out.

Confronted with the fact that he flip-flopped on the border wall and asked about the danger to safety and security in our country if we don't guard our borders, Brad immediately rolls out his go-to talking point.

"Stop pretending this is about safety," he retorts. "Undocumented immigrants commit fewer crimes than people born in the United States!"

His point is that the only reason anybody could want to build a border wall is because they hate Mexicans. But that's ridiculous.

So the proper response here is to remind Brad that he's not the only one who knows what tactic he's using in the debate. We can see it too. Don't just say "that's a talking point." Tell him what he's doing. Nothing puts people on defense quicker than being told what they are doing.

What you're doing, Brad, is using a talking point. You think if you tell us illegal aliens commit fewer crimes that that means the only reason we could want to build a border wall is if we're xenophobic. I see what you're doing. It's a classic debate tactic, but it's not the truth.

Now Brad is fidgeting in his seat. Brad's face begins to turn red.

Once we've called out Brad's talking point and its purpose, thereby defusing the tactic, then we can move on to the truth.

Actually, illegal immigrants make up 3.5 percent of the population in the United States. But illegal immigrants commit 13.6 percent of all crimes. Why the disparity? Illegal immigrants commit 12 percent of all murders and 16 percent of drug trafficking offenses in our country.[29]

More than 40 percent of all federal crimes in 2013 were committed near the Mexican border.[30]

According to the Department of Justice, in fiscal year 2013, 38.6 percent of all federal cases (23,744) involved immigration. Almost 22 percent of those cases were drug-related. That's 13,383 drug-related immigration cases in 2013. Of the twenty-three thousand federal immigration-related crimes, 19.7 percent (12,123) were violent crimes.[31]

In addition, according to the United States Sentencing Commission, illegal immigrants accounted for almost 75 percent of all federal drug-related sentences that same year.[32]

This trend stretches back all the way to when Brad supported border security. In 2003, according to the Government Accountability Office report, there were 55,322 illegal immigrants in prison. They accounted for 459,614 arrests and 700,000 crimes.[33] Basic math tells us that number adds up to thirteen offenses per each illegal alien in prison. And those are only the ones caught and convicted.

■　■　■　■

#9: Flip the argument and call out the contradiction. I promise you, it exists. For every radical leftist position, there is a hypocritical and obvious contradiction.

(We'll cover this tactic at length in Chapter 10, but it would be remiss of me if I didn't include a brief summary here in the "tactics" chapter, since it's such a multi-purpose tool during any debate with the Left.)

This tactic is the most fun. I have never met a liberal argument that didn't come with a side dish of logical inconsistency, hypocrisy, or contradiction. (Pro tip: that's what happens when you build your political stances on a foundation of what will give you the most power and money, rather than building your policy platform on principles).

Less than a month after congressional Republicans passed the tax reform bill and President Trump signed it into law on December 22, 2017, Democratic Minority Leader Nancy Pelosi took a swing at the law, which cut taxes (translation: people got to keep more of the money they earned in their paychecks every week) and resulted in companies giving their employees one thousand dollars in bonuses, citing the tax bill as the reason why.

Pelosi scoffed at the extra one thousand dollars given to workers, saying, "In terms of the bonus that corporate America receives versus the crumbs they are giving to the workers to put the schmooze on is so pathetic."[34]

Oh, if only we were all as filthy rich as you, Nancy! Sadly, not all of us can be the fifth wealthiest woman in Congress with a net worth of sixteen million dollars—the thirtieth richest member of Congress as a whole.[35]

Only a member of Congress as out of touch as Nancy Pelosi would make such an elitist statement.

Here's the thing: Pelosi's position is contradicted *from within her own party.*

Remember Sandra Fluke? The law school student who testified in front of Congress that her Catholic university refused to pay for her birth control as part of their school health plan. Fluke actually stood before the U.S. Congress and America and brazenly cried victim because somebody else wasn't subsidizing her "I-demand-sex-without-consequences" lifestyle.

"When I look around my campus," Fluke said about the health plan at her school, "I see the faces of women affected by this lack of contraceptive coverage."[36]

The Democratic Party supported her, decrying evil Republicans for trying to shove women back into the Dark Ages, claiming that without birth control women have no chance to succeed in life and in their professions, saying the burden of women paying for birth control themselves is simply too great for them to bear.

But wait, you might be saying...*Doesn't birth control cost ten dollars or twenty dollars a month?*[37]

How can the Left claim the Trump tax cuts are "crumbs" (the average tax cut for American households in 2018 is estimated by the Tax Policy Foundation to be approximately twelve hundred dollars—or one hundred dollars per month—plus the one-thousand-dollar bonuses)[38] but also claim that paying ten dollars or twenty dollars a month for your own birth control is oppressive to women?

The answer is: they can't without being the huge hypocrites they are.

I have never met an outraged liberal who didn't bring to the table a hilarious contradiction to his argument.

■　■　■　■

#10: Mirror their tactics. What do I mean when I say mirror their tactics? Picture Bobo the Monkey in front of a mirror. He thinks he's waving to a new friend. But it's himself.

In other words, is there ever a time when you feel as stupid as when you hear your own voice on your voicemail message on your phone? (I never hate myself as much as when I hear a recording of my own voice. Even compared to the time when my necklace, a gaudy piece of costume jewelry, shattered during a solemn U.S. Navy commissioning ceremony and the beads bounced and rolled loudly across the hardwood floor during the quietest part. Still hate the sound of my own voice more.)

Mirroring their tactics shows liberals they won't like what their own medicine tastes like. Campus Reform's Cabot Phillips is a master of using this tactic in his videos. Cabot visited college campuses following the Supreme Court ruling on Masterpiece Cakeshop and asked students if they believed Jack Phillips (no relation to Cabot) should be forced to bake the gay wedding cake.[39] The majority of the students responded emphatically yes. The students said baking cakes is the baker's job, and he shouldn't be allowed to say no to baking a cake just because he doesn't like the cake, since it's his job.

Cabot then asked the students if a black baker should be forced to bake a cake for a Ku Klux Klan rally? Of course, most of the students said no, the baker shouldn't be forced to do *that*.

What Cabot did was not only expose the lack of critical thinking taught on college campuses, but also show the liberal students how silly their arguments are by mirroring their logic. Cabot even used the students' own words! He said, "How is that different? If they are a baker, isn't that their job?"

Several students admitted at the end of Cabot's interview that their negative answer to the second question about the black baker and the KKK cake contradicted their first affirmative answer about Jack Phillips and the cake for the gay wedding.

But would they have seen their lack of consistency if Cabot hadn't mirrored their tactics to show how faulty their logic was when applied to a similar case? Perhaps not.

■   ■   ■   ■

#11: Always reframe the question you are asked so you can answer the question you want to answer.

This tactic is a rhetorical trick to sidestep debate landmines. The radical Left loves to pose lose-lose questions, where if you answer "no" you're a monster, and if you answer "yes" you're giving a thumbs-up to any number of destructive progressive policies.

There are two ways they do this. The first way is with an open-ended question. As follows:

How can you oppose providing a path to citizenship for the millions of undocumented immigrants who have been living here in the U.S. for decades? They came here for a better life, they've been contributing to our society, their children go to school with your children, they work with us, they worship with us, and they pay taxes. It's cruel to keep them in the shadows.

The proper answer there is to reframe the question:

Why do I oppose blanket amnesty to eleven million illegal immigrants, most of whom we don't know who they are? Or what crimes they committed? Who committed a crime just by entering our country illegally? Who essentially shanked legal immigrants waiting in line for legal entry? Most of whom don't pay taxes, but burden our welfare system at taxpayers' expense? Why do I oppose putting Americans at risk—like Kate Steinle, who was killed by an illegal immigrant? Because I care about the safety and security of our people. I'll support some sort of legalization for at least some of the eleven million just as soon as we've stopped the flow of illegal aliens, including cartels and human, sex, and drug traffickers into our country. Otherwise, amnesty not only puts our nation at risk, but it also encourages a mad flow of aliens trying to jump our border knowing they will face no consequences and will probably be legalized by doing it.

The second way the liberals will try to put you in a lose-lose situation is with a direct question, a yes or no.

Are you anti-abortion even in the cases of rape, incest, or to save the life of the mother?

Not an easy question to field when an affirmative answer makes you look like a monster on the side of the rapist and a negative answer amounts to an abandonment of your pro-life principles.

So don't say yes or no until you've reframed the question the way you want to answer it.

Is that baby still a human being created by God? Should that baby be punished for the crimes of her father? Will I defend the sanctity and dignity of life in all circumstances? Yes, I will always celebrate and champion the most vulnerable among us, those who cannot speak for themselves in defense of their own lives—our unborn babies.

Then you can go on and drop your fact bombs about how less than 1.5 percent of abortions as a whole are as a result of rape or incest, or to save the life of the mother,[40] so why do liberals pivot to that talking point—as if abortion policy should be based on the slimmest of minorities of reasons for abortion? You get the idea.

As you can see, reframing a question is a defensive tactic, but it's an excellent way to steer the debate back to your own terms and reposition the conversation so you can shift back to offense.

■ ■ ■ ■

The overarching purpose of these 11 tactics for debating liberals—as I'm sure you've gathered while reading them—is to reframe any debate. These tactics are exactly that. They are tactics. They are tools. They are not a strategy to defeat liberal principles, but tactics to be used to expose the agenda of the radical Left.

Once you disarm the talking points and rhetorical games of the radical Left, you've laid them bare to unbraid their illogical, destructive, or communist policies and prove why conservative principles of limited government and individual liberty are superior. (Trigger warning to the administrators at Bellarmine College in Kentucky. Yes, conservative principles *are* superior to communism. Just crack open a history book and read it for yourself.)

Moreover, each of these tactics is a tool to position the debate in your own terms. When the debate is on home turf, if you know what you're talking about and your position is based on principle, you should handily defeat the radical Left.

Notice the caveat there. *If you know what you're talking about.* We have a responsibility to be educated about that of which we speak. In fact, none of these tactics is worth its weight in horse hockey if we don't know what we're talking about. We'll dive into being the most educated person in the debate in Chapter 6.

Now, you may be thinking, this is all well and good for a serious, contentious debate with a radical leftist, but what about the bleeding-heart liberals we talked about earlier? The other half of liberals, the ones who aren't die-hard progressive closet Marxists? What about my neighbor Lindsay who works hard, supports her kids as a single mother, but has an "I'm With Her" sticker stuck on the back of her car? What about Paul in the cubicle next to me who hates "the man" and hates the fact that the executives who do nothing get paid so much more money than he does?

You might be thinking, I don't want to shank them. How do I genuinely give sight to the blind?

You're right. Bleeding-heart liberals are different. (And great instinct—you shouldn't verbally shank them just to score a point.)

One of the most difficult things for human nature is "losing face" or admitting you're wrong. So when we constantly sneer at the other side, how can they change their mind without feeling like idiots? After all, didn't Thomas Jefferson himself say in the Declaration of Independence, "mankind are more disposed to suffer, while evils are sufferable, than to right themselves by abolishing the forms to which they are accustomed"?[41] Why do you think that is? Well, even men wearing knee breeches and buckles and women who spent their days spinning wool and churning butter had a hard time admitting they were wrong.

Some things never change.

To talk to Lindsay or Paul, you can still use these tactics. Just pick and choose wisely. Listen first to the concerns of the bleeding-heart liberal. Listen, listen, listen. And then ask questions. Don't throw data, but gently ask, "Well, how many people did Obamacare cover? Wasn't it supposed to be universal coverage?" (Of course, it was supposed to do that, according to liberals. Did it? Of course not.)

You'll see small changes if you provide an opportunity for somebody to change his mind without feeling like an idiot for doing so. Like so:

Well, I certainly understand the intentions behind your support of Obamacare. Who doesn't want to help as many people as possible get health insurance? But I think we can see after eight years that intentions notwithstanding, this isn't working. It's time to try something different.

Paul and Lindsay might just agree.

It's a lot easier to change your mind if you position the change as the next evolution…a new turn in the road, versus impugning the original motives behind the position or ridiculing the bleeding-heart liberal for being dumb enough to fall for such a stupid piece of legislation that was obviously set up to fail in the first place.

Chapter 5

Liberty Once Lost

If a leftist asked you why you believe the Second Amendment applies to semi-automatic rifles like the AR-15 when the Founding Fathers only had muskets, could you answer?

If a leftist asked you why we shouldn't punish women for having abortions if you believe abortion is murder, could you answer?

If a bleeding-heart liberal asked how you can justify cutting entitlements when single moms can't afford food and healthcare without government benefits, could you answer?

If a leftist asked you how you can support the outdated Electoral College system we use in electing our presidents when the Electoral College seemingly contradicts the idea of "one person, one vote," could you answer? (By the way, conservatives—this author included—turned out in force to defend the Electoral College after President Donald Trump lost the popular vote but defeated Hillary Clinton in the Electoral College.[1] We ought to know why we believe what we believe.)

Those are some tough questions.

Even questions about basic conservative doctrine are sometimes tricky to answer. We *know* intuitively which positions we support and which we oppose. We know in our heart what is right and what is wrong. (It's called common sense and a conscience.) But what about intellectually? Can we answer for the policies we stand for? Can we articulate those answers clearly? Do we know *why* we believe what we believe?

If so, we need to prove it.

If a radical leftist asks us why we believe capitalism is superior to communism, we need to be able to shred that question in under sixty seconds. If a progressive liberal asks us why liberty is superior to a welfare state, we lose if we stutter over our response and pretend it's so obvious everybody knows the answer.

If Professor Unidentified Blob challenged you on why limited government is necessary to liberty... could you answer?

If not, why not?

If we don't know—or if we can't *articulate* clearly why we conservatives believe what we believe—we're entering dangerous territory. Knowing intuitively what's right and what's wrong may help us determine our vote privately, but if we know what we believe, then we need to prove it verbally. Otherwise the very morals on which our nation was founded will be compromised and ultimately lost.

Never was that clearer than in the immigration fiasco during the summer of 2018.

■　■　■　■

On May 7, 2018, the *Washington Post* ran this headline: "Sessions vows to prosecute all illegal border crossers and separate children from their parents."[2]

That date is very important. May 7, 2018. That's the day the news broke.

Yet it took five weeks after that story dropped before the radical Left started frothing at the mouth. Five weeks later, the Left called President Trump Hitler for holding children separately from their parents in detention centers at the border (after the parents crossed our border illegally). Five weeks later, the Left pretended to be outraged. Five weeks later, the Left pretended they cared about the children. (Funny how these radical leftists who claim to care about kids temporarily separated from their parents at the border don't care about the ONE MILLION kids who are permanently separated from their families by abortion, huh? But I digress.)

Five weeks after that headline dropped, the radical Left suddenly took notice. In fact, the radical Left started caring about the border on the very same day the Department of Justice inspector general Michael Horowitz released his report on the FBI's handling of the Hillary Clinton email investigation. The report revealed biased FBI agents whom the IG found "might be willing to take official action to impact presidential candidate Trump's electoral prospects."[3]

Funny how the radical Left suddenly, on that very same day—five weeks after the immigration story broke—became champions of children, right?

TVs began flashing pictures of children in cages. Children wrapped in foil blankets. Warehouses with barbed wire fences and Port-a-Potties full of kids, teenagers, and even some babies. Trump is Hitler! the Left screamed. These are internment camps for kids! Photos of children lying on pallets on the floor, so close to each other they looked like sardines in a can. It was awful.

But funnily enough, the Left trapped themselves in their own outrage over these photographs. The Left painted President Trump as Hitler for temporality separating parents and children in the detention centers at the border…but President Obama did the same thing! In fact, the policy and many of the photographs of the children in cages happened while Obama was president. Were Democrats outraged when Obama did it? Of course not.

That inconvenient fact doesn't matter to the radical Left. The outrage dominated the news coverage for weeks, culminating in Democratic congresswoman Maxine Waters calling for liberal mobs to attack Republican members of the Trump administration.

Waters told her supporters at a rally, "If you see anybody from that cabinet in a restaurant, in a department store, at a gasoline station, you get out and you create a crowd and you push back on them, and you tell them they're not welcome anymore, anywhere."[4]

Create a crowd. Push back on them. Tell them they're not welcome anymore, anywhere.

Scary stuff, right?

The radical Left inciting violence—actually calling for violence—against Republicans who dare to disagree with the radical leftist ideology.

All because of the fact that President Trump continued a policy of temporarily separating children and parents after the parents illegally crossed our border. A policy President Obama started in the first place.

And here we circle back to our original point. This is why we must be able to articulate why we believe what we believe.

Democrats change their rhetorical tune at the drop of a hat.

Here's what I mean. When this story broke, it seemed like everybody in America—Democrat, Republican, conservative, liberal—was on the same page. Everybody thinks the law that requires kids to be separated from their parents is awful (notwithstanding the fact that the parents are being charged with a crime for illegally crossing our border). We all think it's a bad law. We all want that law changed. Of all the issues that divide our nation, couldn't this be the one where we actually come together?

But no.

Instead, the radical Left exploited the issue. We watched it play out before our very eyes.

The Democrats called for President Trump to issue an executive order to halt the separation. So President Trump did that. After the order was signed and the policy was halted (just like the Democrats asked), the Democrats suddenly didn't like that anymore.

The minute President Trump finished signing the order, the radical Left changed their entire narrative from "We don't want kids and parents detained in separate facilities" to "Actually it's immoral to detain anybody at all."

God forbid we have unity once in a while, right? We have this idea in our country of coming together and working across the aisle. Every politician on the campaign trail promises voters that he or she will stand up for so-and-so values but will also work across the aisle to accomplish XYZ because that is important to voters. In other words, the idea of bipartisanship and "ending the gridlock" is always held up as the ideal. It's like sharing in kindergarten. In politics, we're told we should aspire to compromise and work together. Especially Congress.

I don't think we can do that with Democrats anymore. Here's why.

At the beginning of our nation, back when the Founding Fathers were drafting the Declaration of Independence and our Constitution and then during the first years of our brand-new republic, the men serving in our government were very divided. They had massive disagreements. In that sense, the division in our nation is not as unprecedented as the radical Left would have us believe. More on that later. But the political division back then was different because both sides agreed on the fundamental morality of the thing.

This is what I mean. Thomas Jefferson and John Adams were the primary brains behind the Declaration of Independence, right? They teamed up in the Continental Congress to fight for freedom and justice for all based on the idea that all men were created equal. But after they drafted this document and pledged their lives, fortunes, and sacred honor in defense of what they had written, they spent the next half their lives hating each other because they disagreed about the practical ways to protect the unalienable liberties they had codified into law.

In other words, although Thomas Jefferson and John Adams hated each other's guts for decades afterward, fundamentally and even during their years of animosity, they actually always agreed on the underlying principle.

They both believed that as individuals we are inherently endowed by our Creator with unalienable rights to life, liberty, and the pursuit of happiness. Both Jefferson and Adams believed that God and nature endow us with those rights, and therefore government cannot supersede those rights. They both believed our rights are not on loan from government. They both believed our rights existed before governments were ever instituted among men. Both Jefferson and Adams believed it was the role of government to protect those rights from being violated by other people, by foreign enemies, or by the state.

In other words, the animosity between Jefferson and Adams was over how to protect those rights. Should the federal government be large and sprawling and be the primary guardian of our rights? Adams thought so. Should the state governments wield most of the power in order to protect against a too-powerful centralized government? Jefferson thought so.

Both Jefferson and Adams believed so strongly in their own practical policies, their own prescriptions for what would best protect our rights, that they fought over it for years.

And therein lies the difference between now and then. Between political divisions that prompted the writing of *The Federalist Papers* or some decades of personal feuding between Jefferson and Adams—and the political division now, wherein the radical Left justifies driving secretary of Homeland Security Kirstjen Nielsen out of a restaurant and sending agitators to surround her home because they don't like her immigration policy, or Congresswoman Maxine Waters tells her supporters to attack members of the Trump administration in public.

We can see it for ourselves. Democrats and Republicans don't agree on the fundamentals anymore. How can we work across the aisle with a party whose view of the world justifies physical violence against political opponents and contends that such violence is moral? Our fundamental beliefs are no longer shared.

What do I mean when I say "fundamentals"? This is what I'm talking about.

The idea that every person is endowed with the right to life and liberty is based on Judeo-Christian morality. In fact, our entire idea of right and wrong—our idea of justice—is based on what Jesus Christ taught his disciples in the Bible about right and wrong. You don't have to practice Christianity or Judaism to abide by our laws, but Judeo-Christian mores are the basis of the foundation for our nation.

This used to be a commonly held belief.

Again, this is why we can't compromise with Democrats. They don't agree on these fundamentals anymore. Instead, we have the anti-religion types on the Left who are trying to redefine the definition of right and wrong. Now, instead of right and wrong, they want political correctness. Instead of justice, they want privilege points. They want the entire premise of our justice system based on how people feel at that moment, not based on objective truth.

Isn't that why we saw the Democrats negotiate in bad faith over immigration and the separation of parents and their children at the border? First they wanted an executive order, then they rejected it. They claimed they didn't want parents and children detained separately, but when Trump fixed that, they said they didn't want parents and children, anybody, detained at all.

The radical Left doesn't agree anymore on the fundamental morals and values on which our nation was founded. The immigration debate isn't a Jefferson-Adams intellectual disagreement where both sides agree we should secure our border but disagree on the best policy to do that. Democrats don't want to secure our border anymore.

How can we "work together" and compromise with the radical Left when what's on the negotiating table isn't practical solutions? When it's our morals on the chopping block?

We shouldn't be willing to work together with a party whose goal isn't practical solutions, simply for the sake of compromise. Especially when that party is seeking to implement a radical leftist ideology that seeks to shift our nation away from the Judeo-Christian values on which we were founded.

And now we've come full circle. In order to know whether we can compromise over practical solutions or whether we're bargaining our souls, we have to understand why we believe what we believe.

If we don't know why we believe what we believe, we are at risk of erring on the side of good-heartedness and compromise for the sake of compromise without realizing that we're rolling the dice with the age-old morals and values on which this nation was built.

Chapter 6

If You Know What You Believe, Prove It

So sit down in a chair. Pretend Professor Unidentified Blob is sitting on a stool across from you. Only in this situation, you're allowed to answer his questions without fear of being kicked out of his class. You're allowed to challenge what he's teaching without being sent to the corner to think about your white, cisgender, straight, male, Christian privilege (or whatever immutable characteristic you have that autonomously inflicts suffering on those less privileged). This is your chance. This is your opportunity to tell this radical leftist exactly why you believe what you believe.

The stakes are high. If you can't defend conservative principles, Professor Unidentified Blob will pounce. If you hem and haw and shrug and assume that *everybody* knows the answer to *that*...the genderless radical in front of you will crack a slow smile and methodically pick up the conservative principle *you* couldn't defend, wad it up, and eat it (throwing trash away has long since been illegalized). Once gone, it will be lost forever.

The clock starts ticking. You have one minute for each answer and then your mic is cut off. Are you ready?

If you know what you believe, prove it.

Question: Why are you pro-life?

Answer: Now is not the time for a novel-length dissertation. Now is the time for short, punchy answers that get straight to the heart of this issue. The heart of this issue is, literally…the heart. When does life begin?

#1: Science. Science says life begins at conception. The moment an egg fuses with a sperm, a new life is created. Don't believe me? Look it up for yourself. You remember in Chapter 4 that we saw how the pre-eminent medical textbooks say a new life is formed at the moment of conception.

Actually, forty-one medical textbooks and medical experts say a new human life is formed the moment of conception.

"Human life begins at fertilization." That's from the textbook *Developing Human: Clinically Oriented Embryology*. "Fertilization being the process during which a sperm unites with an ovum to form a single cell called a zygote. A zygote is the beginning of a new human being."[1]

And a textbook called *Patten's Human Embryology* says, "It is the penetration of the ovum by a sperm and the resulting mingling of nuclear material each brings to the union that constitutes the initiation of the life of a new individual."[2]

Just two examples of the forty-one textbooks.

The U.S. government acknowledges the scientific fact that life begins at conception, too.

From the U.S. National Institutes of Health: "Fertilization is the process of union of two gametes, whereby the somatic chromosome number is restored and the development of a new individual is initiated."[3]

If you *don't* believe human life begins at conception, you are ignoring scientific facts. Why are you ignoring science?

#2: Morality. If life begins at conception, what right do we have to end that life?

Why isn't that life—that person—protected under our law? If we can't protect the most vulnerable among us, what kind of society are we?

Our system of freedom and justice for all is unique in that we apply our laws equally to all people, regardless of their race, gender, sexual orientation, age, ethnicity, socioeconomic status, or anything else.

There is no moral exception for certain people who happen to be unable to talk yet. Or certain persons who are unable to care for themselves. Or certain persons just because they are still in their mother's womb.

Unless the radical Left wants to start picking and choosing which classes of people are protected under the law and which are not. Haven't we been there before in our country? Is that something the Left wants us to relive?

Great job. Five seconds to spare. You won. If you want to explain and defend the pro-life worldview, always bring it back to the fundamental reason you believe what you believe about why abortion is wrong: When does life begin? If life begins at conception (per science), what right do we have to end the life of the unborn baby? Science and morality paired together are an undefeatable pair.

■　　■　　■　　■

Question: Why are you pro-gun?

Answer: Sixty seconds on the clock…ready…go! Get to the heart of the matter immediately. All the peripheral statistics that show nations with higher legal gun ownership have lower crime rates,[4] or studies that show more legal gun ownership in an area reduces the violent crime rate,[5] or statistics that show concealed carry permit holders in the state of the Texas have a lower crime rate than police officers,[6] or the fact that two hundred thousand times a year women use firearms to defend themselves against sexual abuse[7]…those statistics can wait. Use them to deflect liberal lies.

The more guns people own, the radical Left says, *the higher the number of murders!* False. They're trying to scare you. Ignore that for now. Get to the heart of the matter. The heart of the matter here is…do you trust the government?

#1: History says we shouldn't trust governments. Before Adolf Hitler killed six million Jews, he took their guns away.[8] Before Pol Pot killed two million people, their guns were taken away.[9] In Soviet Russia, before Stalin killed twenty million people, he took their guns away.[10] Black people in America during our own history of slavery and oppression were not allowed to own firearms.[11] I wonder why? (More on this in Chapter 9.)

In other words, guns are the great equalizer. Without the right to keep and bear firearms, we the people have no recourse against a tyrannical government. Conversely, the government cannot oppress us if we have the means to defend ourselves.

Remember, our Constitution and our government do not endow our rights. They don't give our rights to us or loan our rights to us. Our rights are not privileges. They are *rights*. Our Declaration of Independence *acknowledges* our inherent right to life, liberty, and the pursuit of happiness...rights that existed *before* government.

But as history teaches us, governments become tyrannical. They oppress their citizens. They deprive people of basic human rights and dignity. Look around the world. Point to the most powerful nations in history that have lasted without becoming tyrannical at some point. You can't.

By arming ourselves, we keep the government in its place.

Remember the oft-ignored words of the Second Amendment: "A well regulated militia, being necessary to the security of a free state, the right of the people to keep and bear arms, shall not be infringed."[12]

Being necessary to the security of a free state.

The men who crafted our Second Amendment were smart. They looked at history and they saw what happened. They noted that historically governments that have the opportunity to abuse their power...ultimately abuse their power. The framers of our Constitution were determined that the United States, their brand-new baby nation, would not meet that same tragic end.

Our arms are a deterrent reminding the government that their role is to protect our rights and also a means—in the case of any violation of rights—to defend ourselves should that become necessary. (As it did in 1776.)

#2: Personal self-defense. Let's not forget that the right to defend ourselves against harm is a basic human right. You have a *right* to stop me if I try to hurt you. You have a right to protect yourself and your family (and by extension the fruits of your labor—your property). Your inherent right to self-defense includes arming yourself so you have a realistic possibility of warding off attackers, whether that attacker be the state or a criminal or otherwise hostile person.

Again, guns are the great equalizer. This is true especially for women. If I'm attacked by an angry 250-pound man, I may not have a realistic chance of defending myself with my bare hands…but put a gun in my hands and I'll have a fighting chance.

This is true for anybody who's not Buffy McMuscles. Our rights— and whether other people respect our rights or attempt to violate them— should not be determined by who is strong enough to protect themselves. Otherwise our society would devolve into anarchy where the physically strong ruled the weak, disabled, small, or powerless.

Great job. You were a little long-winded on that one. More than sixty seconds. But we'll let it slide. If you want to explain and defend the pro-gun worldview, always bring it back to the fundamental reason you believe what you believe about why our Second Amendment is necessary to the security of a free state: governments ultimately oppress their people when the people are powerless. If we arm ourselves, we keep the government in its place and protect our basic human rights.

■ ■ ■ ■

Question: Why does the Second Amendment apply to semi-automatic rifles like the AR-15 when the Founding Fathers only had muskets?

Answer: Great question. If the Founding Fathers meant "the right to keep and bear muskets," why didn't they write "the right to keep and bear muskets"?

Well, they must not have meant muskets. It doesn't take a rocket scientist to interpret the language of the Constitution (although maybe a rocket scientist could have explained this concept to the Harvard

J.D. who formerly occupied the Oval Office and never seemed to grasp the obvious).

The point is, the Framers wrote keep and bear "arms." They knew firearm technology would develop. They specifically did *not* want the right to self-defense to become outdated as government firepower progressed. So they protected individuals' rights to possess commonly owned weapons *of our time*. We'll call them "arms."

And yes, our government has tanks and nukes and ballistic missiles and we the people don't. No kidding. Nonetheless, even a citizenry armed with weapons less powerful than the government can inflict a great amount of harm in our own defense. (If you doubt inferior weaponry can inflict enormous amounts of harm on a force with superior firepower, just think about Vietnam and the 58,220 U.S. military servicemembers who were killed despite the superior weaponry of the U.S.)[13]

■   ■   ■   ■

Remember—if you know what you believe, now is the time to prove it. If you can't explain why you believe what you believe, you'll end up losing the whole principle. Radical leftists are looking for that tiny pinpoint of doubt. Any inability to defend your position so they can point to the audience and say, *See? This buffoon doesn't even know what he's talking about. He's just clinging to his guns and religion…and he doesn't even have any reasons why!* As soon as any radical leftist lands that punch, he'll lift the lid off a platter of gun control and explain why his crazy leftist policy is better. Don't let that happen.

■   ■   ■   ■

Question: Why do individuals have the right to bear arms when the Second Amendment says a "well-regulated militia"?

The Founding Fathers wrote militia! the radical Left will argue. (This is a pivot point, but have a little fun! Go ahead and debunk it.) *Why are you as an individual allowed to keep and bear arms?*

The best part of this question is the radical Left thinks this point is a "kill shot." (Pun intended.) Don't worry. The radical leftists are wrong. Put thirty seconds on the clock, please!

Answer: Jump right to the heart of the matter on this question. The heart of the matter is: Does the text of the Second Amendment to our Constitution say "militia" or does it say "people"? Well, both.

Very literally, in the text, it says people. The right of the people to keep and bear arms.

You are people. I am people. If the Framers didn't mean people as individuals, why did they say "the right of the people to keep and bear arms shall not be infringed"? And why would they include both words—militia and people—if they didn't intend to clarify that the right to keep and bear arms extends to both individuals and militias as separate entities?

If the Framers meant to recognize gun rights only for a collective like a militia…a militia regulated by the federal government…why didn't they say "the right of a militia regulated by the federal government to keep and bear arms"?

If the Framers meant to recognize gun rights only for a collective like a militia…a militia regulated by the state governments…why didn't they say "the right of a militia regulated by the state governments to keep and bear arms"?

They didn't. They very specifically did not say that.

So ask Professor Blob, if the Framers were giving the *government* power, why would they have included the Second Amendment in the Bill of Rights? (Spoiler alert: they wouldn't have.)

Look Professor Unidentified Blob in the eyes. Ze thinks ze's trapped you. Ze thinks the "well-regulated militia" argument is going to make your brain smoke down.

So, ask him, why did the framers include the Bill of Rights in our Constitution? Very simple. The framers wanted to make sure that the federal government knew in no uncertain terms what they are *not* allowed to do. The federal government is not allowed to infringe on the right of the people to keep and bear arms.

The Second Amendment provides a check against the standing army of a tyrannical government, right? We established that in the answer to the previous question. That's how a government tyrannizes a nation and oppresses its people. The people's right to bear arms is a check against the firepower of the federal (or state) government. So, why would the power to regulate a check against government power...be given to that same government? It wouldn't.

Bring it back to the heart of the matter every time. Why does the Second Amendment say people if it doesn't mean individuals? And why would the Second Amendment be included in the Bill of Rights, which was meant to limit the powers of the federal government, if the Framers meant the federal government could "regulate" that right? Know why you believe what you believe, and you'll slay the radical Left's gotcha rhetoric every time.

Next up, putting women to death.

■　■　■　■

Question: Why shouldn't we punish women for having abortions if we believe abortion is murder?

Answer: Abortion *is* murder, if you believe in science. Science says a new human life begins at the moment of conception. Abortion ends that human life. Period. Even Planned Parenthood, the largest abortion provider in our country, which commits over three hundred thousand abortions every year,[14] admitted in a pamphlet that abortion kills a baby whose life has already begun.[15]

Make sure you get your opponent to agree on *that* before you engage in hypotheticals.

Then ask: What's the purpose of our justice system? Is the purpose of our justice system revenge? Or vengeance? Making people suffer the punishment they deserve for the crime they committed? No. The purpose of our justice system is to restore order. The purpose of our justice system is to protect the rights of innocent men and women.

We incarcerate people if they have proved they can't be trusted not to violate people's rights after they already violated somebody's rights. That restores order in our society. Not because those lawbreakers "deserve" to spend their lives in prison. (*That* kind of vengeance ought to be left to the Final Judgment, yes?)

So what purpose would it serve to punish women who seek abortions? None. I don't think it would serve our society well to penalize women. Instead, it would further victimize victims.

In one study, 64 percent of women who had abortions reported feeling coerced or pressured into procuring the abortion. Abortion is not a single-victim act. Sixty five percent of these women suffered symptoms of trauma following their abortion.[16] According to a study conducted in Finland, the suicide rate for women skyrocketed in the year following their abortion—to *seven times* the suicide rate of women who gave birth.[17] In other words, both the baby and the mother are victims of abortion and both suffer serious mental and physical consequences from abortion. For the baby, the consequence is death. For the mother, the consequence is increased risk of serious mental health issues, suicide, infertility, and trauma.[18]

The best recourse to protect the rights of the baby and restore order to society? Penalize the abortionists who commit the act knowing the consequences.

In the greater debate, don't get distracted by this hypothetical, though. Know why you believe what you believe so you can quickly explain away the concerns (or pivots) of the radical Left and get to the heart of the matter. The heart of the matter is that we have to establish right and wrong before we can enact a just penalty. We have to establish when life begins and what right we have to end that life before we restore order through our justice system when a wrong is committed and a right violated.

That's the crux of this question. Democrats think it's a gotcha question, but don't worry. It's not. It's usually an effort to deflect away from addressing the *real* question: What right to do we have to abort unborn babies at any stage?

And there you see it for yourself. This is why it's so important to understand why we believe what we believe. If we can't articulate the answers to the trick questions as well as the obvious fundamentals, the radical Left will trip us up. And if we trip, we risk dropping the values we hold dear, and, as John Adams said, "Liberty once lost is lost forever."[19]

■   ■   ■   ■

Question: Why do we believe in border security if we're a nation of immigrants?

We're all immigrants! the radical Left yells. They pound their fists on the table. *We're a melting pot! It's xenophobic to build a wall! You hate brown people! These immigrants are fleeing oppression, domestic violence, cartel killings, and extreme poverty!*

Answer: Great. And the immigrants who are fleeing cartel killings, domestic violence, and government oppression are welcomed into our nation via our generous asylum program. That's not what a border wall is about, and the Left knows it.

#1: A border wall saves taxpayers money. Without a border wall and border security, we aren't a nation. Without a secure border, our people aren't safe. Without a secure border, criminals, cartels, traffickers, and terrorists enter our country and hurt our people. More on that in a moment. First, let's start with the money issues.

Robert Rector and Jason Richwine of the Heritage Foundation calculated in 2013 that illegal immigrants in the United States cost taxpayers an estimated fifty-four billion dollars every year.[20]

But illegal immigrants pay taxes! the Left will be quick to yell.

First of all, this fifty-four billion dollars is the net burden, calculated by tallying the cost of taxpayer-funded government services used by illegal immigrant households minus the tax contributions of the illegal immigrant households.

Rector and Richwine point out, "In 2010, the average unlawful immigrant household received around $24,721 in government benefits and services while paying some $10,334 in taxes. This generated an average annual fiscal deficit (benefits received minus taxes paid) of around $14,387 per household."

Consider just one of the largest expenditures paid out by American taxpayers on illegal immigration: public school education for the children of illegal immigrants, which costs $12,300 per pupil per year. Any child in our nation regardless of immigration status is eligible for free public-school education, whether or not their parents have paid into the system.

Now let's look at the number of illegal aliens in our country costing taxpayers all this money. There were 521,090 border apprehensions reported by U.S. Customs and Border Patrol in 2018. (Repeated on a yearly basis.)[21]

According to a 2017 Department of Homeland Security (DHS) report, between 55 and 85 percent of illegal aliens attempting to cross the border were apprehended.[22]

So let's do the math. We'll split the difference. Let's say 70 percent of illegal aliens attempting to cross our border are apprehended (that's midway between the 55 percent low and 85 percent high estimate by DHS).

If the 521,090 illegals who were apprehended trying to cross the border in 2018 are 70 percent of the total number who attempted the crossing…basic math tells us that 744,414 total attempted and 223,324 were successful.

Then, let's plug in Rector and Richwine's number from above. If 11.5 million illegals cost U.S. taxpayers a net fifty-four billion dollars every year, then adding a quarter million more illegals (just from border crossings; this does not count the illegals who overstay their visas) because of the 30 percent rate the Border Patrol does not catch crossing the border would result in over ONE BILLION dollars per year in taxpayer money spent on just illegal aliens who cross our border. Again, this is not a one-time price tag. This is an annual fee.

Finally, let's look at the cost of a border wall. Generous estimates predict a comprehensive wall and border security package would cost between fifteen billion and twenty billion dollars. So how quickly would a border wall pay for itself? Do the math. Pretty darn quick. And remember, that's *only* the money related to the border crossers themselves; that doesn't take into consideration the cost of law enforcement, crime, or drugs.

#2: A border wall keeps people safe. The radical Left tells us that illegal aliens commit crimes at a lower rate than native border citizens. That is egregiously false.

We talked about some of the statistics in Chapter 4. Illegal aliens make up approximately 3.5 percent of our population in the United States. Yet, illegal aliens commit 13.6 percent of all crimes here. That includes 12 percent of murders and 16 percent of trafficking offenses.[23] That's what the Left calls a "disproportionate rate."

Then we have transnational gang activity. Between 2005 and 2014, U.S. Customs and Immigration Enforcement arrested nearly four thousand members of the violent gang MS-13 here in the United States.[24] MS-13 has committed crimes on U.S. soil so horrific and demonic that it's hard to write about them. These crimes include beheading, ripping out the hearts of live victims, sexual torture, amputating the hands of victims, running over victims with a car, gunshots to the back of the head, mutilation by machete, and slashing victims' stomachs open—in addition, of course, to plain old murder.

Ninety-two percent of the four thousand MS-13 gang members arrested in that ten-year span were illegal aliens. That's astounding, and it's not safe for American citizens (or for legal immigrants residing in the U.S.).

That is why we need a border wall.

The heart of the matter when it comes to border security is keeping citizens safe and saving taxpayers money. If you want to explain and defend a border wall, bring it back to the fundamental reason you believe our border should be secure: What keeps people safest? And what is the most cost-effective way do that?

As we've seen, without a border we have no nation. Without border security, the amount of money taxpayers are forced to spend on illegal immigration is untenable, and a border wall ends up paying for itself almost immediately. The first role of government is to protect the safety and security of its people. Without border security, government is failing in its primary role.

Keep it short, concise, and you'll obliterate this talking point in no time.

■　■　■　■

Question: Why shouldn't we bring democratic socialism like they have in Sweden here to the U.S., since Swedes are happier[25] and have less poverty[26] than we do?[27]

Answer: You don't even need thirty seconds on the clock for this one. Get to the heart of the matter immediately: What's the difference between "democratic socialism" like Bernie Sanders peddles and "regular old socialism" the likes of which Cuba, Venezuela, and the Soviet Union peddle? Well? Spoiler alert: There is no difference. Or at the very least, it's a difference without distinction.

Socialism is one of the deadliest ideologies the world has ever known. President Jimmy Carter once said our country suffers from an "inordinate fear" of communism.[28] He was wrong. Fear of rattlesnakes is not inordinate. It's prudent.

Over one hundred *million* innocent people were killed at the hands of socialist and communist governments in the twentieth century.[29] Do radical leftists who praise democratic socialism want that to happen here in the United States? Ask them.

The Scandinavia comparison is stupid. Denmark and Sweden and the other Scandinavian nations are not "socialist utopias" like Bernie Sanders claims. Finland discontinued its universal basic income experiment in 2018 because it didn't work.[30] (Shocker!) Sweden turned its economy back toward capitalism decades ago because its socialist policies were driving wealthy people and business out of the country and threatening to tank the economy.[31] Sweden also has a population of 9.9 million people, compared to the 325 million people in America. Collectivism on a small scale is a whole different ballgame (and it still doesn't work well even in tiny countries).

In Venezuela, a socialist utopia conveniently overlooked by the radical Left, parents are bargaining for antibiotics for their kids in hospitals. One mother got antibiotics for her child after another mother whose child died didn't need the medication anymore.[32] The government in Venezuela has expropriated over 1,400 businesses in the past twenty years in an effort to "stabilize" the economy.[33] And when that didn't work—shocker!—Venezuela nationalized even more industries. (More on this in Chapter 9.)

In Cuba, the universal healthcare system is so great that people have to bring their own blankets and lightbulbs to the hospital.[34] Surgical instruments are filthy.[35] And the elites fly to free market nations for their own healthcare needs.[36]

The heart of the matter is that socialism is wholly contradictory to the idea that individuals were made in God's image or endowed by Nature with unalienable rights. Socialism puts government first and squashes the people under the power of a few elites who think they know better than people about people's own lives.

Socialism also just doesn't work. Promising free stuff to people is foolish. Free healthcare. Free college tuition. Free housing. Free jobs guarantee. Free living wage. Free universal basic income. Who pays for all that?

Rich people? Even if you taxed the top 1 percent at a 100 percent tax rate, it still couldn't cover the costs of those enormous programs.[37] So guess what happens? The government takes from the rich...until the rich aren't rich anymore. Then the government takes from the kinda-rich...until the kinda-rich aren't kinda-rich anymore. Then the government takes from the middle class...until the middle class aren't middle class anymore. And so on and so on...until the socialist government takes control of *everything* in order to redistribute it "fairly." Then, lo and behold, we end up like Cuba or the Soviet Union or Venezuela. Oppressed. Starving. Poor.

So-called democratic socialism is just another name for regular old socialism. Socialism isn't fair. Socialism isn't just. Socialism is authoritarianism at its best, a mass murder machine at its worst. And it's the absolute antithesis to freedom and liberty and the idea of government of the people, by the people, and for the people.

■   ■   ■   ■

Question: Why *is* capitalism superior to communism? Isn't capitalism a breeding ground for greedy imperialists who don't mind if they exploit the working man as long as they make another buck? Why do conservatives claim capitalism is the best system of economics the world has ever known?

Answer: Did you buy this book on Amazon? If so, thank a capitalist. Look down at your feet. Are you wearing brand name shoes or custom orthotics? If so, thank a capitalist. Has your cell phone pinged at you since you started this chapter? Have you checked your Facebook lately? Are you wearing a smart watch? If the answer to any of these questions is yes, thank a capitalist.

Now for the real reason why capitalism is superior to communism: capitalistic free market economies lifted more people out of poverty in the twentieth century than any other economic system in the history of the world. Think that's just a talking point? We have proof.

In 1820, 94 percent of the world's population lived in poverty (84 percent in extreme poverty). By 1992, 172 years later, only 24 percent of the world's population live in extreme poverty.[38] What changed between 1820 and 1992? The Industrial Revolution. The onset of global trade, *free* trade.

When the radical Left castigates capitalism as being centered on "self-interest," they are missing a critical point. Self-interest doesn't mean the sin of selfishness. Self-interest is a healthy human instinct to take care of oneself and one's own as a matter of self-preservation. In other words, if we didn't think about getting ourselves food, we'd die. If we didn't think about building ourselves shelter, we'd freeze to death. If we didn't think about not walking through a dark alley at night, we quite likely could be attacked, robbed, raped, or killed.

Self-interest is not selfish when your interest is mutually beneficial to another's interest. That's the whole idea of the free market. When you bring a product to the market to sell it (for—gasp—profit!) so that you can buy food or shelter or health care for your family, that product also helps somebody else take care of themselves or their family. And vice versa.

Sounds too good to be true, right? Wrong. Look at the numbers. Thanks in part to the capacity to trade freely, from 2001 to 2011 nearly seven hundred million people around the world exited poverty[39] (people who had been living on two dollars or less a day).

Contrast that with communism—the radical ideology that the Left claims is "fair" to everybody. In the twentieth century, as seven hundred million people exited poverty thanks to capitalism, over one hundred million people worldwide were killed as a result of communism and socialism.

(And I'm not even talking about the freedom variable here. More on that later.)

Why would anybody who cares about people's lives and standard of living support communism?

■   ■   ■   ■

Question: How can you support the outdated Electoral College system we use in electing our presidents when the Electoral College is seemingly contradictory to the idea of "one person, one vote"?

Answer: Keep it short and punchy. Get right to the heart of the matter. Do you care about the voices of minorities or not?

If you do, you'll support the Electoral College.

#1: The electoral college prevents mob rule. We don't have to see the liberal mobs harassing Sarah Huckabee Sanders or attacking transgender conservatives wearing MAGA hats[40] to know that mobs are dangerous. Our Founding Fathers wanted to avoid that.

Remember, the Founding Fathers originally intended for a representative republic where the people's representatives (in Congress) elected a president amongst themselves.[41] (Similar to how Congress elects their Speaker of the House.)

But the Founders worried about corruption and collusion in our nation's government. (I like to say our Founders worried about "the original swamp creatures in knee breeches.")

So, they settled on this compromise: the Electoral College. Combining the original idea of electing a president via the Congress (only, they swapped this out for electors) and taking into account the voices of the people. The Founders called it avoiding the "tyranny of the majority" inherent in pure democracies but allowing the "sense of the people" to impact the government.

In other words, the Founding Fathers wanted to create a government that avoided corrupt congressional representatives electing a president, but also avoided the mob rule of a pure democracy.

As Madison said, a "common passion or interest will, in almost every case, be felt by a majority of the whole; a communication and concert result from the form of government itself; and there is nothing to check the inducements to sacrifice the weaker party or an obnoxious individual. Hence it is that such democracies have ever been spectacles of turbulence and contention; have ever been found incompatible with personal security or the rights of property; and have in general been as short in their lives as they have been violent in their deaths."[42]

John Adams reiterated the same point about pure democracies: "Remember democracy never lasts long. It soon wastes, exhausts and murders itself. There never was a democracy yet, that did not commit suicide."[43]

But George Mason argued that even though history shows that pure democracies self-destruct because of the emotional mob, the people have a right to choose their leader: "Notwithstanding the oppressions and injustice experienced among us from democracy; the genius of the people is in favor of it, and the genius of the people must be consulted."[44]

Hence the compromise that created the Electoral College, which takes into account the voice of the people while guarding against the emotional whims of a pure democracy.

#2: The Electoral College gives minorities a voice. How many presidential candidates would visit Kansas or Oklahoma if the goal of the campaign was winning the popular vote? (Ask Hillary Clinton: How did it work out for her ignoring Michigan in 2016? She ignored a pivotal state to her detriment... in pursuit of the popular vote.) The answer is none. All presidential candidates would only visit highly populated cities on the coasts like New York City, Los Angeles, Chicago, Houston, Philadelphia, and San Francisco because that's where the people are. In a pure democracy, people = votes. So, sensibly, presidential candidates would ignore the majority of states and the interests of the people in those states... simply because the states aren't populated as densely as the coastal cities like New York and Los Angeles.

Compare that to the Electoral College system, in which states are given one elector for each representative in Congress for a total of 538 electors. This gives the states themselves power. It's called federalism. Federalism gives minority states a voice—a stake in the election even when their cities aren't densely populated—so they aren't drowned out by the loud voices of the populous states like California and New York.

That brings us back to the heart of the matter. If you care about giving minorities a voice, the Electoral College is a stunningly clever solution to the problem. After all, what other system in a free nation protects minorities, prevents the chaos of mob rule, protects against the tyranny inherent to pure democracy, and grants definitive outcomes in elections? The answer to that is none. (Somebody please send this chapter to Hillary Clinton.)

■ ■ ■ ■

If you sat down in a chair facing yourself in a mirror to conduct an interview, would you be nervous if you asked yourself why you believe what you believe?

Good afternoon, thank you for joining me, you're looking especially beautiful today. My first question is the simplest and the most complex of them all. Why are you…conservative?"

After all, the very word "conservative" has a stingy connotation. *Conservative.* Miserly. It brings to mind old Aunt Maude doling out just *one* dollop of mashed potatoes on your plate so that you don't get fat. But you're starving! Old Aunt Maude eyes you up and down as she serves you a measly portion, hoarding the rest. (This didn't happen. Old Aunt Maude is fictitious.)

Then we have the word liberal. The word liberal is a different story. *Liberal.* It sounds like an invitation, doesn't it? Generous. Open. We love you for who you are. *Liberal.* A night of liberal food and drink, a liberal splash of vodka in your soda, a generous uncle hands you a crisp one-hundred-dollar bill for your birthday. How liberal he is with his money!

That's the picture the Left paints of conservatives versus liberals. Except worse. Toss in racism, sexism, misogyny, homophobia, xenophobia, and all the rest of the isms and ias, and *that's* what the Left tells the world conservative principles are all about. (Is it any wonder that the majority of millennials are liberal?)

Except that vision of conservative principles is not true. It's a lie. (Fake news, if you will.) You know that intuitively. But can you *explain* why?

Can you explain why are you conservative? Do you know what you believe?

If so, I'll repeat: prove it.

We have to prove it because the radical Left doesn't want to compromise. Remember the last chapter? Conservatives and radical leftists no longer agree on the fundamental values on which our nation was built. Conservatives and radical leftists are no longer debating which solution best achieves the same goal. Not anymore. Conservatives and radical leftists have fundamentally different philosophies of right and wrong, moral and immoral, justice and equality.

We can see examples of this everywhere if we look at the actions of the radical Left.

Take immigration. Not too long ago, Speaker of the House Nancy Pelosi and Senate Minority Leader Chuck Schumer condemned illegal immigration and called for securing our border, with Pelosi saying, "we certainly do not want any more [illegal immigrants] coming in."[45] Now Minnesota attorney general Keith Ellison, the former deputy chair of the Democratic National Committee, wears a t-shirt that reads (in Spanish), "I don't believe in borders."[46] Prominent liberal senators with presidential hopes—like Kirsten Gillibrand—are calling to "abolish ICE."[47] Democrats and the radical Left no longer want to secure our borders. They don't care about the cost of the border wall. They want open borders.

Scary stuff, right?

We can't compromise with radical leftists who are trying to play poker with our principles. Our values should not be on the negotiating table.

We have to know what we believe because the stakes are higher than ever. If we negotiate with the radical Left and lose, we lose our liberty, and as we established at the beginning of this chapter, liberty once lost is lost forever.

The first line of defense against the radical Left hijacking our conservative principles is knowing how to answer with the right information and the right tactics. That is the material point of this chapter. When the radical Left attacks our values (and the political policies that are the extension of our values), can we defend ourselves? If not, why not?

It's critical for all of us in the conservative movement to understand the *why* behind our party platform. Otherwise, the Left will bulldoze us and the values we treasure—life, liberty, and the pursuit of happiness, our right to free speech and freedom of the press, our Second Amendment right to bear arms, our family and parental rights, our religious beliefs, and our right to practice our faith in the public sphere and determine the course of our own lives, our businesses, and our property.

So, I challenge you. If you know what you believe, prove it.

Or lose it.

Chapter 7

Read and Improve Your Mind, My Son

"**N**ot all readers are leaders, but all leaders are readers."

A million people have co-opted that quote, but it originated with the thirty-third president of the United States, Harry S. Truman.[1] I would only add to it the following nuance: all *good* leaders are readers. A list of books, resources, conservative thought, liberal philosophy, and literature for the well-read individual is the most powerful arsenal we have against the radical leftist progressive agenda.

It's also the most frequent question I'm asked via email and in person: What should we be reading?

When people ask me, "How did you get to where you are now?" I always have the same answer. I tell people, "Under all this hairspray and lipstick, I'm just a huge dork." In fact, my best friend since my freshman year of high school told me during college that I have the hobbies of a middle-aged man. (Hey, she's the one who's friends with me.) I assume that means voracious consumption of the news and books, because I loathe gardening.

The point is that the purpose of this chapter is to put into practice the theory of the previous two chapters. 1) If you know what you're talking about, prove it. 2) If you *don't* know what you're talking about, you run the risk of losing your liberties to a radical leftist version of the Democratic Party that no longer shares the core values on which America was built.

Don't forget that these radical leftists want biological men to think they are women if the men *feel* like women. Straight men are now being told by the radical Left that if they (straight men) don't want to have sex with transgender women (biological men who identify as women, whether or not they've had the genital surgery), those straight men are "transphobic."[2] Because transgender women, according to the radical Left, are just as much "real women" as biological women.

Except that common sense and biology tells us that's ridiculously false.

These radical leftists think they're justified in breaking down businesses,[3] throwing rocks at police officers,[4] and assaulting Republicans[5] because they don't like law enforcement or they don't like Donald Trump.

In San Antonio, Texas, a teenaged boy wearing a Make America Great Again hat at a restaurant was attacked by a radical leftist who hates Trump.[6] The thirty-year-old attacker stole the kid's hat, hurled profanities at him, and threw a drink in the kid's face. Then, instead of condemning the violence, former CNN commentator Marc Lamont Hill (a radical leftist if there ever was one) *laughed* at the attack. He tweeted crying-laughing emojis in response to the story, and when somebody called him out for it, Hill responded, "I actually don't advocate throwing drinks on people. Not at all. But yes, I think MAGA hats (deliberately) reflect a movement that conjures racism, homophobia, xenophobia, etc. So yes, it's a little harder to feel sympathy when someone gets Coca Cola thrown on him."[7]

In other words, Hill doesn't endorse attacking political opponents...unless they're Republicans.

The radical Left uses our money to fund their agenda, too. They want the government (a.k.a. money from your wallet) to fund emotional support unicorns for any snowflakes whose feelings get hurt.

A state-funded university in California—Cal Poly, San Luis Obispo—admitted in summer of 2018 that they are actively trying to reduce the number of white people on their campus.[8] The school said they want the number of white students and faculty to match the percentage of white people in the state. And 39.7 percent of people in the state of California are white, while 55 percent of students on the campus of Cal Poly, San Luis Obispo are white. (The horror!) So the school spent money on a project—a thirty-page report on how to reduce the number of white people on their campus. They said, "In 2011, the campus was 63 percent Caucasian. In fall of 2017, it was less than 55 percent…but there is still much work to do."[9]

To be clear, this school is not looking for ways to boost underprivilege kids—poor kids from the inner city or kids from broken families. No. Instead, Cal Poly is targeting white students because of the color of their skin, *discriminating* against white students because Cal Poly doesn't like their skin color.

That's racism, plain and simple. Targeting somebody based on the color of their skin—no matter what color that skin is—is racism.

Yet the Left calls this perverted philosophy *fair*. The radical Left calls this racial discrimination aimed at white people *justice*. The radical Left calls this version of America *utopia*.

I call it hell.

We've established that we want to avoid that. We've proved that the radical Left is waging a quiet insurgency in our society to implement their fundamentally different vision for America. We can see it for ourselves in the insane policies they push in state governments and on college campuses. We understand the strategy of the radical Left is dependent on tearing down the social fabric of our nation, which they do by targeting the cultural cornerstones of family, education, and religion.

The bill we discussed in Chapter 1, California's AB-2943, could have made it illegal for Catholic teachers to teach kids the Catechism, since the Catechism calls individuals with same-sex attraction to chastity,[10] and the language in AB-2943 would have made it illegal to engage in any practice that seeks to change somebody's "behavior or romantic feelings" toward another person of the same sex. That "practice" is not limited to the counselor's office. It could apply to the religious-ed classroom at a Catholic church, too.

In previous chapters, we've discussed "how-to" tactics to parry with radical leftists in conversations so that we don't fall prey to their rhetorical tricks. We've outlined the basics of what we believe as conservatives and how we can champion those principles even in the face of tricky questions from radical leftists that are intended to trap us in our own values.

But something is still missing.

We agree it's critical to know *why* we believe what we believe because knowledge is power, right? We know that part of understanding "why" is simply learning how to frame the argument—the rhetorical tricks. All well and good. But even rhetorical tricks are useless if we don't have the fuel to fill the rhetorical engine. So what next?

This all leads me to the point of this chapter: *How* do we know what we're talking about?

Don't worry—it doesn't require a Ph.D. in economics or a law degree, conversion from ISIS, or experience living in a communist nation. Acquiring this knowledge doesn't entail decades of service in the U.S. government or a career in the military. (Although any of the above certainly wouldn't hurt.)

How to know what we're talking about is something anybody and everybody can do.

It simply requires…books.

Below is a collection of books that have helped me know what I'm talking about and understand the *why* and *how* behind the policies I support and defend on my show every night. This is neither a complete list (my editors strong-armed me into whittling my original 235-book list down into a chewable 50-ish book starting point), nor is it the only route to gain the knowledge you need to be more educated than the Left. It's simply (part of) the list I used.

This is why I picked these 50-ish books. I will use a flow chart for illustration.

Religion → right and wrong and justice → philosophy → human nature → history → the fundamentals → what they believe → what we believe → issue-specific reads

Religion. I'm a practicing Catholic. I'm open about my faith on my show because my political views are informed neither solely by my moral and religious beliefs nor solely by the secular practicality of the policy, but rather by the combination of both...and that is completely irrelevant here. (Didn't see that coming, did you?) Regardless of your personal religious beliefs or mine, the fundamental definitions of **right and wrong and justice** in our nation are informed by the Bible and Judeo-Christian teachings. Whether or not you believe in God or Jesus, you ought to understand what they taught in order to understand the building blocks upon which our nation was built.

That brings us to **philosophy.** Some of the greatest minds in recorded history grappled with the same questions we do. What's the right thing to do? What is the purpose of life? What *is* life? What is justice? What is the purpose of government?

It's impossible to understand philosophy fully without some sort of grasp of universal **human nature.** It's fascinating to study human nature because no matter where you're from, no matter your educational background, no matter your family history or the culture or era in which you grew up...every person on this earth feels hungry. And sleepy. And angry. And happy. And craves human interaction and love. At some point in their life, at least, no matter their circumstances.

That brings us to **history,** which is nothing more than the application of human nature in real world situations (both good and bad). Hence the wisdom of "history repeats itself." Well, of course it does, since human nature remains the same, constant throughout time and culture. Imagine then what we can learn if we study history—exactly how certain behaviors and laws and certain political, religious, and social policies impact people and nations.

Then we have government here in the United States. **The fundamentals** of which are based upon the above study of history, human nature, philosophy, justice, and religious and moral values. We will see in this the application of universal truths and inherent rights formed into a fallible but inspired form of human government.

And that brings us to **what they believe,** since evidently the radical Left has drawn different conclusions than we have from history. Likewise, at the core of their political philosophy, the Left holds different moral values from the Judeo-Christian values that America was founded on and in which we as conservatives still believe. It's critically important that we know why *they* believe what they believe, too.

Of course, the purpose of all this study is so we know why we believe **what we believe** . . . right and wrong, justice, human nature, and history, how those principles apply to our governmental structure, and finally, how all of that forms the basis for our policy positions on specific issues. These are **issue-specific reads.**

Let's get started at the beginning.

■   ■   ■   ■

Religion

The book: the Bible

Why read it: *GQ* magazine published a list of "books you don't have to read" in April of 2018, and the Bible was one of those books. According-ing to the pretentious upstart who wrote the *GQ* piece, "The Holy Bible is rated very highly by all the people who supposedly live by it but who in actuality have not read it. Those who have read it know there are some good parts, but overall it is certainly not the finest thing that man has ever produced. It is repetitive, self-contradictory, sententious, fool-ish, and even at times ill-intentioned."[11]

(I'm Catholic. I crossed myself. God have mercy on his soul. Seriously.)

When the radical Left tells us the Bible is foolish, all the more reason to read it, right? The Left claims they are not waging a war on religion, then they encourage people not to read the Bible. (This is it. This *is* the War on Religion.) Talk about foolish.

I once read a book that said, "A fool takes no pleasure in understand-ing, but only in expressing his opinion."[12] Can you guess what book offered that wisdom? (If you guessed Proverbs 18:2, you were correct. That's from the Bible, *GQ*.)

That verse could be the thesis of this chapter. After all, the Bible is the reason why we have laws against murder and rape and kidnap-ping and assault and robbery. It's the reason why we have laws protect-ing liberty and individual rights. It's the reason why we believe in dignity for all people no matter their race, origin, age, gender, sexual orientation, or whether or not they are born. It's the reason why our ancestors came to America, the reason why our Founding Fathers broke away from the tyrant King George, and the reason why our government was formed with the primary purpose of protecting liberty and justice for all.

These values, Judeo-Christian morals, are woven deeply into the fabric of our nation, and how can we understand them without an understanding of Jesus Christ and His life and His teachings? How can we understand *our* lives without knowing that God so loved the world, that He gave His only Begotten Son, so that whosoever believes in Him shall not perish, but have eternal life?[13]

The Bible is foundational to every aspect of my life and the life of our nation, and I highly encourage you to read it.

■   ■   ■   ■

The book: *Rome Sweet Home* by Scott Hahn

Why read it: The second most common question people ask me, after "What books should we be reading?" is how I deal with the hatred and vitriol that's flung at me for being a happy, young, Catholic, conservative female. Full disclosure: The first answer to that question is my family. My husband, my parents, my sisters, and my brother, and my best friends who have been as close as family since we were children are a protective bubble around me that's essentially impenetrable. (Think about one of those invisible electric fences Midwesterners used to keep their dogs in their yard...the fences that zap the pup with an electric shock if he crosses the line...but stronger.)

The second reason is my faith. Jesus says in the Gospel of Mark, "And you will be hated by all on account of My name, but the one who endures to the end, he shall be saved." (Mark 13:13)[14]

Okay, well Jesus said it, right? So be it. I must be doing something right.

If my principles and my deep faith in God weren't rock solid, I frankly don't know how I'd weather the constant assault from the radical Left. Jumping into the cutthroat and sometimes dangerous political melee without the full armor of God is...scary. But with Him, I am protected.

Put on the full armor of God, so that you will be able to stand firm against the schemes of the devil. (Ephesians 6:11)[15]

Think about the proverbial fool who built his house on sand.

"The rain fell, and the floods came, and the winds blew and slammed against that house; and it fell—and great was its fall." (Matthew 7:27)[16]

And now picture a fool—a politico, pundit, or elected official—who enters politics for the sake of fame, argues for the sake of notoriety, and pushes political policies for money and power. See the resemblance?

But the man who built his house on a rock (get the analogy?)…he weathered the beating.

"And the rain fell, and the floods came, and the winds blew and slammed against that house; and yet it did not fall, for it had been founded on the rock."[17] (Matthew 7:25)

In other words, for me it's critically important to know what I believe about my faith so that my words and my actions and my public defense of conservative principles are built on the rock.

Reasons to Believe by Scott Hahn is another wonderful explanation of faith, and in *Hail, Holy Queen,* Hahn explains the Catholic views on Mary, the Mother of God (which so many non-Catholic Christians email me about!) *Mere Christianity* by C. S. Lewis is one of the most reasonable explorations of why it's stupid *not* to believe in God. And *St. John Paul the Great* by Jason Evert is a stunning portrait of the modern Church and the man who helped fell Communism in Europe, Pope John Paul II.

■ ■ ■ ■

Philosophy

The book: *Democracy in America* by Alexis de Tocqueville

Why read it: In July of 2018, Gallup released a new poll showing that a record low 47 percent of Americans are extremely proud to be Americans.[18] Perhaps unsurprisingly, the poll illuminated a big split between Republicans and Democrats. Seventy-four percent of Republicans said they are extremely proud to be Americans, but just 32 percent of Democrats said they felt that way.

Yet the number of legal immigrants in the United States is above thirty-seven million. These are people who were born elsewhere and voluntarily chose to relocate in order to live in our nation. According to the Department of State, the line of people waiting overseas for entrance to our country is approximately five million people. In other words, Democrats in America might not like our country, but people all over the world do!

Democracy in America exemplifies this perfectly. Sometimes it's hard to see the forest for the trees, right? Alexis de Tocqueville was French. He was an outsider. He was young. He came to the United States for nine months and spent the entire visit traveling and observing and speaking with the American people about their relatively new republic built on the radical idea that all men were created equal...and that government exists to protect our rights—not endow them. And what Tocqueville wrote is one of the most thorough analyses of American liberty and our constitutional republic that's ever been written. Read it.

■　■　■　■

The book: *Second Treatise of Government* by John Locke

Why read it: In the Declaration of Independence, Thomas Jefferson's most famous phrase—"life, liberty, and the pursuit of happiness"—was directly derived from Jefferson's study of John Locke and Locke's three inalienable rights of "life, liberty, and property."

In fact, the idea that government should protect the inalienable rights of citizens rather than bestow rights (or privileges) on subjects is the philosophy upon which our government was built. Once you read Locke, you will see his influence in much of Jefferson's writing, and therefore on the makeup of our nation.

■　■　■　■

The book: *The Republic* by Plato

Why read it: Once you get past the first ten pages and acclimate to the style in which it was written (the way the characters talk), it's fascinating. This is the epic dialogue of Socrates in which the ancient philosopher explores the brainy questions: What *is* ideal? What *is* utopia (on Earth)? And how does that apply to government and mankind? Without looking at these questions, it's essentially impossible to know what we're trying to achieve in life and with government, right?

And when we don't know what we're trying to achieve or whom we serve, all manner of vices become our master. (All we have to do is look to the godless Hollywood culture or the Sexual Revolution in the 1960s to see that for ourselves.)

■　■　■　■

The book: *The Nichomachean Ethics* by Aristotle

Why read it: Aristotle was the student of Plato. This book is the perfect companion to Plato's *Republic*. Full disclosure: this book is dense. Read it one chapter at a time or risk brain smokedown.

A Harris Poll in 2017 found that only one out of three Americans say they are happy.[19] Yet happiness is something for which we all strive. Our entire advertising industry in this country is based on people trying to use products or services or medication to make themselves happy, right?

Aristotle unpacks this universal human emotion (and the universal desire for it) by going a step deeper and asking: what is the best thing for man? He then concludes that happiness is the best thing for man, but not happiness the *emotion*. I'll let you discover the rest.

■　■　■　■

Human nature

The books: *For Men Only* and *For Women Only* by Shaunti Feldhahn

Why read them: Human nature is universal. Whether you wear a nose ring in a naked tribal culture in the rainforest or a beanie in a hipster coffee shop in Portland, Oregon, every person on this earth feels hungry. And sleepy. And angry. And happy. Everyone craves human interaction and love, no matter where you're from or where you went to school, regardless of your family history or the era or culture in which you grew up.

These books are two of my favorite books of all time. They're packaged as relationship books, but don't worry. These books are an *extremely* useful study on human nature in general, whether you apply it to a romantic relationship or just to relating to other people—male and female—at your workplace, in friendships, or in your own family.

Shaunti Feldhahn uses survey data to show how men feel when women act a certain way and how women interpret men's behavior. And I kid you not, no matter how expert you think you are at relating to the opposite sex, these books will open your eyes. Get ready to read your own soul. And once you read both these books, you'll see the truth of her surveys everywhere. (Important: read the one about your *own* gender first so you can see how accurate her analysis is. Otherwise, you'll never believe what she writes about the opposite gender.)

I also recommend *The Surprising Secrets of Highly Happy Marriages* by Shaunti Feldhahn, another survey-based commentary on human nature habits, how men and women interpret the same actions and the same words differently, and what makes us happy as humans.

■　■　■　■

The book: *Never Split the Difference* by Chris Voss

Why read it: I couldn't put this one down, which I've heard is the highest compliment you can pay to an author. I've read this book multiple times—some parts more than multiple times. It's a template on how to win arguments and negotiations. I've read tons of books like this, but this one is different. This guy is a former FBI hostage negotiator. He relies on…you guessed it…universal human nature in all his tactics. Every time I've used the tactics in this book, I've won the argument. It's a quick read, too.

■ ■ ■ ■

The book: *Pride and Prejudice* by Jane Austen

Why read it: What's the first line of this outstanding work of fiction? "It is a truth universally acknowledged...." Also known as: human nature. Jane Austen was a student of human nature. That's why her works are beloved by so many people two centuries after they were first published. We see ourselves in Austen's characters. We see people we love in the people her characters love. We see people we hate in the people who disrupt their lives. We desire our partners to be like Austen's romantic interests. Why is that? The answer: Austen captures the universal truths about us that make us our best and our worst all at the same time.

■ ■ ■ ■

The books: I will categorize this shelf of books with a sweeping generalization: The Classics. *The Complete Works of William Shakespeare* by himself. *The Adventures of Tom Sawyer* by Mark Twain and its companion book, *Huckleberry Finn*.

Why read them: Fiction is food for the imagination and a peek into worlds unknown to us. What can we see in fiction besides human nature? (And there's plenty of that in these book collections...think Tom Sawyer's clever fence-painting scheme.) An opportunity to see situations and experiences different from our own. To feel the impacts of social policies and cultural norms that we wouldn't otherwise *feel*.

For example, take Elizabeth George Speare's *The Witch of Blackbird Pond*, which contains insights both into human nature and into life in the New England colonies and the origins of the tradition of liberty in America.

Fiction is powerful and important. It's an age-old medium to convey messages—political, religious, and social—that impact all of us. I'm not talking about drivel like *Fifty Shades of Grey*. I'm taking about the jewels of literature. Books that remain relevant long after the era in which they were written because of how expertly and compellingly they convey the timeless truths of human nature…to which we relate no matter if we're wearing hoop skirts or cut-off jean shorts.

■   ■   ■   ■

History

The book: *John Adams* by David McCullough.

Why read it: This is another book that *GQ* magazine listed as "you don't have to read anymore." I'd be lying if I said it doesn't give me some measure of satisfaction to recommend books the radical Left is afraid for you to read.

This book is fat. It's long. It's detailed. It's *so* good.

If you turn on any cable news channel, within approximately five minutes you'll hear some bloviating radical leftist whining about "how divided" our nation has become. (Blame Trump, you dolt! is essentially their ultimate point.) This cliché complaint shows us exactly how ignorant of history the radical Left truly is. Read *John Adams*. Learn about the radical divisions that pervaded the founding of our nation. The anger. Animosity. Hyperbole. Fear. Insults. It was a battle between liberty and tyranny, between the self-interest of the few and the freedom of many.

■   ■   ■   ■

The book: *The Letters of John and Abigail Adams*

Why read it: The correspondence between Adams and his wife personalizes the founding of our nation and the infant years of our brand-new republic. From the attacks on the man himself, John Adams, to his unwavering stubbornness when it came to standing up for the principles he believed to be right and moral, these letters provide insights into both human nature and history.

■ ■ ■ ■

The book: *Marine Sniper: 93 Confirmed Kills by Charles Henderson.*

Why read it: Sergeant Carlos Hathcock should be a name every child knows. Hathcock was a hero, a U.S. Marine, and a "regular, everyday American." He is one of the deadliest snipers in U.S. military history, serving during the Vietnam War in the height of the action. The story is a personal one, a biography of the man, and a view of the Vietnam War through the eyes of those who fought. That's important. The consequences of political decisions at home in Washington, D.C., are evident in this book, and it's not the lives of the politicians who made those decisions that were on the line. It was men like Carlos Hathcock.

■ ■ ■ ■

The book: *Spy Handler* by Victor Cherkashin.

Why read it: This is a Cold War Soviet spy book and it's a true story...but told from the perspective of a Soviet spy, rather than an American spy. Cherkashin was the handler for some of America's worst traitors—Aldrich Ames of the CIA and Robert Hanssen of the FBI. There's a smidge of Soviet politicking in there, but it's a fascinating look at the other side. Know thine enemy, right?

Moscow Station by Ronald Kessler is another great Soviet-era spy thriller. A true story, not a novel, showcasing exactly what the other side—the Socialists—were trying to achieve, and what the U.S. did to defend our liberty. In Russia. It's a thrilling read.

I Pledge Allegiance by Howard Blum is a third perspective. *Spy Handler* covers the Soviets. *Moscow Station* covers the Americans. *I Pledge Allegiance* covers Americans who betrayed our nation and turned into Soviet spies. Soak up the history; enjoy the electrifying adventures. Revile the traitors. Love America.

■ ■ ■ ■

The book: *Night* by Elie Wiesel

Why read it: Full disclosure—I had a very difficult time reading this book. It's graphic and it's other-worldly (not in a good way). This is a true story, all the more shocking and horrifying because it is true. Elie Wiesel survived the Nazi concentration camp Auschwitz as a teenager, but his family and eleven million other people did not. Elie watched his father die, crying out to Elie for help, but Elie was frozen by fear of being noticed by the camp guards and ignored his father's dying pleas.

I got an upset stomach reading this book. What happened in Germany during the reign of Adolf Hitler will only be an aberration in history if we study what led to the rise of Nazism and stop it before it starts in our nation or any other nation in the world. Because make no mistake—if we don't learn from history, we will repeat it.

■ ■ ■ ■

The fundamentals

The books: the Declaration of Independence and the Constitution of the United States of America

Why read them: Because the radical Left haven't. And if they have, they haven't understood them.

After President Trump nominated Judge Brett Kavanaugh to the Supreme Court to replace retiring Justice Anthony Kennedy, MSBNC's Katy Tur asked on air on her show, "Based on where Americans stand on the issues, Americans have really moved in a much more progressive direction over the years. Do you think it's appropriate to continue to take such a strict originalist view of the Constitution, given it's 2018 and not 1776?"[20]

(Who wants to tell Katy the Constitution was not written in 1776? Anybody? Anybody?)

This is an example not only of how badly the radical Left wants a progressive judicial activist seated on the bench of the highest court in our land, but also of the utter ignorance of the Left on why our Constitution was framed the way it was framed.

Liberty never goes out of style. Freedom is timeless. It doesn't matter if it's 1789 or 2018—the self-evident truth that all men are created equal and endowed by their Creator with certain unalienable rights, among these life, liberty, and the pursuit of happiness…that was, is, and always will be true.

That's the beauty of our founding documents.

In any case, the other timeless aspect of our Constitution is that if we the people decide we don't like part of our Constitution, we can change it. (They're called "amendments" for a reason.) We don't have to ditch the whole thing if we recognize that slavery is a violation of human rights or that women have the same right as men to vote. We simply amend what is already written.

And the beauty of our Constitution is in the language—broad and all-encompassing. There's a reason our Founders said "the right to bear arms" and not the "right to bear muskets" (as we discussed in Chapter 4).

Similarly, the First Amendment protects our right to free speech and freedom of the press, whether it's a quill and parchment or the Internet (something I doubt even Benjamin Franklin—for all his forward thinking—could have conceived in his wildest imagination).

The Constitution was written to be timeless and to apply to changing times…but guess what's not changing? Human nature. The nature of man is both universal and constant, and the way in which our Constitution was written protects man from man and man's rights from government usurpation—no matter the era.

■　■　■　■

The book: *The Federalist Papers* by Alexander Hamilton, James Madison, and John Jay

Why read it: Confused about a certain phrase in the Constitution? Wonder why the framers of the Constitution formed our government in the very specific way that they did? Question whether a different provision would have worked better in how we make our laws, or why we have three separate branches of government, or why we are a republic and not a democracy, or why our Congress suffers partisan gridlock? Wonder no more—every single minute detail was hashed out between the framers and argued publicly before the people in *The Federalist Papers*.

In other words, if ever there is a disagreement about the interpretation of parts of the Constitution or the intention of the Founders, one of the parties involved in the debate did not do their homework. Because all the answers lie in *The Federalist Papers*.

■ ■ ■ ■

The books: *A Debt Against the Living* by Ilan Wurman and *The Law* by Frédéric Bastiat

Why read them: Be forewarned—these are two of the nerdiest books in this chapter. But both rank in the top five best political philosophy books I've read.

The Law talks about the basis of a free society, why it's necessary to live in a nation of laws, and what underpins the idea of justice.

A Debt Against the Living—the most energetic book, by the way, on interpreting the Constitution that I've ever read—persuasively presents an airtight case for originalism, which is judicially interpreting the Constitution the way it was intended by the Founders and framers. Both books are must-reads.

■ ■ ■ ■

What they believe (more on this in the next chapter).
The book: *The Communist Manifesto*
Why read it: I've read this book about five times. I reread it again this year, and I was struck by how the tactics and the arguments for

Communism proposed by Karl Marx are shockingly similar to the arguments and tactics being used by the radical leftists in the Democratic Party today.

Marx says the best way to overthrow capitalism is to erase the class structure. The radical Left tells us the only *fair* way to do business is to spread the wealth around—until there is no "disparity" between the richest and the poorest.

Marx discards the stability and influence religion plays in our society and in our history. The radical Left actively tries to eliminate the influence (and existence) of religion in our culture.

See the shocking similarity?

I could go on and on. It doesn't matter if you read this book in high school or college. It's a super short read and worth rereading.

■　■　■　■

The book: *Rules for Radicals* by Saul Alinsky

Why read it: Know thine enemy. If you know the tactics used by the radical Left to advance their agenda, you will recognize them when they are used. When you recognize the tactics used, you can more easily disrupt them. When you disrupt the tactics, the radical Left are less successful in advancing their agenda.

Rules for Radicals is the playbook of the radical Left. (And fun fact: Alinsky gave a shout-out in the first pages of his book to Lucifer. The Devil.[21] Scary, right?)

Hillary Clinton wrote her college thesis on Saul Alinsky and his tactics.[22]

Barack Obama started his political career in the home of a domestic terrorist, Bill Ayers, who lived the tactics of Alinsky to the extreme.[23] Obama also taught a class at community-organizing workshops in Chicago that could have been titled "Alinsky 101."[24] It was an introduction to Alinsky's agitation tactics.

Read the book and you'll see the tactics everywhere in Democrats' rhetoric, campaigning, and overall political strategy (and that isn't a compliment).

■   ■   ■   ■

The book: *Don't Think of an Elephant* by George Lakoff

Why read it: This book is an extraordinary peek into the mind of the radical Left. Lakoff lays out exactly what they believe on policy, not just politics (that is, not just opposition to Trump).

Also read *The Political Mind* by George Lakoff. He's far, far left. And he's a good writer.

■   ■   ■   ■

The book: *The Handmaid's Tale* by Margaret Atwood

Why read it: Groups of women dressed in blood-red prairie dresses with white bonnets on their heads followed behind Vice President Mike Pence at events across the country leading up to the midterm elections. Their message: Republicans are going to turn the United States into the Republic of Gilead—the fictional nation formed after the U.S. falls, per the storyline of *The Handmaid's Tale*. Because Pence is faithful to his wife and avoids being alone with other women. Obviously. And because he's pro-life. Duh.

This book starts with an utterly stupid premise suggesting that if Republicans take political control, then women—"handmaids"—will be forced to bear children at the hands of oppressive men. And to wear red prairie dresses with white bonnets. Hence the attire of the Pence protesters.

This book is frustrating. It's disrespectful to people of faith. And it's entirely ignorant of Christianity, conservatism, and the political policies that Republicans actually champion. So watch out. Prepare to be annoyed. It's also juicy, clever, and easy to keep reading from the first page to the last without putting down the book.

And the reason I'm including it in this chapter is because it's a great peek inside crazy feminists' minds. This is actually what they think. It's nuts.

■   ■   ■   ■

The book: *Lean In* by Sheryl Sandberg

Why read it: I don't agree much politically with Sheryl Sandberg. That's exactly why this book is so valuable. Much of the subject matter in this book transcends politics. (Not all of it. I don't think Sandberg is correct about legislating equal pay. And the "seventy-two cents on the dollar" narrative is a whole bunch of baloney.) But the fact that the premise of the book is non-political, yet it shows the thought process Sandberg takes to arrive at a political conclusion—and a liberal political conclusion, at that—is extremely useful. Sandberg is an incredibly successful businesswoman. I liked this book a lot.

■   ■   ■   ■

What we believe

This builds on all of the above. What we believe is a manifestation of right and wrong, justice, human nature, history, and how they apply to practical policy platforms we champion as conservatives.

These are issue-specific reads.

The book: *Hillbilly Elegy* by J. D. Vance

Why read it: Nobody who's lived it has ever written about the white working class before in this way, or about how their unique life experience impacts how they vote. White working-class Americans feel forgotten. What an awful human emotion. When you get a peek into Vance's life, you'll know why.

(Also, while my childhood experience was very different than Vance's, every place he describes in his book, I recognize. I grew up about fifteen minutes away from Vance in suburban Ohio right outside Cincinnati.)

Why did the white working class reject Hillary Clinton—who claimed she was a champion for the working man—and instead embrace President Trump? The answer lies within this book.

■　■　■　■

The book: *Things That Matter* by Charles Krauthammer

Why read it: This is a fantastic book. You'll learn one hundred new vocabulary words, but it's an easy read because it's set up in vignettes or essays (a compilation of his columns through the years). Krauthammer was wrong about abortion and when life begins to have value enough to be protected by the law, but this book is wonderfully insightful and funny.

Krauthammer also had an incredible life story. In medical school he was paralyzed from the waist down by an accident in which he dove into a shallow swimming pool and broke his neck. He continued with medical school from his hospital bed, graduated, and became a doctor and a leading psychiatrist at Massachusetts General Hospital before turning to journalism and political commentary. He was one of the brightest minds of his generation, and a beacon of what it means to live life with hope and succeed—regardless of tragedy.

■　■　■　■

The book: *The Conservative Heart* by Arthur Brooks

Why read it: Hillary Clinton claimed she championed the working class. Then she said she hadn't driven a car since 1996[25] and was "far removed from the struggles of the middle class."[26]

Bernie Sanders promised students they wouldn't have to pay for college, and if they had any outstanding student loan debt Uncle Sam would pay that off through taxes on the vilified Top 1 percent. (Meanwhile, Bernie owns multiple houses.)

Alexandria Ocasio-Cortez—the Democrats' favorite young socialist who upset the fourth-ranking Democrat in the House, Representative

Joe Crowley—said everybody is entitled to free housing, free health care, free college, a free job, and a free paycheck.

There's so much politicking in our country when it comes to poverty (and the votes of the lowest income citizens in our nation) that we forget the moral imperative to *solve* the issue of poverty. Arthur Brooks in *The Conservative Heart* lays out practical solutions to ending poverty in our country—in a book that's quite interesting (not boring like a lot of policy books can be).

Brooks's *Road to Freedom* and *Poverty in America and What to Do about It* are good companion reads. His ideas are tried and tested. And they work. Why aren't we implementing them across the board?

■　■　■　■

The book: *Stonewalled* by Sharyl Attkisson

Why read it: Great, great book. *Stonewalled* reads like a thriller…but it's all entirely true. Investigative journalism, government spying, and corruption…Sharyl discovered that the government had hacked into her laptop to plant classified information on her computer in an effort to frame her. All because the Obama administration was terrified about what Sharyl's stellar reporting was about to expose. (Hint: the Fast and Furious scandal.) The government *spied* on her. And then they stonewalled her investigations into who hacked her laptop. Highly recommend reading. You'll never think of government bureaucracy the same way again. And that's a good thing.

■　■　■　■

The book: *Reagan's War* by Peter Schweizer

Why read it: Did you know Ronald Reagan had his first taste of fighting Communism when he was an actor in Hollywood? Did you know Reagan was the *only* actor to cross the Communist-inspired picket line after Hollywood went on strike? Reagan's fight against

Communism started almost a half century before he entered the Oval Office.

This book tells the whole story of the formation of Reagan's views on Communism. It's fascinating and illuminating. Before "Mr. Gorbachev, tear down this wall," Ronald Reagan told John Paul II that he was put on this earth to defeat Communism. That's a pretty heady claim to make to the pope.

And Reagan designed his strategy to defeat the Soviet Union himself. This book shows you exactly how and why.

■　■　■　■

The book: *Clinton Cash* by Peter Schweizer

Why read it: Follow the money and you'll find the truth, right? The Clintons have done a diabolically intricate job of hiding the receipts from years of doing business with the world's worst people. Hillary and Bill Clinton have made bank off dictators and thugs, and they have exploited tragedy and poverty and the AIDs epidemic...all in an effort to line their own pockets with cash.

It's hard to believe until you see the proof. This book is the proof. No longer can Democrats scoff, *Those are wild accusations you're hurling at Hillary.* This book is the evidence that Hillary sold favors at the State Department in exchange for cash flowing to her husband in obscene quantities.

■　■　■　■

The book: *Extortion* by Peter Schweizer

Why read it: Ever wonder how politicians get so filthy rich serving in Congress when their salaries are under two hundred thousand dollars per year? How do they accumulate millions? These politicians are no "millionaires next door." (Fist bump if you catch *that* book reference.)

We always say "politicians are bought off by special interests"—and that's true. But what if our politicians operated like...the Mafia? What if it's the politicians who are *extorting* special interest groups? Making lobbyists pay up before the politicians consider or advance any kind of bill or cast any vote?

This is what I mean. Imagine a politician. Her name is Senator X. Senator X is fictional. When a Supreme Court justice announces his retirement and it's time for the president—he's also fictional—to nominate a new justice, Senator X picks up her fictional phone and tells an abortion lobbyist who wants to meet with her to make sure she's on their side that sure, she'll meet with them...but weren't they going to make a small donation to her? Then Senator X probably calls a pro-life lobbyist who wants to talk to her about the importance of protecting life that she'd be happy to meet with them...but her fundraising needs just a little boost. Again, this is fictitious. It's also simplified. But what if our entire Congress was run under that premise? That every time there is gridlock...it means Congress is shaking down lobbyists for money?

Then we have *Secret Empires*, also by Peter Schweizer. This is where the Mafia analogy really comes to life. The families. How are the dumb kids of politicians so darn rich and successful? Could it be because it's legal for the children of U.S. politicians to do business with private businesses tied to foreign governments—which have interests that just so happen to coincide with the votes of the politician whose children they are making rich?

Read and see. You will never look at Congress the same way again, nor will you ever view gridlock the same again. It will all make sense, and it's chilling.

■   ■   ■   ■

The book: *The Truth about the Black Lives Matter Movement and the War on Police* by Ron Martinelli

Why read it: This book comes from a law enforcement perspective, not a political perspective, which is an interesting take on the Black Lives Matter movement. (A movement, as you recall, that started on a lie...a lie told by the radical Left accusing Officer Darren Wilson of murdering Michael Brown in Ferguson, Missouri, in cold blood. That is false. Even the FBI says they have proof Brown was attacking Officer Wilson before Wilson shot him. But I digress). This book, written by a forensic criminologist who analyzes many crime scenes of police-involved shootings, reveals who the founders of BLM are—three lesbians radicals—what their goals are—a Marxist America—and why they've picked an assault on police as their means of starting a revolution.

This is not a long read; it's not written particularly glamorously (that's my polite way of saying the value here is the content, not the writing style), but it's informative.

■   ■   ■   ■

The book: *Courting Disaster* by Marc Thiessen

Why read it: Is enhanced interrogation torture? Was it unnecessary and evil? Or was waterboarding necessary and relatively humane compared to actual torture? (Hint: our servicemen and women historically have been required to undergo waterboarding as part of their training in certain areas of the military.)[27] Once you read this book and see inside the world of the CIA, Al Qaeda, and Gitmo...once you get a glimpse inside the minds of the actual terrorists who want to kill us...you won't ask that question anymore. You'll know the answer.

Thiessen lays out the proof—as only the speechwriter for President Bush with access to the highly classified information can—that the enhanced interrogation program implemented after the September 11, 2001, terror attacks prevented another such attack. Without the waterboarding and other enhanced techniques, Thiessen contends, our country would have been attacked again. Isn't that the most important consideration of them all? Highly recommend. Fact-filled and fascinating.

Then we have *Enhanced Interrogation* by James E. Mitchell. Mitchell is the man who interrogated Khalid Sheikh Mohammed, the mastermind of the 9/11 terror attacks. Mitchell spent hundreds of hours with the terrorist who plotted the strategy to attack the U.S. with jetliners. Mitchell paints a picture of the day-to-day life in the CIA black sites where the world's worst terrorists were housed, interrogated, and waterboarded and details how they were interrogated and what subsequent plots for attack were disrupted because of those interrogations.

Both Thiessen and Mitchell debunk many of the claims in *The Dark Side* by Jane Mayer (also a great read...I always advocate for reading what the other side has to say). Many of the inaccurate claims by Mayer are still echoed by Democrats today.

■　■　■　■

The book: *When Harry Became Sally* by Ryan T. Anderson

Why read it: I feel like this one should be read simply based on the pun-tastic title. But the content is solid, too.

Remember in Chapter 3 that we talked about the judge in Cincinnati, Ohio, who stripped custody of a seventeen-year-old girl from her parents.[28] The teenager claimed she was transgender and wanted to transition to a man (and demanded everyone call her by a boy's name and use male pronouns when referring to her). She wanted to take puberty-suppressing hormones to begin her transition. Her parents said no. They told the judge that their daughter suffered from diagnosed gender dysphoria and that they did not believe the best treatment for her medically, scientifically, or spiritually was to transition to a man. She would have to wait a few more months to turn eighteen and make that decision herself. Because of this, the girl was threatening suicide.

As we discussed, the judge removed the girl from her parents and gave custody to her grandparents, who agreed to facilitate the girl's transgender transition.

Yet the judge never cited the statistics that show upward of 80 percent of the time, children under eighteen who suffer from gender dysphoria grow out of it when their parents don't facilitate transition. Scientific studies show that a majority of the time, gender dysphoria is just a phase in children. But the judge usurped the parental rights of these people anyway and allowed a seventeen-year-old child with a diagnosed mental disorder to dictate her own life-altering plastic surgery.

Dr. Ryan T. Anderson breaks down the actual science behind gender dysphoria. He encourages compassion for people suffering from this unimaginable burden, but presents research often ignored by the Left and the mainstream media—and even the mainstream medical community—about the risks of "transitioning" via irreversible surgeries and hormone treatments.

This book is everything you need to know about the facts of the transgender movement, and it is written in such a compassionate way. (That's why the Left hated it so much.)

■　■　■　■

The book: *Gosnell: The Untold Story of America's Most Prolific Serial Killer* by Ann McElhinney and Phelim McAleer

Why read it: Read this book in small doses. It's the hardest book I've ever read. In fact, it made me sick to my stomach while I was reading it. The pro-abortion lobby and the radical leftists who are bought off by the pro-abortion lobby nearly tripped over themselves telling voters that Dr. Kermit Gosnell, the abortionist who was convicted of killing babies and women (and keeping severed baby feet in jars in his office as "souvenirs"), was not representative of the abortion industry as a whole. Gosnell was not, the radical Left told us, a regular abortionist. He was disgusting and deranged and inhumane. The latter is certainly true.

But were the abortions performed by Kermit Gosnell any different from the abortions that kill almost a million unborn babies in America ever year? Was the brutality and the blood really that dissimilar to "regular" abortion? The radical Left was terrified you would ask that question…and then answer it. So they stifled press coverage of the trial of the most prolific serial killer in our nation's history. This, after the government officials responsible for oversight of such facilities knew what Gosnell was doing and covered up for this killer for decades. This is a traumatizing and true read, and you'll never think of abortion the same way after you read it.

■　■　■　■

So, there it is. The whole list (minus the other two hundred books I ruthlessly cut, thanks to an editor who shall not be named). Think of this as a starting point. Once you're read these books, you'll know where to go next. You'll be inside the head of the radical Left. You'll know *why* you believe what you believe. You'll understand the context of our history, our country, the Judeo-Christian morals on which our country was built (and on which our system of law and justice was created), you'll have a grasp of human nature and its universal constancy throughout different eras and cultures in our world, and you'll begin to apply all of the above to specific political issues we face in our country today.

With that ammunition, you won't be susceptible to the tactics of the Left—whether they be rhetorical traps, guilt, trick questions, phony accusations, or simply talking points that seem difficult to debunk. Armed with knowledge, you'll know *why* we believe what we believe and why we as conservatives cannot sacrifice our principles simply for the sake of "compromise" with the Left. Because at the end of the day the Left doesn't want compromise; they want their radical, leftist ideology imposed on we the people, no matter what.

That's what we'll talk about next.

Part 3

What They Believe (and Why They're Wrong)

Chapter 8

Facts Liberals Ignore

The radical Left tells us there is an epidemic of murders with assault rifles in our nation. Did you know only 3 percent of homicides in our country are committed with rifles (and even fewer with semi-automatic or "assault"-style rifles)?[1]

The Left tells us that voter fraud is virtually nonexistent, and therefore we don't need to enact protections against it. Did you know that according to a university study, 14 percent of non-citizens—who are therefore ineligible to vote in our nation—self-report that they are registered to vote?[2]

The radical Left tells us that if the top 1 percent paid their "fair share" in taxes, we could have free stuff. Did you know that even if we taxed the top 1 percent at a 100 percent tax rate for an entire year, that wouldn't pay off even the outstanding student loan debt in our country, let alone fund free college or pay for universal healthcare?[3] (The Left is counting on you *not* knowing those numbers.)

Liberals don't like facts. They assume you don't *know* the facts. This chapter contains all the facts and figures and data and statistics you need to call out the radical Left on their fictitious claims.

■ ■ ■ ■

In February of 2018, Dick's Sporting Goods announced they would no longer sell so-called assault rifles or sell any firearm to any person under the age of twenty-one.[4] The store revealed they planned to destroy the assault rifles they had in their stores already. The reason they gave: if refusing to sell so-called assault weapons saves just one life....

First of all, this is a stupid argument. If only one life could be saved by prohibiting children from going outside in the front yard by themselves because then they won't be near the street or risk being hit by a car, would we do that?

If only one life could be saved by banning McDonald's since the garbage they serve is so catastrophically damaging to people's health, would we do that?

If only one life could be saved by outlawing stiletto high heels since that one time a psycho woman murdered a man with the pointy heel, would we do that?[5]

(Dear God, don't give the radical Left any ideas.)

You get the idea. The Left's claim about banning assault rifles in an effort "to save just one life" is equally dumb.

Fictitious claim: There is an epidemic of murders with assault rifles in our country!

Facts liberals ignore: False. This claim can be broken down on multiple levels and proven false with data. Let's start with the FBI statistics from the year 2016.

During 2016, there were 15,070 homicides committed in our country. 11,004 of those 15,070 homicides were committed with a firearm.[6]

Of the 11,004 firearm-related homicides in our country in 2016, handguns accounted for 7,105 (64 percent), shotguns accounted for 262 (2.3 percent), and rifles accounted for only 374 (3.3 percent). (So-called "assault rifles" are a subset of that 3.3 percent.)

Or look at it this way. Of the 15,070 total murders in the U.S. in 2016, 656 were committed with people's hands and feet. That's 4.4 percent of total murders where the murderer killed his victim by using bare hands. Compare that to how many murders were committed with a rifle: 2.5 percent. Nearly twice as many people were killed with hands and feet than with a rifle (and don't forget, a rifle doesn't mean an "assault rifle").

The radical Left ignores those facts.

Clearly the Left's paranoia about assault rifles is based on their anti-gun agenda, not on FBI crime statistics. We can see this for ourselves when we look at the numbers.

In March of 2018, the radical Left staged a protest called "The March for Our Lives." They advertised the rally as a memorial for the seventeen students and teachers killed in the shooting at Marjory Stoneman Douglas High School in Parkland, Florida, but that was false advertising. Instead, the Left used the platform to push radical gun control measures, with one student saying, "when they [Republicans] give us that inch [on gun control] we will take a mile."[7]

In other words, the Left stopped hiding their anti-gun agenda. Now they are telling us to our face: we want to ban your guns.

They blame their anti-gun agenda on the "epidemic of gun violence." They blame the weapon for the murders and pretend they want to enact unconstitutional gun control "if it will save even one life."

But the radical Left ignores the facts. Firearms are used eighty times more often to save a life than to take a life in our country.[8] In Texas, concealed carry permit holders have a lower crime rate than police officers.[9] And schools are safer now in regard to gun violence on campus than they were twenty years ago.[10]

The point is that any time a radical leftist tells you guns make you less safe, they're ignoring the data that prove them wrong. In fact, more legal concealed carry gun ownership reduces the crime rates.[11] According to an analysis of FBI statistics, states with concealed carry laws reduced their murder rates by 8.5 percent, reduced rape rates by

5 percent, reduced aggravated assaults by 7 percent, and reduced rob-
beries by 3 percent.[12]

It's hard to argue with the facts, isn't it? Unfortunately, that doesn't
stop the Left.

■ ■ ■ ■

In 2013, the University of Colorado at Colorado Springs released
an advisory on campus telling students how to defend themselves from
sexual assault. The school counseled female students to deter attackers
and potential rapists by...urinating on themselves. To gross out the
rapists, apparently. Then if peeing your pants doesn't work, the advisory
encouraged women to say they were menstruating or had a venereal
disease. If that still doesn't work, maybe vomit.[13]

The outrage over this horrendous policy was swift and warranted.
The advisory itself was posted during Colorado's debate about banning
firearms on all college campuses. (You know, because posting a sign
that says "No Guns Allowed" is the best way to keep criminals from
committing crimes: *Come attack us! We don't have any guns to stop
you!* Criminals typically follow the law, right? Obviously not.)

Fictitious claim: Gun-free zones keep people safe!

Facts liberals ignore: False. The radical Left ignores the fact that 98
percent of mass shootings in the United States in the past sixty years
have occurred in areas where firearms are prohibited.[14] (A.k.a. gun free
zones.) Think about the most hideous examples of mass shootings in
recent years. The shootings that have drawn the loudest cries of "gun
control" from the Left.

Parkland, Florida. Gun-free zone. No guns allowed in that high
school. Not even the Physical Education teacher Coach Aaron Feis, who
was a certified security guard.[15] He died protecting his students...because
he wasn't allowed to carry his firearm.

Pulse Nightclub in Orlando, Florida. Gun-free zone. Not even concealed carry permit holders were allowed to arm themselves in that
establishment, per state law.

Santa Fe High School in Texas. Gun-free zone.

Virginia Tech. A college. Gun-free zone.

Sandy Hook. An elementary school. Gun-free zone.

Sutherland Springs. A church. Gun-free zone.

San Bernardino, California. A holiday party in an office building. Gun-free zone.

The list goes on and on. The radical Left continues to push a dangerous policy that makes innocent people sitting ducks to criminals who know their easiest shot at getting away with rape, murder, or mass shootings is committing that crime in an area where nobody *else* is armed. And the radical Left ignores the facts.

■　■　■　■

In fact, the Left points to Australia: Australia did it right! After the Port Authority massacre, Australia confiscated firearms, and they haven't had another comparable mass shooting since!

(You remember from Chapter 4. This is the argument we might use if we're thinking like a liberal. Unfortunately, we'd be wrong.)

Fictitious claim: Australia's gun confiscation worked!

Facts liberals ignore: False. There are more firearms in Australia now than before the "buyback" program. In 1996, there were 3.2 million firearms in circulation in Australia. By 2015, that number was up to 3.77 million, despite the government forcing law-abiding citizens to turn over their firearms for destruction.[16]

The firearm homicide rate in Australia did decline after the 1996 confiscation; that's technically true. But it declined at much the same rate as it was already declining at before the government took away citizens' firearms.[17] (In other words, the gun ban had no statistical impact on this declining rate.)

The firearm suicide rate likewise dropped following the gun ban, but at the same time the overall suicide rate dropped at a greater rate than the firearm suicide rate.[18] In other words, again, no statistical correlation between the gun ban and this declining rate.

In fact, America's firearm suicide and homicide rate declined during this same time period, but America wasn't confiscating guns; we were manufacturing firearms at a record pace.[19]

And that brings us to the heart of the matter. Following the 1996 gun confiscation in Australia, the violent crime rate in Australia skyrocketed. Sexual assault, kidnapping, manslaughter, and robbery (armed and unarmed) increased directly after the government confiscated people's means of self-defense.

The crime rates of most of those categories of violent crime remain higher today than before the gun ban.[20]

But the radical Left ignores these facts.

■　　■　　■　　■

The radical Left ignores evidence of crime (or the potential for crime) in our country, too.

In July of 2018, the city of San Francisco began to register illegal immigrants to vote in the 2018 midterm elections. (This is different from allowing illegal aliens allowed to serve in state government–appointed positions in California, which we discussed in Chapter 1.) In this case, the Left said these non-citizens wouldn't be allowed to cast a ballot in the state elections or the federal elections (since federal law prohibits non-citizens from voting in state or federal elections.) But these illegal immigrants and non–U.S. citizens were registered to vote in local school board elections, per a 2016 ballot initiative in San Francisco.

Just the local school board elections. Not federal elections.

Right.

A San Francisco City supervisor named Sandra Lee Fewer said, "As a parent myself and a former member of the SF Board of Education, it's critical that the voices of all parents are at the table, particularly those that have historically been denied a voice in the process."

But another city supervisor named Norman Yee was more honest: "We want to give immigrants the right to vote."[21]

And there you have the truth about the agenda of the radical Left. Make no mistake, the Left is pulling out all the stops to circumvent federal law (which prohibits non-citizens from voting) and exploit vulnerabilities in our voting infrastructure (such as a lack of voter ID) in order to give illegal immigrants a vote. They do this because when illegal immigrants vote, studies show illegal immigrants vote for Democrats.[22]

Fictitious claim: Voter fraud is rare and insignificant and therefore not worth spending taxpayer money to investigate!

Facts liberals ignore: How do we know how much voter fraud is committed every election if we don't investigate?

The San Francisco example is one of a hundred similar circumstances where the opportunity for widespread voter fraud exists. Illegal immigrants and non-citizens could easily take advantage of the law and vote in a presidential election. How many actually cast fraudulent votes? We don't know, because we don't study it.

But there is ample data to show the need to investigate voter fraud because the opportunity certainly exists for any lawless persons to exploit.

For example, two professors at Old Dominion University and one professor from George Mason University collaborated on a study in 2014 that found in the 2008 and 2010 elections that 14 percent of non-citizens self-reported that they were registered to vote.[23] (That's self-reporting too, which makes the real number likely even higher.) Keep in mind, even if you are a legal permanent resident, a legal immigrant, you are prohibited under federal law from voting. Citizens of the U.S. are the only eligible voters in our state and federal elections.

Nonetheless, these professors found 14 percent of non-citizens said they were registered voters. How many of those registered actually cast a vote? We don't know. How many potentially could have cast an illegal vote? Well, let's do the math. For the sake of simplicity, let's ignore the legal residents (non-citizens) for a moment and just deal with illegal immigrants.

There are approximately twelve million illegal immigrants in the United States at any given time.[24] Fourteen percent of twelve million = 1.6 million. Therefore, potentially 1.6 million illegal immigrants who reported they were illegally registered to vote could have cast an illegal vote. That's a whole heck of a lot of votes. More than enough to swing any election, up to and including a presidential election.

So, that's one area: the potential for illegal immigrants to cast votes. Then, we have dead people. According to a Pew study from 2012, there are 1.8 million deceased Americans still registered to vote who haven't been purged from the voter rolls.[25]

The point is, did all of these people fraudulently cast votes in our elections? Of course not. But the potential for abuse is there. We can see for ourselves how many other government institutions are the victims of fraud. Our own government reports on the huge number of fake ID papers circulating among illegal aliens, including fake (or stolen) Social Security numbers and forged birth certificates.

Between 2012 and 2016, according to the Immigration Reform Law Institute, thirty-nine million Americans potentially had their Social Security numbers stolen or used by illegal immigrants.[26]

In 2010, 1.8 million illegal immigrants worked with Social Security numbers that did not match their real names. An additional seven hundred thousand obtained Social Security numbers with forged birth certificates.[27]

The radical Left ignores all these facts. But these facts debunk the faulty leftist narrative that voter fraud is so scarce we don't need to waste money studying or investigating it.

■   ■   ■   ■

In fact, most of the problems with voter fraud and the potential for voter fraud could be fixed with voter ID laws. But if we say the phrase "voter ID," Democrats melt down like the Wicked Witch of the West faced with a bucket of water. Their false claim about voter ID goes as follows:

Fictitious claim: Voter ID causes voter suppression of minorities!

Facts liberals ignore: False. According to a Reuters poll, 2 percent of white people don't have government-issued IDs compared to 3 percent of black people who don't have government-issued IDs.[28] Do the math. Given the total number of white people in our country and the total number of black people in our country, 2 percent of white people is a much larger number than 3 percent of black people.

But the radical Left ignores that fact. The Left also ignores the fact that people of all races need government-issued IDs to do all sorts of everyday activities in our country. You need a government ID to drive a car, buy an M-rated video game, get a job, fly on an airplane, open a bank account, apply for a credit card, secure a loan, buy alcohol or cigarettes, sign up for food stamps, apply for Medicaid, file for unemployment, rent a car, get married, adopt a pet, rent a hotel room, obtain a fishing license, buy a cell phone, pick up a prescription, or donate blood. The list goes on and on.

But nobody on the Left complains that minorities are "suppressed" trying to buy cigarettes because of ID laws, do they? No, they don't.

Besides, this is a fundamentally insulting argument from the Left. Why does the radical Left assume minority voters are somehow less capable of obtaining a government ID? Does the Left think people of color are stupid?

In the case of voter ID, nearly every state with such laws also has provisions to pay for free IDs for people who cannot afford one.[29] So, the radical Left doesn't have any valid argument there.

In regard to voter suppression, the facts destroy the leftist argument. A study by the University of Missouri found voter turnout in Indiana *increased* after the state passed a voter ID law.[30] There is no statistical proof that voter ID suppresses or prevents voters of any demographic from turning out to vote.

In fact, here's a story liberals love to ignore. The state of Alabama has some of the toughest voter ID laws in the nation.[31] Yet during the 2017 special election for Senate to replace former attorney general Jeff

Sessions, African Americans made up 29 percent of the voters, according to the *Washington Post*. Why is that significant? Because African Americans make up only 26 percent of the population there.[32] That means minority turnout was higher percentagewise than white turnout.

If voter ID laws deter minorities from voting, why was there such incredibly high turnout of black voters in Alabama when the state has such strong voter ID laws?

The radical Left ignores those facts.

Finally, the majority of non-white voters support voter ID, according to a Gallup poll.[33] But of course, the radical Left still thinks they know best—better than minorities know themselves. Isn't that insulting?

■ ■ ■ ■

It's not just black Americans the Left exploits. The radical Left exploits women, too.

Every year on approximately April 10, the gate of the feminist castle opens wide, and over the pink-knitted drawbridge tumble scores of oppressed and angry feminists. Hair flying, scowls bristling, buzzing rabidly, this mob of victimized daffodils races to sniff out their male prey....

See, according to the radical Left, women in America have to work until April 10 every year to catch up to the amount of money that men make in the previous year.

Fictitious claim: The gender pay gap: women earn seventy-nine cents on the dollar compared to men.

Facts liberals ignore: This claim is a load of statistical nonsense. Here's why.

There *is* a gender pay gap. That part is true. Men do typically make more money than women every year. That's statistically accurate. But the *reason* men typically make more money than women is not because men are misogynistic beasts actively seeking to reduce women to slave labor by refusing to pay them a fair and equal salary.

Not at all.

The gender pay gap is not because of sexism. The gender pay gap is primarily due to the different choices men and women make in their lives and their careers. The numbers back this up.

Let start with career choices. Different jobs pay different salaries, right? Careers like teachers and nurses pay less than fields like engineering or finance. And women are more likely to choose careers like teaching or nursing, while men are more likely to choose engineering or finance. In other words, of their own volition, women tend to choose lower paying jobs than men do.

This starts as early as college. Of the ten lowest-paying college majors, six are majority female.[34] Of the ten highest-paying college majors, only one is majority female, and eight of those ten are 80 percent male.[35] Obviously, that factors into salary.

So choices about college majors and choices about career fields set up the difference is salary. Then we have the actual hours worked. According to the Bureau of Labor Statistics, men who work full time work on average three hours longer each week than women who work full time.[36] Naturally, that factors into salary.

Women also leave the workforce more often than men (for reasons such as maternity leave), which impacts experience. Women choose to work part time more often than men. Women choose flexibility in our jobs more than men—to prioritize our families. Women are less likely than men to accept overtime or business trips. And women choose jobs with shorter commutes than men do. All of those choices impact salary, particularly in the long run when the cumulative effects of all those choices build up.

But the radical Left ignores these facts. The Left also ignores the data showing that if women choose the same college major as men, choose the same career, make the same life choices as men, work the same number of hours as men, commute as long as men, travel for business as often and as willingly as men—then women will make, on average, the same amount of money as men.[37]

For example, if you're a chemical engineer, you'll earn approximately the same as your male counterparts. If you work as a social worker or an architect, you'll earn on average more than your male counterparts in those positions,[38] (if the experience between the men and women employees is equal).

In other words, no sexist-pig-man is sitting at his desk cutting seventy-nine percent off a one-dollar bill to give to a woman because she's a woman. That's as ridiculous as it sounds, and the data back it up.

If you look at the salary data before choices—particularly choices about family—are factored in, the pay is not equal: the salary data *favors* women. In 98 percent of America's largest 150 cities, single women under thirty earn 8 percent more than their male counterparts.[39]

But the radical Left ignores those facts.

■   ■   ■   ■

The Left ignores the facts about the cost of Obamacare, too. Let's sketch it out. (And yes, this is satirical.)

Picture a radical leftist. Let's call him Hogan. Hogan loves Obamacare. Hogan is on his parents' insurance at age twenty-six. Hogan does not have a job because he's exploring himself by attending #resistance rallies (as long as he wakes up early enough to get there by noon). But Hogan thinks Obamacare is great. He acknowledges that there are still some problems with the law (he's open-minded like that), some areas that need improvement. (Most of the things that need improving are President Trumps' fault, am I right? So says Hogan.) But Hogan says Obamacare did what no health care system in the U.S. had ever done before—provided health care to everybody who could ever want or need it at an affordable cost.

Fictitious claim: Obamacare is universal coverage at an affordable cost!

Facts liberals ignore: This is statistically false. A report from the IRS in the spring of 2018 showed that a majority of the people paying the

Obamacare individual mandate penalty instead of purchasing the health insurance are low-income and middle-income Americans.

In 2017 there were 6,665,480 households in America that chose to pay the Obamacare penalty. This totaled $3,079,255,000 paid in fines. Ninety-two percent of these households (6.1 million households) earned less than $75,000 that year.[40]

In other words, the government forced low-income and middle-income Americans to fork over three *billion* dollars as punishment for not buying the health insurance plan government bureaucrats think people should buy...all the while claiming Obamacare gave people universal coverage.

These people paying the penalty are some of the nearly twenty-eight million Americans who still don't have health insurance, despite Obamacare. You remember them from Chapter 4.

How many times did the Left promise Obamacare would be universal coverage for all Americans? Almost as many times as the number of Americans who still don't have health insurance.

There are still nearly twenty-eight MILLION Americans who don't have health insurance coverage even after Obamacare was signed into law.[41] (And this number was before President Trump and Republicans in Congress nixed the individual mandate in the tax reform bill of December 2017. Just wait until the next round of numbers is released. Then we'll see how many Americans *really* didn't want "comprehensive" coverage. They were just forced by Obama to buy a product they didn't want. But I digress.)

Besides the almost twenty-eight million Americans who are still uninsured despite the "universal" access to health care promised by the Left, thirty million Americans were kicked off their health care plans due to Obamacare regulations because the plans weren't "good enough."[42]

But the radical Left ignores those facts.

Even if we play the liberals' game and accept the faulty claim that twenty million gained coverage (remember, we debunked that claim in Chapter 4), that still leaves a ten million-person deficit when we factor in the thirty million who lost their plans because of Obamacare regulations. So, it's a lose-lose for Democrats. (Not such a "big f—ing deal" now, huh, Joe Biden?)[43]

Clearly, the radical Left doesn't care about the facts.

■   ■   ■   ■

The radical Left doesn't care about scientific facts either. Every time there is a hurricane or a tornado or a flood or a drought or any other type of devastating severe weather event, the Left trips over themselves trying to be the first to inform us superciliously that this tragedy is due to climate change.

You silly little hillbillies. If only you had given us more of your money to fight climate change, you wouldn't be watching a funnel cloud suck the barn right off your farm!

But the Left is ignoring the facts.

Instead, the Left hijack emotions in order to push their agenda. (We'll talk more in Chapter 11 about how the Left use the liberal mainstream media to frame issues and events in order to play on our emotions and push a radically leftist agenda. It's remarkable. Once you know the bias framework the Left use to frame all their stories in an effort to get you to feel and think a certain way about the issue, you'll recognize each element of the framework every time you see it. Stay tuned for that.)

Fictitious claim: Severe weather, hurricanes, and tornados are caused by climate change! At the very least, climate change makes these severe weather disasters worse!

Facts liberals ignore: False. Look at the scientific data.

Since 1950, wildfires have plummeted by 15 percent, according to analysis by climate expert Bjørn Lomborg.[44]

According to the United Nations, droughts in North America have become less frequent, less intense, and shorter.[45]

The frequency of devastating tornados has declined since the 1950s, according to data gathered from the National Oceanographic and

Atmospheric Administration (NOAA).[46] In fact, 2012, 2013, and 2014 were all record low years for tornado counts in the United States.[47]

Until Hurricane Maria in 2018, according to NOAA, the United States saw eleven straight years without a Category 3+ hurricane. This was the longest streak since NOAA began tracking this data in 1851.[48]

To put it bluntly, there is no scientific evidence that the radical Left's version of climate change has increased the severity or the frequency of severe weather events. Even the United Nations Intergovernmental Panel on Climate Change admits it, according to scientist Roger Pielke Jr.[49]

But the radical Left ignore these facts, which isn't surprising. Historically, since the Left began to push their radical environmentalist agenda, their claims and predictions have been horribly false. Thirty years after many of the hysterically dire predictions were first proclaimed, we can see the prophecies were wrong.

Take polar bears, for example.

In 2018, we still have polar bears, contrary to predictions from the Left. In fact, the *National Geographic* photographer who took the viral photo of the polar bear dying from climate change in 2017 admitted that they knew the bear was not dying from climate change, but they were comfortable with the false narrative because it helped them push their agenda.[50]

The first line of the accompanying video from *National Geographic* was, "This is what climate change looks like." There were 2.5 *billion* people who watched the poor polar bear struggling to walk and find food. Contrary to the narrative from *National Geographic*, conservative experts said at the time that they believed the bear was simply dying from old age and disease, but the Left scoffed and called conservatives climate change deniers. Now we know for a fact that the claim from *National Geographic* and the Left was a lie.

Moreover, the polar ice caps are still floating, despite the predictions that they would be melted by now. The fifty million climate refugees the Left expected to be fleeing the Pacific Islands and flooding the West are still nowhere to be seen.[51] Entire nations that were supposed to be wiped

off the map (according to the Left) are still here.[52] The Himalayan glaciers are not on their way to be melted by the year 2035, as the Left has
prophesied.[53] California shows no signs of being flooded with inland
seas.[54] (I'm in California as I write. I am not sitting in a row boat. I
checked to make sure.) The Netherlands are still habitable. Children still
know what snow is. The Arctic still enjoys ice in the summer.

And no, we have suffered no devastating increases in raging fires,
crippling droughts, or powerful storms due to climate change. Those are
the facts. But the radical Left ignores the facts.

■ ■ ■ ■

The Left told us in 2017 that if Republicans passed their tax reform
bill and repealed the Obamacare individual mandate, people would die.[55]
Yet we're still alive. The Left told us if we pulled out of the Paris Climate
Accords, people would die.[56] Yet we're still alive. The Left told us if we
repealed Net Neutrality, people would die.[57] Yet we're still alive. They
warned if Judge Brett Kavanaugh was confirmed to the Supreme Court,
we would die.[58] Nonetheless, last time I checked, we're all still alive. And
yet the Left persist with their fear-mongering, warning us that if we don't
raise the minimum wage to a fifteen dollars an hour "living wage," you
guessed it…people all across our nation won't have enough money to
buy food to stay alive![59]

Fictitious claim: A fifteen dollar per hour minimum wage is a necessary "living wage."

Facts liberals ignore: Wrong. Hiking the minimum wage doesn't do
what the radical Left says it will do. A fifteen dollar per hour minimum
wage doesn't help low-income workers. Here's why.

San Diego, California, lost four thousand restaurant jobs since they
hiked the minimum wage. (And that's a hike to just eleven dollars and
fifty cents, not all the way to fifteen dollars.)[60]

In Seattle, low-wage workers have been hurt (they make less money
per month) since the minimum wage hikes took effect.[61] Small business

owners have been forced to shut down their shops, citing the minimum wage hikes as the reason they can't afford to stay in business.

In Minnesota, people have suffered significant job losses and stagnant growth since the state began hiking the minimum wage in 2014. In fact, employment of youth in Minnesota dropped by 9 percent (thirty-five thousand workers) in the past three years since the wage hike took effect. Compare that to neighboring Wisconsin, where young employment grew by 10.6 percent (forty-three thousand jobs) over the same time period. Unsurprisingly, Wisconsin doesn't have the same crippling minimum wage laws as Minnesota.[62]

In other words, small businesses can't afford to pay their employees outrageous minimum wages, so the businesses are forced to lay off workers. That hurts people. Fifty percent of workers in the private sector in America are employed by small businesses.[63]

The idea of a "living wage" itself is a flawed premise. According to the Bureau of Labor Statistics, in 2016 only 2.2 million hourly paid workers in America earned wages at or below the federal minimum wage. That's 2.7 percent of all hourly paid workers in our country.[64]

Second of all, in 57 percent of poor families in America, nobody has a job.[65] It's a false narrative to suggest that most families in poverty are working minimum wage jobs. In truth, most people in poverty don't work at all. And hiking the minimum wage actually hurts these people in poverty—making it harder for them to get any job, which makes it more difficult to break the cycle of poverty.

In fact, the Federal Reserve did a study about the impact of raising the minimum wage and found that if we raise the minimum wage to ten dollars and ten cents per hour (not even the fifteen dollars per hour the radical Left is advocating for), only 18 percent of the increase in income would go to families in poverty. Thirty-two percent of that increase in income would go to families in the top half of the income distribution because lots of minimum wage workers are secondary earners in high-income families (moms working part time and teenagers working summer jobs).[66]

Workers in poverty actually suffer from minimum wage hikes as consumers too, because products become more expensive as companies pass on to consumers the increased cost of minimum wages they're forced to pay.

But the radial Left ignores these facts.

■   ■   ■   ■

Instead, they tell us that if the wealthy, the top 1 percent, paid their "fair share" in taxes, we wouldn't suffer from such stark income inequality and we could fund the progressive welfare programs Democrats have been promising to their voters: free healthcare, free housing, free college, free guaranteed income, and so forth.

Fictitious claim: If the top 1 percent paid their fair share of taxes, we could have free stuff.

Facts liberals ignore: This is just bad math. As we have already seen, even if we taxed the top 1 percent at a 100 percent tax rate for a year (perhaps about as long as it would take rich people to stop working if they weren't making a profit, yes?), the entire pile of money wouldn't pay off the outstanding amount of student loan debt in our country (which currently stands at over $1.5 *trillion* dollars).[67] Yet the radical Left wants to tell you they can pay off those student loans...and pay for free college. And free healthcare. And free housing. If we would just make the rich pay more taxes.

But the radical Left doesn't like math. So they ignore these facts.

Actually, the idea that the rich don't pay their "fair share" of taxes is false, too. The so-called top 1 percent, whom the radical Left loathes so fearsomely, collectively earn approximately 20 percent of all dollars earned in America. Yet, they pay 39 percent of all taxes in our country.[68] That doesn't sound very fair to me.

But the Left ignores that fact, too. The Left ignores the estimates from libertarian and non-partisan think tanks like the Urban Institute and the Mercatus Center at George Mason University, who predict "universal healthcare" would cost upwards of $32.6 trillion in the first ten years.[69]

Vox, a notoriously left-leaning media outlet, priced the democratic socialist promises coming from the likes of Bernie Sanders—free health care, free college, free housing, free jobs, free guaranteed income.

The price tag amounted to $42.5 trillion just to start these programs![70]

Single-payer healthcare: an estimated $30 trillion.

Guaranteed minimum wage jobs: $6.8 trillion.

Free college: $807 billion. (And that doesn't even take into account the $1.5 trillion in outstanding student loan debt the Left has promised to pay off with these socialist programs.)

But the radical Left ignores these facts. In fact, Senator Bernie Sanders called such estimates biased and wrong—but he refuses to tell us how much he thinks his plans would cost. Perhaps we won't find out until we check our bank account to see if Bernie extracted *his* definition of "fair share."

Meanwhile, the Left will continue to ignore the data and the facts.

■　■　■　■

These are just some of the most popular liberal talking points. We hear these claims from the Left during debates, in campaign ads, on Twitter, or if we accidentally turn our televisions to MSNBC. This isn't an exhaustive list, but you get the idea.

And here are a few more.

According to the Left, it's "Islamophobic" to say "radical Islamic terrorism." After radical Islamists bombed the Ariana Grande concert in Manchester, England, in May of 2017, killing twenty-two innocent people, the Left told us that terrorism has no religion. The religion of Islam is peaceful, they say. It's bigoted to associate Muslim terrorists with Islam, the Left proclaims.

Fictitious.

According to a Pew Research Poll from 2006, 35 percent of young Muslims in the U.K. believe suicide bombings can be justified.[71] A poll from the Federation of Student Islamic Societies in 2005 shows that one in five Muslim students residing in Britain would not report a fellow Muslim planning a terror attack.[72] Expand that group beyond students, and according to a 2016 poll from ICM Research, two out of three Muslims in Britain say they would not report a terror plot to the police.[73] This same poll found that 25 percent of British Muslims don't think that a Muslim has an obligation to report terrorists to the police.[74]

Another ICM poll, from 2006, found that 20 percent of British Muslims sympathize with the terrorists who killed fifty-two people in London on July 7, 2005, in the name of Islam.[75]

A BBC Radio survey in 2015 found that 45 percent of British Muslims indicated that clerics who preach violence against the West represent "mainstream Islam."[76]

In America, a Pew Research poll from 2007 found that 26 percent of young Muslims in the U.S. believe suicide bombings are justified.[77] A 2015 survey from the Polling Company found that 19 percent of Muslim-Americans say violence is justified in order to make Sharia the law of the land in the U.S. Twenty-five percent of Muslim Americans say violence against Americans in the U.S. is justified as part of the "global Jihad."[78]

But the radical Left ignores these facts.

Instead, they tell us Muslims are persecuted in America. The Left claims hate crimes against Muslims have skyrocketed since President Trump announced his campaign for the presidency. Again, fictitious.

In fact, many of the so-called hate crimes against Muslims the liberal media reported (and blamed on President Trump) have turned out to be hoaxes.[79] In December 2016, shortly after the election of President Donald Trump, a teenaged Muslim girl in New York reported to law enforcement that she was harassed on the subway by men who tried to remove her hijab and yelled "Donald Trump!" at her.[80] This story made national news. It was exactly what the radical Left was hoping would happen. They had made so many false allegations of racism against

Donald Trump, and they wanted their lies to be proved true. Too bad for the Left—the teenaged Muslim girl confessed to authorities weeks later that she had fabricated the hate crime because she had broken her curfew and didn't want to get in trouble. She was arrested for making the false report.

In August of the same year, a Muslim professor at a college in Indiana claimed he was attacked and received anti-Muslim hate mail.[81] This professor later pled guilty to a misdemeanor for lying to the cops about this fabricated hate crime. It never happened.

Months before that, in June of 2016, a mosque had been set on fire in Iowa in an apparent hate crime against the Muslims who worship there. At least, that's what the headlines said—until authorities found security footage showing a young Muslim woman pouring lighter fluid into the carpet and setting the fire. There was no hate crime, just a hoax.

In Louisiana, a Muslim teenager told police she had been attacked by two white men who stole her wallet.[82] The teenager told police the men yelled slurs at her and stole her hijab. She said one of the robbers was wearing a Trump hat. Turns out, the Muslim girl was lying. The attack never happened.

All lies.

Furthermore, according to the FBI 2016 hate crime report, the fastest growing category of racial hate crimes in our country are crimes committed against white people for being white.[83] And the number of hate crimes against Jews is always the top category of religious hate crimes. There are twice as many hate crimes committed against Jews in America every year as there are hate crimes against Muslims.[84]

But the radical Left ignores those facts.

Almost any talking point we hear from the Left directly contradicts the facts. They're simply counting on you not knowing the facts.

Ignorant voters are compliant voters. That's what the radical Left wants you to be. But if you learn the facts, the numbers, the data, and the scientific research, then the entire structure of the Left's platform, built on a lie, comes tumbling down.

Chapter 9

A Comprehensive List of Liberal Lies—and How to Call Them Out

If we don't learn our history, we will be doomed to repeat it.

The original of that well-known maxim comes from novelist and philosopher George Santayana, who wrote, "Those who cannot remember the past are condemned to repeat it."[1]

The radical Left desperately needs the American people to forget history. Or at least to fall for a distorted and twisted version of the events from our past (in order to draw inaccurate conclusions from the mistakes of our ancestors).

For example, the radical Left loves to tell us that socialism isn't the problem in failed socialist countries. It's simply that no country or political party or authoritarian dictator has done socialism *correctly*. If *we* did socialism, the Left tells us, it wouldn't end in destruction, starvation, oppression, and death like it has in every other country in the history of the world where it was forced on the people. *We'll* do socialism right, the Left says.

A ridiculous claim, right?

We conservatives point to Venezuela as a textbook example of the destructive nature of socialism. As we have seen, Venezuela was once one of the richest nations in South America, but its citizens are now living in abject poverty while their economy collapses in on itself. Even Venezuelan dictator Nicolás Maduro admitted in August 2018, "The production models we've tried so far have failed, and the responsibility is ours—mine and yours."[2] He was talking to his own political party.

So, the Left conveniently denies that Venezuela is a socialist nation. *That's* not socialism, they say. I once observed on Twitter that Venezuelans are starving thanks to socialism. Liberal trolls immediately descended on me, scoffing, labeling me as an "enormous moron" for insinuating that Venezuela's collapse was related in any way to socialist policies.

Open a dictionary.

The definition of socialism is a government seizing control of the means of production and distribution in its country.

Now look at the history of Venezuela. In the past twenty years, the socialist government of Venezuela has seized more than fourteen hundred businesses from the private sector and placed those businesses under government control.[3] It's no coincidence that the government expropriating private industry and engaging in price tampering led to economic disaster. It's also no coincidence that during this downfall, the government took away any number of other liberties from the people—including the people's power over their legislature and courts—and violently stifled dissent from the citizens.

That's called socialism.

The Left, however, says it's moronic to call that socialism.

Both statements cannot be true; therefore, at least one is false.

The point is, this is what the Left does. It's called revisionist history. They twist and distort historical fact until it's unrecognizable. The new, butchered version of history that emerges is full of cosmetic changes of the kind that rendered Bruce Jenner into Caitlyn Jenner.

This revisionist history is taught as truth, propagated in talking points, repeated often enough until liberal lackeys believe the lies they tell. (What's that principle of marketing? A consumer needs to see an advertisement five to seven times before she acts on it? Once an advertise-ment—or a lie—has been repeated seven times, it becomes truth in people's minds.) This is what the Left is counting on.

The platform of the Left is rife with inaccurate historical facts. In fact, the Left has built their platform on a foundation of twisted reality. Without these faulty premises (which are easily debunked), what do they have left? (Spoiler alert: nothing but hot air.)

That's why the Left rewrites history. They need fuel to power their agenda, otherwise logical people will reject their insane big government ideas.

Or you can think of revisionist history like this:

Revisionist history is like the bank robber who was worried about leaving fingerprints in the vault at the bank. So he burned off his fin-gerprints. That way no matter what he touched, the police wouldn't be able to dust the smudges, run his prints through their database, identity him, catch him, arrest him, and convict him.

That's what the Left does to history. They send important historical events into the operating room and burn off history's fingertips so we don't recognize the prints they've left behind.

The problem is, burning off fingerprints doesn't exonerate the rob-ber. He still committed the crime; it just makes it harder to find him after he makes his getaway. That's the same with history. Mutilating historical fact doesn't change the reality of history. It just makes it harder for us to peel back the layers of the onion and find the truth.

That's what this chapter is about. The five big historical lies peddled by the Left. Once we debunk the lies of revisionist history, the Left's entire nar-rative and the reasons they tell people to vote for their policies crumble.

So, let's take a look at the pre-op x-rays. The fingers before the prints were scorched off. Let's start with the Left's favorite narrative: accusing all Republicans of being racist.

Historical lie: The Republican party is the party of racism.

Now, this argument is patently absurd to conservatives. The party of racism? What are you talking about, Republicans ask. The Republican party itself was formed in Ripon, Wisconsin, in 1854 as an opposition party to slavery.[4]

It doesn't get more anti-racism than that. Abraham Lincoln, arguably the man most influential in securing liberty for black people in America, was a Republican.[5]

The first twenty-one black Americans elected to serve in the United States Congress were all Republicans.[6] (Guess who didn't elect a black congressman until 1935? That's right—the Democrats.)[7]

The first black Republican was elected to the Senate in 1870.[8] (Guess who didn't elect a black senator until 1993? That's right—the Democrats.[9] You could say the Democrats were 123 years behind the Republicans on minority representation in the United States Congress.)

On the flip side, the KKK was originally founded as a club for former Confederate soldiers and quickly evolved to serve the interests of the Southern Democratic Party.[10] The purpose of the KKK as a wing of the Democrats was to terrorize freed slaves and harass Republicans who helped free slaves.

Seems pretty obvious that this narrative from the Left accusing the Republican party of being inherently racist is false, right?

That's where the fingerprint butchering comes into play. The radical Left knows everything I just said about the Republican party is true. There is no nuance to the fact that the Republican party was literally formed as an opposition party to slavery. How could the Left possibly distort that historical truth?

(Don't underestimate the dishonesty of the radical Left. They'll find a way.)

Enter the surgeon.

Oh, this man? He's not the bank robber; he couldn't possibly be. See, the robber you're looking for has fingerprints. The surgeon holds up the hand with the newly mutilated fingertips. *This man has no fingerprints; you must be looking for somebody else!*

So the radical Left twists the history. *The Republican party was formed to oppose slavery? Republicans historically championed the rights of black people in America? Well, yes,* the Left tells us...*but* the *parties switched in the 1960s and 70s—didn't you know that? The Republicans of old (the ones who fought against slavery and fought for equal rights for black Americans) are actually equivalent to the Democratic party now. The Democratic party of old (the ones who invented the KKK and refused to elect black people to Congress for decades)? That's the Republicans now. The parties just...traded places. They changed their labels and reversed their ideology.*

Get it? If the parties switched per this leftist narrative, then it's *Republicans* who historically oppressed black people and *Democrats* who fought for equal rights for black Americans.

This narrative peddled by the radical Left is pure fiction. It's revisionist history.

The radical Left claims this switcheroo occurred starting in the 1960s. The radical leftist narrative goes as follows: The Republicans couldn't win elections in the South, so President Richard Nixon concocted the so-called "Southern Strategy" to win the Southern States. According to this leftist narrative, instead of selling Southern voters on Republican principles in order to win elections, the Republican Southern Strategy was simple: appeal to the racists in the South. *Voilà!* Republicans = racists.

Get out your magnifying glass and bring your fingerprint dust. That whole narrative is a lie.

In fact, the Southern Strategy narrative is composed of several lies. Press the mute button on the Left's rhetoric and look at the historical facts. Dr. Carol Swain, a former law and political science professor at Vanderbilt University, thoroughly debunks this myth.

As Swain points out at PragerU, Republicans actually began to compete in the South in 1928 when Republican Herbert Hoover defeated Democrat Al Smith. (Note: 1928 is approximately forty years before Democrats tell us Republicans started winning Southern states.) Hoover won that election with 47 percent of Southern voters.

In 1952, Republican Dwight Eisenhower won Tennessee, Florida, and Virginia in the presidential election. All Southern states. In 1956,

Eisenhower also won Louisiana, Kentucky, and West Virginia. (This second victory happened after Eisenhower had championed the desegregation of schools in the South.)

So you can see for yourself, if you look at historical facts, that Republican candidates were not only competitive in the South long before the 1960s, but a Republican president won the Southern states twice before this so-called Southern Strategy was ever concocted. That's the first thing.[11]

Then we had the Civil Rights Act in 1964. The House of Representatives passed the bill on February 10, 1964, and the Senate followed suit on June 19, 1964.

Guess who voted to pass the law? That's right—Republicans. Eighty percent of Republicans in the House of Representatives voted in favor. Only 61 percent of Democrats did the same. Eighty-two percent of Republicans in the Senate voted in favor of the bill, while just 69 percent of Democrats did.[12]

The radical Left claims Democrats in the South were so incensed by the passage of the Civil Rights Act that they left the Democratic Party and joined the Republicans. (That argument doesn't make a lot of sense given the vote counts to pass the bill, does it?)

As Dr. Swain also points out, twenty-one Democratic senators voted against the Civil Rights Act—and only one of those twenty-one became a Republican. The remaining twenty continued to serve as Democrats. In fact, those twenty seats didn't switch to Republican seats for another twenty-five years.

Thirdly, Swain points out that President Nixon is the Republican president accused of concocting the Southern Strategy in order to win the South—and yet in 1968, Nixon lost the Deep South.

Then, after this so-called Southern Strategy supposedly took effect (and turned the racist South Republican by appealing to racists), Democratic presidential nominee Jimmy Carter handily won the South in 1976.

In 1992—long after the South had supposedly turned solid Republican because Republicans were appealing to racists—Bill Clinton, a Democrat, won six Southern states.

So when did Republicans actually start dominating in the South? According to historical fact, the GOP didn't win a majority of Congressional seats in Southern states until 1994.

Do the math. That's *thirty years* after the radical Left claims racist Southern Democrats "switched" and turned Republican.

In other words, it didn't happen. The narrative peddled by the Left is a lie. The reason the South eventually turned Republican, according to Dr. Swain, has nothing to do with racism—except for the fact that the defining value of the South was no longer racism. The voters in the South began to focus on other political policies, such as lower taxes and gun rights, and the Republican party best protected those values. So Southerners switched their votes to the Republican party.

Just dust off the smudges left by the bank robber. You'll start to recognize his prints by the fact that all he leaves behind are smudges.

The Left mutilates history to push their radical agenda.

Just look at the outrage from the Left every year on Columbus Day.

Historical lie: *Christopher Columbus committed mass genocide! The colonialist white settlers led by Columbus stole America from the Natives by brutally murdering everybody who didn't have white skin! For shame, white people!*

In fact, as I sit here writing this book, four states and more than fifty-five cities across America (run by Democrats) have replaced Columbus Day with Indigenous Peoples' Day.[13] And that number continues to grow.

Remember from Chapter 5 that we demonstrated how the Left wants to redefine the idea of right and wrong? Instead of right and wrong, they want political correctness. Instead of justice, the Left wants privilege points. Instead of objective truth, the Left wants feelings valued higher than fact.

The Left vilifies Christopher Columbus in order to denigrate America and shame white people in an effort to pass progressive, redistributive, big government policies where government bureaucrats pick winners and losers and certain people are afforded special treatment and opportunities (think: the so-called victims) and others are excluded (think: the so-called oppressors).

We aren't living in a meritocracy anymore, Toto.

This is how the Left imposes their system of privilege points on us. By burning off the fingertips of history and erasing the prints.

The truth is that it's historically ignorant to claim Christopher Columbus was a mass murderer and brutal tyrant responsible for the death of millions of Native Americans (and we'll get to the claims about Columbus enslaving natives in a moment).

First of all, historians estimate the population of North America was approximately twenty million people in 1492 when Columbus first discovered America. Within two centuries, approximately 95 percent of the twenty million were dead.[14] That part is historically accurate. But what killed the Native Americans? What wiped out nearly twenty million people in the space of just two hundred years? How did Christopher Columbus and his men carry out such mass extermination?

The answer to that question is, they didn't. Nearly all of the nineteen million natives who died following the arrival of European settlers were killed by diseases. Smallpox. Flu. Tuberculosis. Malaria. The Plague. Measles. Cholera.[15] You name it. The European settlers brought with them viruses and diseases to which the Natives had no immunities. Those diseases sadly wiped out the native populations.

In fact, a professor at Stanford University named Carol Delaney says most of the deaths came after Columbus's time in the Americas. Delaney says, "They are blaming Columbus for the things he didn't do. It was mostly the people who came after, the settlers. I just think he's been terribly maligned."[16]

In other words, most of the mass deaths happened after Columbus because of disease, and most of the mistreatment of the Native Americans was perpetrated by people who came after Columbus.

In fact, Columbus specifically forbade his men from taking advantage of natives they encountered on San Salvador. In his own accounts of his journeys, Columbus described friendly relations and adopted the son of a chief.[17]

The Left claims they have proof that Columbus was evil,[18] but the document supposedly proving his crimes and bad character was written by Columbus's chief political rival, a man named Francisco de Bobadilla, who hated Columbus.[19] It's as if somebody claimed that Hillary Clinton had written a true historical account of the 2016 election of Donald Trump...

He stole the presidency from me—and it was rightfully mine! I won the popular vote, the people wanted me! I was robbed!

Only, the presidency is won by winning the electoral college, not the popular vote, and Donald Trump did nothing to "steal" the election from Hillary Clinton. Trump beat Hillary fair and square. Because Hillary was a terrible, corrupt candidate with terrible, destructive policies.

See the similarity? The document about Columbus written by Columbus's enemy is itself a piece of revisionist history concocted by a man who wanted to use that disinformation to push his own agenda for his own gain. Fast forward to modern times, and the narrative in that letter also boosts the agenda of the modern Left, so they grabbed hold and ran with it.

It's nothing more than revisionist history from the fifteenth century, recycled by the radical Left five centuries later.

(It's also hilariously ironic that the radical Left condemns Columbus for coming to America to find a better life for his people back home and plundering the Native Americans...you would think using the logic of the Left, the natives would owe Columbus free health care, free housing, and free welfare after he jumped their border and declared residency in their country, right? But I digress.)

It's true that Columbus took natives as slaves. There is no excuse for that. It's unequivocally wrong to enslave another human being for any reason. But the Left misrepresents the historical context of Columbus's actions. The Native Americans were also famous for enslaving each other,[20] and even the pope sanctioned slavery of certain pagans at the time.[21] None of that makes slavery right. It's hideous and immoral. But the Left conveniently leaves out historical context in order to push their radical leftist narrative that Columbus was evil, and therefore white men in 2018 should pay the price.

It's revisionist history and it's a lie.

It's like a kid with chocolate frosting on his face denying that he ate the cake. We know he ate the cake. Denying reality doesn't mean he's not the culprit. It just means he's lying.

The radical Left denies historical reality with lies at every turn.

In order to push gun control in America, the radical Left denies the historical fact that dictators and authoritarian regimes in not too distant history have disarmed their people before subjugating them.

Historical lie: Adolf Hitler didn't disarm his people before the Holocaust.

That's simply false. Before Hitler killed six million Jews, he took their guns away.

We established that fact in Chapter 6. We talked about how history demonstrates why we shouldn't trust governments and how gun registries have served as a precursor to disarming, oppressing, and killing millions of people. That's why the Left doesn't want us to look at history. Now, let's talk about how authoritarian governments morph gun control into tyranny.

Let's look at Germany first. The Germans had already implemented a gun registry before the rise of Hitler in the early 1930s.[22]

Unsurprisingly, when Hitler seized power in 1933, the Nazis used the existing gun registry to identify and disarm Jewish gun owners. The Gestapo issued orders prohibiting Jews from obtaining firearm permits. Hitler also disarmed political opponents and anybody the Nazis deemed politically unreliable.

After Kristallnacht in November 1938, SS Chief Heinrich Himmler dictated that any Jew in possession of a firearm would face twenty years in a concentration camp.

Likewise, in France after the Nazis invaded in 1940, the French people were prohibited from possessing firearms and were subject to the death penalty at the hands of the Nazis if they refused to turn over their firearms to the Germans.

Hitler and the Nazis went on to kill over eleven million people. But first, Hitler disarmed them.

In Cambodia, before the dictator Pol Pot killed two million people, the government took away the people's guns (and their means to self-defense against a murderous dictator).[23]

The Khmer Rouge regime prohibited private citizens from possessing firearms and ordered people to turn over their weapons to the government. The private firearms of the people were then added to the stockpile of the tyrannical government.

The radical Left claims Pol Pot's regime didn't enact any gun control laws. The Left is technically correct. The French had *already* established gun control in Cambodia. Pol Pot and the Khmer Rouge regime then confiscated firearms and prohibited citizens from owning guns. They forced citizens to turn over their weapons, or else die. It's a difference without a distinction.

In Soviet Russia too, before Joseph Stalin killed twenty MILLION people, he took their guns away.[24] In the late 1920s, Stalin enacted laws forcing universal registration of firearms and only allowed hunters to possess weapons (and only then after the hunters obtained permission from the local police department). Then after 1930, the Soviet government conducted mass gun confiscation targeting "socially dangerous elements." In other words, the Soviet government disarmed any populations they believed might resist the Stalin dictatorship and his destructive socialist policies. In particular, the Soviet government targeted the peasant population to force the peasant class to comply with collectivist agricultural policies. Then, once the people were disarmed, Stalin committed his mass genocide virtually unimpeded.

Black people in America during our own history of slavery and racial oppression were likewise not allowed to own firearms. I wonder why. The state of Virginia not only prohibited free black people from owning firearms, but even made it a criminal offense for a black person to be in possession of lead or powder. Tennessee altered their state constitution after a slave uprising to remove the provision that allowed "freemen" to own firearms and changed the language to "free white men." North Carolina's state constitution said the same thing. (In fact, before the Civil War, black Americans in Maryland weren't even allowed to own dogs for fear that they would use dogs as a weapon to rebel against slavery.)[25]

Fast forward to the Jim Crow era in the South. Former secretary of state Condoleezza Rice, who was raised in the segregated South, says her family protected themselves against white supremacists with firearms.[26]

In other words, time and time again as history illustrates for us, gun control, gun registries, and gun confiscation were used by tyrants as tools of oppression to enslave, demean, oppress, starve, abuse, and ultimately kill millions and millions of people. Even in nations like Cambodia, where the gun control laws were already on the books before the dictator ascended to power, the fact that the people had no means for their own self-defense left them vulnerable to abuse, oppression, and ultimately, mass genocide.

It's simply historical fact.

But whenever historical fact exposes the radical leftist agenda to be dangerous, destructive, or deadly, the Left haul out their surgical instruments and begins a complete reconstruction. Burn off the fingertips. Scorch off the prints. Dust off the windowsill. And then shrug your shoulders when the bank teller sounds the alarm that the vault has been violated.

Or let's try another bank robber analogy. I recently read a fascinating article about an *Ocean's Eleven*–style diamond heist that took place in Britain in 2009.[27] The bank robbers didn't cover their faces with the traditional hood or scarf or pantyhose during the assault, even though the diamond exchange shop was dripping with closed-circuit TVs. Why not? Why wouldn't these criminals attempt to disguise their appearance since they were committing an enormously illegal crime? Surely they knew the entire law enforcement power of the United Kingdom would turn out to search for them. The police would hunt them down. Based on their photographs and videos, of course.

Turns out just hours earlier, both criminals had spent the afternoon in the chair of a local makeup artist who specialized in theater arts. The unsuspecting makeup artist completely reconstructed the robbers' appearance to the extent that one robber commented to the other, "My own mother wouldn't recognize me now."[28]

Sound familiar?

That's what the radical Left does with history. They do it with *recent* history too, so we don't recognize what's in front of our eyes.

Take, for example, the Supreme Court ruling on Jack Phillips, his bakery Masterpiece Cakeshop, and Phillips's freedom of religion. Rather than admit the historically accurate facts about religious freedom in our nation, the Left presents revisionist history of an event that occurred just last year.

In fact, the radical Left is so anti-religion (which is the reason they present a revisionist version of the history of religious freedom in our nation), that late night comedian and liberal mouthpiece Jimmy Kimmel resorted to using a homophobic slur against the Christian baker.

You remember the Jack Phillips case. In Chapter 1, we talked about how Phillips declined to design a custom cake for a gay wedding because gay marriage violates his religious beliefs. Thanks to his First Amendment freedom to practice his religion, the Supreme Court ruled in Phillips's favor. But on the very same day in 2017 when the Supreme Court initially agreed to hear Phillips's case, a transgender lawyer in Colorado telephoned Masterpiece Cakeshop and requested that Phillips bake a "gender transition cake." (A cake that is pink on the inside and blue on the outside.) Phillips declined, citing his religious objections, but offered to let the individual purchase any pre-made product in his store. (In other words, to reiterate the important distinction drawn in Chapter 1, Phillips did not refuse service to the trans lawyer because of the lawyer's gender identity. Phillips simply declined to use his First Amendment right to free expression to create art that celebrates something to which he is religiously opposed.)

Fast forward to August 2018, when Jimmy Kimmel responded on late night TV to this second lawsuit against Phillips by saying that Phillips looks like a woman. Kimmel said Phillips spends his days baking flowers made of icing, therefore Phillips's entire job is gay. Kimmel suggested that perhaps Phillips declined to bake that gender transition cake because it would bring to light gay feelings...in Phillips.[29]

In other words, Jimmy Kimmel hurled a homophobic slur at Phillips because Phillips is Christian, and Kimmel didn't want to talk about the history of religious freedom in America. So, he distorted the history of the Masterpiece Cakeshop lawsuit. It's as simple as that.

That brings us to our next historical lie.

Historical lie: The Founding Fathers didn't want religion to influence our government.

Heard that argument before from the Left? *Don't impose your religion on us! Keep it in your house! If you don't subsidize birth control, you're shoving your religious views down our throat!*

Yada, yada, yada.

I have good news for you. That leftist talking point is revisionist history and it's a lie.

There is no line in the Constitution or any of our founding documents mandating that our moral and religious beliefs be restricted to the inside of our own home or in our house of worship.

In fact, quite the contrary. The First Amendment to the Constitution reads, "Congress shall make no law respecting an establishment of religion, or prohibiting the free exercise thereof...."[30]

Let's be clear: our Constitution does not say "free exercise of religion in your garage" or "not outside the boundary of the church parking lot." That is an invention by the Left.

Likewise, the religious freedom clause in the First Amendment does not dictate Congress create no law "based on accepted cultural norms of Judeo-Christian values." The First Amendment says quite clearly that the government can't dictate to you that you must follow a state-mandated religion, nor can the government prohibit you from worshiping the God you choose in the way you see fit (even if the government or other people think it's weird).

In fact, the entire premise of our Declaration of Independence is that all men are created equal and are inherently in possession of rights the government cannot supersede, among those being life, liberty, and the pursuit of happiness—because we are endowed with those rights by our Creator.

Not by the Big Blue Blob. Not in a random explosion of nature. Not because Nancy Pelosi says it's okay to feed the peasants crumbs. We are endowed by our *Creator* with unalienable rights.

That universal truth is based on religious belief, and it's at the core of our nation and our system of law and justice.

When the radical Left claims pro-life Americans should be forced to fund abortions with our taxpayer dollars, or when the Left sues Christians for declining to bake a wedding cake for a gay wedding, they're telling us that we can't use our religious beliefs as a factor in our life decisions. They say that is a violation of the separation of church and state.

That is unconstitutional, illogical—and not what the Founding Fathers intended anyway. Our Founding Fathers knew America would not survive unless the people embraced our Creator, specifically, unless the people embraced Christianity and Judeo-Christian morals.

Let's look at the words from our Founders about religion.

Our Founding Fathers never intended the elimination of religion from the public square (or from our government). One of the first acts of the first Congress was to institute a congressional chaplain and pay him with taxpayer money. With the exception of only one man, all the Supreme Court Justices prior to Justice John Marshall supported the idea that the Supreme Court could invalidate congressional legislation if that act from Congress violated natural law. The Founders actively encouraged Christianity and religion and morality among the people. They did this through government action. (This, of course, is different than mandating religion.)[31]

The Father of our nation, George Washington, declared in his Farewell Address that of "all the dispositions and habits which lead to political prosperity, religion and morality are indispensable supports."[32]

Furthermore, Washington declared in his 1798 Thanksgiving Day Proclamation:

> Whereas it is the duty of all Nations to acknowledge the providence of Almighty God, to obey his will, to be grateful for his benefits, and humbly to implore His protection and favor...I do recommend...the People of these States to the service of that great and glorious Being, who is the beneficent Author of all the good that was, that is, or that will be.... And also that we may then unite in most humbly offering our prayers and supplications to the great Lord and Ruler of Nations and beseech Him to pardon our national and other transgressions, to enable us all, whether in public or private stations, to perform our several and relative duties properly and punctually; to render our national government a blessing to all the People....[33]

In 1789, John Adams said, "Our Constitution was made only for a moral and religious people. It is wholly inadequate for a government of any other."

In 1799, Patrick Henry said, "The great pillars of all government...[are] virtue, morality, and religion. This is the armor, my friend, and this alone, that renders us invincible."

The first chief justice of the Supreme Court of the United State of America, John Jay, said in 1797, "Providence has given to our people the choice of their rulers, and it is the duty, as well as the privilege and interest of our Christian nation to select and prefer Christians for their rulers."

George Mason said, "The laws of nature are the laws of God, whose authority can be superseded by no power on earth."

Clearly, the men who constructed the government of our nation believed that religion had a place in the public sphere and used the government to encourage religious observance.

In fact, the phrase "separation of church and state" is found only once in the writings of the Founders, in a letter Thomas Jefferson wrote to a Baptist Association in 1802 in which he assured them of the government's role in protecting their right to practice their religion. The exact quote: "I contemplate with sovereign reverence that act of the whole American people which declared that their legislature should 'make no law respecting an establishment of religion, or prohibiting the free exercise thereof,' thus building a wall of separation between Church and State."

Jefferson is actually a perfect example of my overall point. Jefferson was by no means a practicing Christian by the standards of any denomination of the religion. Yet he drew the universal truth on which our nation was founded from the fundamental Christian belief in the inherent dignity and liberty of all men.

As you can see, the revisionist history peddled by the Left that the Founding Fathers of our nation created a nation in which religion had no place is simply a lie. If you look at history, you can see that for yourself. There is a critical difference between government mandating religion or outlawing religion (both of which are abuses of government power and a violation of the fundamental rights of people to practice their religion the way they see fit), and acknowledging that our system of law and justice and the morals and principles and the definition of right and wrong on which our nation was founded is decidedly of the Judeo-Christian variety.

This is the strategy the radical Left employ to make their sacred cow issues untouchable. They warp history. They tell us a story about the past that isn't true.

My favorite novel describes a character about halfway through the book. He's a peripheral character. We never meet him in person, though he is spoken about quite a bit. The novel is set in the early 1800s in French *Ouisconsin* in the home of a family of French-Canadian *voyageurs* and backwoodsmen.

The peripheral character I mention is a friend of the family, supposed to be a trapper and trader by the name of St. Paul. Why the name? Because, we are told, this trapper had the rhetorical ability to explain how the blanket he wore around his own shoulders was *not* a blanket of the very same appearance that was stolen just moments ago from the saddlebags of a fellow woodsman. Such rhetorical prowess rivaled that of the saint for whom he was nicknamed (though Trapper St. Paul's holy namesake certainly used his eloquence for a higher purpose).

This is how the radical Left distort history in their defense of *Roe v. Wade*, the Supreme Court ruling from 1973 that prohibits states from outlawing abortion.

Historical lie: Abortion is a constitutional right.

This is false and a perfect example of revisionist history.

Let's start with the Constitution itself. The text of Section 1 of the Fourteenth Amendment reads as follows:

"All persons born or naturalized in the United States, and subject to the jurisdiction thereof, are citizens of the United States and of the State wherein they reside. No State shall make or enforce any law which shall abridge the privileges or immunities of citizens of the United States; nor shall any State deprive any person of life, liberty, or property, without due process of law; nor deny to any person within its jurisdiction the equal protection of the laws."[34]

Roe v. Wade, which prohibits states from outlawing abortion, contends that the Fourteenth Amendment Due Process Clause above—"nor shall any State deprive any person of life, liberty, or property, without due process of law"—somehow contains a right to privacy that encompasses a right to unrestricted, unfettered access to abortion.

In other words, according to the Blackmun ruling in *Roe*, the word "liberty" protects the right of one person to kill another person (as long as the second person is unborn).

Sounds like a stretch, right?

Even a former clerk for Justice Harry Blackmun named Edward Lazarus, who says he is "utterly committed" to keeping abortion legal in the United States, has written, "As a matter of constitutional interpretation and judicial method, *Roe* borders on the indefensible. Justice Blackmun's opinion provides essentially no reasoning in support of its holding. And in the years since *Roe*'s announcement, no one has produced a convincing defense of *Roe* on its own terms."[35]

Yale law professor John Hart Ely (who, like Lazarus, supports legalized abortion) agrees. Ely says, "What's frightening about *Roe* is that this super-protected right is not inferable from the language of the Constitution, the framers' thinking respecting the specific problem in issue, any general value derivable from the provisions they included, or the nation's governmental structure." Ely goes on to say about *Roe*, "It's bad because it's bad constitutional law, or rather because it's not constitutional law and gives almost no sense of obligation to try to be."[36]

In fact, some legal scholars, such as Ramesh Ponnuru, argue that the same Due Process Clause in the Fourteenth Amendment actually gives Congress the constitutional authority at the federal level to outlaw abortion.

Ponnuru writes that the Fourteenth Amendment "requires states to give 'any person' the equal protection of the law, and empowers Congress to 'enforce' that guarantee. The protection against being deliberately killed is the most basic legal protection a person can have, and it is not being provided to all persons. If a state does not offer that protection to persons, Congress may intervene either by forcing states to perform this duty or by stepping in itself."[37]

The radical Left won't hear these arguments. They refuse to debate. They won't allow the conversation. They demean and degrade and hurl accusations of misogyny at anybody who questions the constitutionality of abortion and *Roe v. Wade*.

Roe is settled law, the radical Left contends. *It's precedent*. Therefore, *Roe v. Wade* is untouchable. A sacred cow to the radical Left.

Again, false. Revisionist history. The scorched fingerprints strike again.

Even if *Roe* is settled law, that doesn't make it constitutional.

There is a long history of egregious unconstitutional Supreme Court rulings that were later rightly overturned. In *Dred Scott v. Sanford*, the Court ruled black people were not citizens. It took (ironically to this discussion), the Fourteenth Amendment to overrule *Dred Scott* and guarantee all Americans equal protection under the law. In *Plessy v. Ferguson*, the Court upheld racial segregation. And *Plessy* was precedent for sixty years—a decade longer than *Roe v. Wade* has been law in our nation. Then, *in Brown v. Board of Education, Plessy* was rightly overturned for being the constitutional travesty it was. Just like *Roe* should be overturned for the constitutional travesty it is.

Revisionist history is an oft-used tool in the toolbelt of the radical Left. And it's an all too effective tool, because it's not easy to debunk without research and study. The five historical lies we just discussed are some of the most common peddled by the radical Left on some of their pet issues.

Republicans are racist.

Christopher Columbus committed mass genocide.

Hitler did not disarm his people before he killed them.

The Founding Fathers didn't want religion to influence our government.

Abortion is a constitutional right.

False, false, false, false, and false.

Yet the Left uses these claims to justify their attacks on conservatives, their ongoing war on white men, their efforts to codify political correctness into law, their push for gun control and gun confiscation, their war on Christianity, their intolerance of religious liberty and of any religion practiced in the public sphere, and their worship of abortion at all costs (as long as the cost is paid for by you and me).

When we unravel their claims... there's no historical evidence any of it is true. In fact, we find that the Left has invented fiction about *back then* to justify their agenda *now*. But unless we do our due diligence and studiously dig through the real history of the thing... we risk falling in the radical leftist trap or falling short in debunking the leftist nonsense and leaving other people with no reason to disbelieve the claims coming from a party who scorched off their own fingertips to hide the true history.

Chapter 10

For Every Liberal Position, There Is an Equal and Opposite Contradiction

Every single Democratic talking point I can think of directly contradicts...another Democratic talking point.

(It's almost as if the radical Left cares more about forcing their agenda down our throats by feeding us trite talking points instead of telling us what they really stand for...which makes sense, doesn't it? Since the Democrats stand for nothing but their own political gain. But I digress.)

I call it Newton's most overlooked principle. For every liberal position, there is a hypocritical and obvious contradiction. (I swear, Sir Isaac wrote that himself! Then Sir Isaac asked me to write a comprehensive list of the contradictions and call them out. True story.)

In this chapter, we'll demonstrate the quickest way to punch a hole in the leftist platform.

This is a useful (and easy) tactic to expose the fact that radical leftists built their ideological foundation on sand. No consistency, no underpinning of moral principle, a conglomeration of policies that help advance their ultimate goal—government control.

In other words, the underlying principle of the radical Left is imposing their agenda at any cost. And we can expose that diabolical agenda by laying out the contradictions and falsehoods we see in every liberal argument.

What happens to these leftist arguments when we flip them on their head? (If you're picturing a WWE gif, you're right on the money.) They unravel and implode. The contradictory arguments of the Left are exposed for what they are: a political farce. (And isn't it fun to catch the leftist grifters in their own net? I think that's called self-destruction.)

This is how it works.

Picture two magnets, the north end of one and the north end of the other forced together, touching despite the opposing nature of their similar charges. *Voilà!* the Left displays the phenomenon like a magician on a stage. *They fit! It works!*

Meanwhile, a skeptic in the front row jumps up and points to the white gloves of the magician holding the magnets together. "Take your hand off the magnets," the skeptic orders. Magician White Gloves does as he's told. The magnets spring apart—repelled from each other by natural law that cannot be altered.

The skeptic bows.

The magnets are the arguments of the radical Left—the north end of one magnet (one leftist argument) repelled and contradicted by the north end of the other magnet (another leftist argument)...all the while the magician (the radical Left) artificially forces them together, proclaiming a breakthrough of the natural law that has bound magnets (logical arguments) for millennia.

The magician booms, *"All those who believe are woke!"*

Sound familiar?

Talking point: *We Democrats are the party of science!*

Contradiction: How can the Left claim to be the party of science but also proclaim that some men have uteruses?

This really happened.

On March 1, 2018, Planned Parenthood of Indiana and Kentucky tweeted the following:

Some men have a uterus.
Some men have a uterus.
Some men have a uterus.
Some men have a uterus.
Some men have a uterus.
Some men have a uterus.
Some men have a uterus.
Some men have a uterus.
Some men have a uterus.
Some men have a uterus.
Some men have a uterus.[1]

That's eleven repetitions, in case you were wondering. Because, obviously, repetition makes it true.

I jest. PP's tweet is not true, no matter how many times they repeat it. No men have uteruses.

Planned Parenthood is not talking about hermaphroditic physiology disorders—the tiny, tiny fraction of people born with a rare disorder of sexual development that includes parts of both male and female reproductive organs. They're referring to "trans men"—in other words, women living under the delusion that they are men.

The radical Left claims to be the party of science, but ignores basic biology in an effort to advance their political agenda: destroying the family by decimating gender. (As we discussed in depth in Chapters 3 and 4.)

They claim to be the party of science, yet they tell women born with female reproductive organs, female genitalia, and two X chromosomes that if you *feel* like a man (despite your biology), you *are* a man.

That's not science. That's not reality. That's ideology and delusion.

And those two talking points from the Left add up to one giant contradiction.

Or, as Planned Parenthood might tweet, in order to make it truer:
Contradiction.
Contradiction.
Contradiction.
Contradiction.
Contradiction.
Contradiction.
Contradiction.
Contradiction.
Contradiction.
Contradiction.
Contradiction.

■ ■ ■ ■

Talking point: Donald Trump is an authoritarian dictator!

Contradiction: If Donald Trump is actually an authoritarian dictator, how can the Left advocate for the government to confiscate so-called
assault weapons from the people? (Remember, this so-called dictator is
the chief executive at the head of the government.)

This isn't hyperbole. The Left actually peddles the narrative that
President Trump is a dictator. In August of 2018, a writer for the New
York Times named Michelle Goldberg appeared on MSNBC and called
Trump "a sort of junior player in a bloc of authoritarian countries. He's
part of a bloc that includes Vladimir Putin, [Rodrigo] Duterte."[2]

The host, Katy Tur, responded, "Well, he's not rounding people up
and murdering them without any, you know, due process."

Goldberg retorted, "He'd certainly like to."

To her credit, Tur demurred, saying, "I don't think you can say that
definitively."

So the Left contends that President Trump is on par with authoritarian dictators and wants to round up people and kill them…yet these

same radical leftists cheer for walk-outs at high schools to advocate for the government to confiscate AR-15s from the people.

This one is worse than a contradiction. It's utter stupidity. If the Left truly believes Trump is a dictator (which is completely absurd), why would they want such a dictator to be the only one with firepower?

■　■　■　■

Talking point: Cops are racist!

Contradiction: This is the same as the previous contradiction. If cops are racist, why does the Left want only cops to have AR-15s?

The radical Left tells us cops are racists who target black people "for being black." We can see this narrative for ourselves when we turn on NFL football games. NFL players kneel during the national anthem. They turn their backs on the American flag. Colin Kaepernick even wore socks that depicted police officers as pigs.[3] The Left pushes the false narrative that police officers are racists who systemically engage in police brutality against black Americans. And yet at the same time, the Left argues that only "trained law enforcement" (a.k.a. police!) should have AR-15s.

If cops are racist killers, why would we want only cops to have assault rifles?

(Try asking the leftists that question. Their heads will explode.)

■　■　■　■

Talking point: Republicans are racists! We Democrats are the party that condemns racism!

Contradiction: How can the Left claim their party rejects racism while they refuse to condemn radical leftist hate preacher Louis Farrakhan?

We hear this talking point from the Left every time they're backed into a corner. The radical Left constantly invokes the names of KKK

Grand Wizard David Duke or white supremacist Richard Spencer in a pathetic effort to conflate a smattering of evil, racist losers (known as the alt-right) with mainstream conservatives. (Keep in mind, mainstream conservatives routinely and rightly condemn evil, racist white supremacist ideology.)

Meanwhile, twenty-one Democratic members of the Congressional Black Caucus in the House of Representatives—and even former president Barack Obama himself—have palled around with virulent racist and anti-Semite Louis Farrakhan. More shockingly, these leftists refuse to condemn Farrakhan.

All twenty-one members of the Congressional Black Caucus who invited Farrakhan to their meeting in 2005—and who are still in Congress—were later asked to condemn Farrakhan's racism. They all refused.[4] Farrakhan has called Adolf Hitler "a very great man."[5] Farrakhan calls for the death of white people.[6] Farrakhan blamed the 9/11 terror attacks on Jews.[7] Farrakhan calls Jews termites.[8] Still, the twenty-one Democrats who literally embraced Farrakhan refuse to condemn or disavow him.

How can the Left claim to reject racism when they refuse to disavow the racist Louis Farrakhan? After they've embraced him for so long.

■　■　■　■

Talking point: Donald Trump is racist!

Contradiction: How can the Left hurl unfounded accusations of racism at President Trump while the radical leftists in the Senate refused to confirm a judicial nominee because of the nominee's skin color?

The nominee's name was Marvin Quattlebaum. He was nominated by President Trump. During the confirmation process, Senate Minority Leader Chuck Schumer, a Democrat, said a vote to confirm Quattlebaum was a "giant step backwards" in regard to diversity of skin color on the bench.[9]

(Who's the racist now, Schumer? What happened to judging a man by his character and not the color of his skin?)

Quattlebaum was eventually confirmed by a 69–29 vote. Schumer did not vote in favor.

How can the Left accuse Trump of racism but attempt to block a federal judicial nominee because of the color of the man's skin?

■ ■ ■ ■

Talking point: Refusing to bake a gay wedding cake is discrimination against LGBTQ people!

Contradiction: How can the Left claim that it's illegal discrimination for Masterpiece Cakeshop to decline to bake a gay wedding cake, but also argue that it's not illegal for a coffee shop in Oakland, California to refuse service to cops?

In March of 2018, a hippie coffee collective in Oakland, California, called Hasta Muerte Coffee (Spanish for "until death") refused to serve coffee to a police officer. The café said, "We have a policy of asking police to leave for the physical and emotional safety of our customers and ourselves."[10]

The police officer respected this dictate and politely left the shop. The officer said he hoped to build a better relationship between the collective owners and law enforcement. The radical leftists sent him away anyway.

We talked about Masterpiece Cakeshop earlier in the book. The owner, Jack Phillips, declined to build a custom wedding cake for a gay wedding because gay marriage violates his religious beliefs. But he didn't send the gay couple out of his store because they are gay. He offered them any pre-made item in his shop. He just didn't want to participate in a gay wedding, since gay marriage violates his religious beliefs.

According to the Left, that's unlawful discrimination—but the refusal to serve a cop at the coffee collective was a-okay.

How is it okay for Hasta Muerte to refuse service to cops, but it's not okay for Masterpiece Cakeshop to decline to build a custom gay wedding cake?

. . . .

Talking point: We Democrats champion women! We champion women's autonomy!

Contradiction: How can the radical Left claim to champion women, but at the same time celebrate abortion, which has killed thirty million unborn women since 1973?

Since 1973, when Roe v. Wade became the law of the land, sixty million unborn babies have been aborted.[11] Approximately half of all pregnancies are baby girls. Therefore, thirty million unborn women have been killed by abortion in the past forty-five years.

Does the Left really champion women? Or does the radical Left only champion certain women who are useful to their radical leftist agenda? Meanwhile ignoring the genocide of unborn women?

How can the Left claim to champion women while they celebrate abortion, which kills almost half a million unborn women every year?

. . . .

Talking point: We Democrats support a woman's right to choose! Her body, her choice! A women's autonomy is sacred! Nobody tells a woman what to do with her own body!

Contradiction: How can the Left claim to support a woman's right to choose what happens to her own body while also proclaiming that women should not have a right to choose to defend themselves with a firearm (if that firearm looks scary to the Left)?

Is there anything more inherent to bodily autonomy than protecting one's own life?

Women use firearms to defend themselves against sexual abuse two hundred thousand times a year. (And that doesn't even include instances where women don't report their use of a firearm in self-defense.)[12]

Yet the Left denounces women's exercise of our right to bear arms (if the firearm looks scary) and peddles an ignorant and naïve narrative claiming that if we ban all guns that will eliminate murders. (Clearly the Left doesn't understand how crime works.)

The Left also ignores women who were not armed at the time of their attack, like Mollie Tibbets, a twenty-year-old college student from Iowa who was kidnapped and murdered (by an illegal alien) in the summer of 2018.[13] Or Kate Steinle, the thirty-two-year-old from San Francisco who was shot and killed (also by an illegal alien) while walking with her father on the wharf in 2015.[14]

Kimberly Corban, a rape survivor, is now a passionate advocate for concealed carry for women. She says the one thing she wished for during her brutal assault and rape (which occurred in her own home) was a firearm to defend herself.[15]

Self-defense is the most basic measure of bodily autonomy.

So how can the radical Left claim to champion a women's bodily autonomy and a woman's right to choose while also attacking the choice of many women to defend ourselves and our bodies with the firearms of our choice?

■ ■ ■ ■

Talking point: Donald Trump won the 2016 election because of Russian meddling! Russian meddling is a threat to our democracy!

Contradiction: How can the Left claim to care about foreign meddling in our elections by the Russians while the Left also completely ignores foreign meddling by illegal immigrants (a.k.a foreign nationals) casting fraudulent votes in our elections?

Every top intelligence official who's been asked has testified that no votes were altered by Russian meddling. Zero votes.

Earlier in the book, we discussed the enormous number of non-citizens who are ineligible to vote in U.S. elections who self-report that they are registered to vote, nonetheless. In fact, 14 percent of non-citizens in our country self-report that they are illegally registered to vote. (That's approximately 1.6 million non-citizens illegally registered to vote in our elections.)[16]

We have also discussed the new initiative in San Francisco where the radical Left passed a ballot measure to allow illegal aliens to vote.

So how can the Left claim foreign meddling in our elections by Russians is a threat to democracy (actually, America is a republic), but also claim voter fraud and foreign meddling in our elections by illegal aliens is not a threat?

■   ■   ■   ■

Talking point: Voter fraud is so rare and insignificant; it's an irresponsible waste of money to conduct expensive investigations.

Contradiction: How can the Left proclaim it's too expensive to investigate voter fraud (foreign meddling by illegal aliens in our elections) while spending over twenty-five million dollars of taxpayer money on the Russia investigation?

After two years of investigation, the final report from Special Counsel Robert Mueller's office concluded there was no collusion between Donald Trump and the Russians, no criminal conspiracy between the Trump campaign and the Russians, and no proof of a crime of obstruction. A big, fat nothing-burger that cost American taxpayers twenty-five million dollars.

Meanwhile, the radical Left tells us voter fraud (foreign meddling by illegal aliens) isn't worth investigating because it would cost too much money and there is no evidence (there is) that it's widespread?

■   ■   ■   ■

Talking point: Fight for fifteen dollars! Everybody deserves a living wage! Raise the minimum wage to fifteen dollars per hour!

Contradiction: How can the Left claim they want a mandatory fifteen dollars per hour minimum wage for workers, but also condemn the Republican tax reform law that led to companies voluntarily raising their minimum wage to fifteen dollars an hour?

In May 2018, thousands of leftist protesters blocked roads in Chicago trying to grab attention for their "Fight for $15" campaign.[17] Their target that particular day was McDonald's, but their agenda is universal. The radical Left wants a federally mandated fifteen dollars per hour minimum wage. They call it a "living wage," and they claim that it's immoral for companies to pay employees anything less. In fact, the radical Left claims every person has a "right" to a living wage. Regardless of whether an employer can afford a fifteen dollars per hour minimum wage and stay in business or not, the Left wants the federal government to mandate that all employers pay all employees at least fifteen dollars an hour.

Five months before this protest, in December of 2017, Republicans in the House and Senate passed a tax reform bill. After President Trump signed the bill into law, 400+ companies presented their employees with one thousand dollars in bonuses or pay raises, or voluntarily raised their company-wide minimum wage to fifteen dollars per hour.[18]

To this day, the Left threatens to repeal these tax cut "crumbs."[19]

How can the Left claim they want a government-mandated fifteen dollars per hour minimum wage, but when companies voluntarily raise their minimum wage to fifteen dollars an hour, the Left refuses to celebrate?

■　■　■　■

Talking point: The wealthy should pay their fair share of taxes! It's immoral for so few people to own so much!

Contradiction: How can Senator Bernie Sanders claim it's immoral for the top 1 percent to hoard that much wealth, while he owns three homes?

Self-avowed socialist Senator Sanders once proposed a tax rate of 90 percent for wealthy Americans.[20] (That's "fair," according to Sanders.)

Furthermore, in April of 2017, Sanders tweeted, "How many yachts do billionaires need? How many cars do they need? Give us a break. You can't have it all."[21]

Senator Sanders owns three houses. One in Burlington, Vermont. One in Washington, D.C. And a $575,000 vacation home on the beach in Vermont.[22]

Senator Sanders, according to his reported income, is in the top 4 percent of wealthiest people in our nation. The top 1 percent are greedy and evil with their yachts and cars and luxury purchases. The government should forcibly take away the excess wealth of those greedy top 1 percenters, according to Sanders. But when Mr. Top 4 Percent Sanders owns three very expensive homes? No moral problem there.

How can Senator Sanders and his leftist allies demonize the wealthy and advocate for socialism and redistribution of wealth while he himself owns three homes?

Nobody is stopping the senator from giving away his wealth and one or two of his homes to people less fortunate. (Spoiler alert: he won't do it.) But Sanders is quick to push laws that will force us to give our money and possessions away, whether we like it or not.

(Side note: this is the inevitable side effect of socialism. Government bureaucrats grow wealthier while sorry people like you and me grow poorer. Funny how that happens.)

■　■　■　■

Talking point: Capitalism is evil.

Contradiction: How can the Left demonize capitalism while plotting #resistance from iPhones and wearing designer jeans?

In October of 2018, Teen Vogue magazine posted a headline on Twitter that read, "Can't #endpoverty without ending capitalism!"[23]

A Gallup poll from August 2018 showed that 57 percent of Democrats (or those who lean Democrat) have a positive view of socialism. Only 47 percent of Democrats (or those who lean Democrat) had a positive view of capitalism.[24]

Remember Occupy Wall Street? Human waste, filth, anarchy galore on the streets of New York City. Angry millennials protesting capitalism and "big money" while using the finest innovations and creature comforts the free market can offer.

These so-called anti-capitalists plotted their #resistance from their iPhones and used celebrity spokespeople who earned their riches selling movies in our wonderful free market economy to push their anti-capitalism cause. These anti-capitalist keyboard warriors camped out in the filthy tent city that was Occupy Wall Street...while wearing designer jeans, coats, boots, and shoes.

How can the Left demonize capitalism while enjoying all the benefits and blessings only available thanks to the capitalistic free market?

■ ■ ■ ■

Talking point: Uber and Lyft are killing taxis!

Contradiction: How can democratic socialist Alexandria Ocasio-Cortez demonize Uber (a capitalistic free market innovation) for destroying the taxi monopoly, while she uses Uber herself?[25]

According to Ocasio-Cortez's campaign finance reports, she and her team frequently use Uber and other ride-share services that were invented (and are thriving) because of good, old-fashioned capitalism.

Meanwhile, Ocasio-Cortez claims to stand in solidarity with the New York City cab drivers. But actions speak louder than words. Apparently, the superior products and services that capitalism provides at more affordable prices are evil for you and me...but okay for her and her team.

■ ■ ■ ■

Talking point: The government should stay out of our bedrooms.

Contradiction: How can the Left claim they want government to get out of their bedrooms while they also demand that the government pay for their birth control?

When Republicans in Congress rolled back the Obamacare contraceptive mandate, the radical Left promoted a hashtag on Twitter: #HandsOffMyBirthControl.

Well, which is it? Does the radical Left want government to take their hands off birth control? Or does the radical Left want taxpayers to dig our hands into our wallets so the government can hand them birth control pills for "free"? You can't have it both ways.

■　■　■　■

Talking point: We Democrats are leading the fight against sexism!

Contradiction: Really? How come the party who claims to fight sexism accuses former U.S. ambassador to the UN Nikki Haley of sleeping her way to the top?

How else would she be so successful? Talk about sexist!

In other words, how come the party who claims to fight sexism is the same party that hurled misogynistic allegations at the most successful conservative woman in the country...just because she's conservative?

During an appearance on Bill Maher's *Real Time* show on HBO, Michael Wolff, the author of *Fire and Fury: Inside the Trump White House*, insinuated that President Trump was having an affair with Nikki Haley. Wolf admitted he didn't have enough proof of such an affair to put it in the book.[26] (Instead, he broadcast such slanderous allegations on national television.) Not sexist at all.

Ambassador Haley vehemently denied the baseless allegations.

Nikki Haley, formerly the governor of South Carolina, is the most liked politician in the United States. According to an April 2018 Quinnipiac poll, 63 percent of American voters had a positive opinion of Haley. Seventy-five percent of Republicans approved of Haley. Fifty-five percent of Democrats approved of Haley. Sixty-three percent of independents. Only 17 percent of people overall disapproved of her.[27]

But Nikki Haley is conservative. Pro-life. Pro-family. Pro-free market. Pro-Israel. Pro-America. Everything the radical Left loathes and fears. So they hurl malicious and misogynistic accusations at her, since she refuses to toe their radical leftist ideological line. That's the definition of sexism.

How can the Left claim to fight sexism...but accuse Nikki Haley, a successful woman, of sleeping her way to the top just because she's conservative?

■   ■   ■   ■

Talking point: Just because you're born with a penis doesn't mean you're a man! If you feel like a woman, you can be a woman...even if you have a penis! Genitalia have no bearing on gender!

Contradiction: How can the Left claim that bodily characteristics such as male or female genitalia have no bearing on whether one is a man or woman (that's up to how you "identify"), yet the cure for gender dysphoria is to physically alter your outward body...which we were just told has no bearing on your gender?

The Left claims it doesn't matter what body parts you have...the biological makeup of your DNA doesn't matter. That doesn't determine your gender, according to the Left. (Though if you're Elizabeth Warren, your 1/1024 Native American DNA makes you Cherokee—even though you're 99.99 percent white. But I digress.) Regardless of your body parts, you're whatever gender you want to be, according to the Left.

In Chapter 7, we talked about the parents in Cincinnati who had custody of their daughter stripped away by a judge who condemned them for not allowing their daughter, who suffers from gender dysphoria, to begin transgender hormone therapy (the first step toward gender reassignment surgery). The judge essentially ruled that it was a medical necessity to perform this intervention to prevent the seventeen-year-old child from committing suicide because she was so unhappy in her body.

How can the Left claim we need to align our body with our "true gender identity" by major medical interventions, but also tell us our outward body has no bearing on what gender we truly are in the first place?

■ ■ ■ ■

Talking point: We Democrats fight against the patriarchy!

Contradiction: How can the Left claim to fight against the patriarchy while they ignore five hundred thousand mostly Muslim women here in the United States who are vulnerable to honor killings, female genital mutilation (FGM), and other abuse at the hands of oppressive and sometimes murderous Muslim men?[28]

The Left demonizes Republican men. The Left demonizes white men. The Left loves to demonize old, white, Republican men (because they are old, white, Republican, and male).

Meanwhile, women who are subject to female genital mutilation are not given anesthesia. They have not given permission or consent. They are brutalized anyway. They are forcibly subjected to an unsterile procedure in which their clitoris is cut off with a razor blade. Many times, young girls are told to lie about whether they've been subjected to this torture. As a result, they are deprived of their sexual capacity. Sexual intercourse is painful. Menstruation can be dangerous. And some women need to be cut open in order to give birth.

According to the Centers for Disease Control, one out of every three Muslim women in the United States is at risk of FGM until she is eighteen years old.

Twenty-four states in the U.S. don't have laws against FGM.[29] In 2018, Democrats in Maine voted against a law that would ban this brutal practice.[30]

Isn't that the most brutal, oppressive, and sexist form of systemic patriarchy possible?

How can the Left claim to be fighting "systemic patriarchy" while they ignore this systemic, horrific crime being inflicted on women by the Muslim patriarchy—including in the United States?

■ ■ ■ ■

Talking point: President Trump is a threat to the free press! He attacks journalists, he calls the media fake news, and soon he'll try to shut down the free press altogether.

Contradiction: How can the Left condemn Trump for so-called attacks on the free press...while they ignore democratic socialist Alexandria Ocasio-Cortez banning press from her townhalls?

On August 15, 2018, the *Boston Globe* and 350 other newspapers across the United States published coordinated editorials decrying President Trump's so-called assault on the free press. The title of the article was "Journalists Are Not the Enemy."[31] The very first line of the article read, "A central pillar of President Trump's politics is a sustained assault on the free press."

But there was no actual assault. Liberal reporters and media honchos were offended the president called them fake news. Nothing more. No actions. No violation of any constitutional right.

In fact, the contentious dynamic between the president and left-wing news outlets proves that freedom of the press in our nation is alive and well. Thriving. Kicking.

If it weren't, a president who so dislikes the way the media covers him would surely silence them, right?

President Trump did not do that. President Trump openly criticizes the slanted, biased coverage and the lies told by left-wing news outlets, yet the purveyors of that coverage are still free to publish whatever they want and to criticize the president as harshly as they want...and suffer no consequences to their safety, security, or livelihood at the hands of the government they criticize.

(Meanwhile, I'm still waiting for the coordinated editorials condemning the Obama administration for targeting journalist Sharyl Attkisson and hacking her computer. And for the coordinated editorials condemning the Obama administration for wiretapping the phones—even the personal cell phones—of Associated Press journalists. I'm waiting for the coordinated editorials decrying the Obama administration for spying on former

Fox News reporter James Rosen, seizing his phone records and emails, and tracking his physical movements. But once again, I digress.)

Three days after the *Boston Globe* pushed this coordinated editorial, democratic socialist Alexandria Ocasio-Cortez banned press from covering her townhall events as she campaigned in New York's fourteenth district.

Banned the media.

Ocasio-Cortez defended the action, saying, "To be honest, the event was very successful. People were much more comfortable sharing their personal issues with healthcare, housing, and immigration. It was a safe + powerful environment for change. My apologies if the situation upset or alarmed journalists or constituents."[32]

She asked, "How should we label a free campaign event, open to all, that's a sanctuary space?"[33]

Sanctuary spaces. Free to all—except the free press.

The harshest condemnation from the liberal media was a piece from CNN gently informing Ocasio-Cortez that banning the press from her events was a "mistake."

Oh my. What a comeuppance. A mistake.

A candidate for public office barring the free press from covering her events. Refusing to allow the media to ask questions about her policies—including how she will pay for the wildly unrealistic socialist policies she's promising voters.

That's a "mistake." Not an assault on the free press, according to the Left.

How can the Left claim to care about freedom of the press when it comes to the president's criticism of the liberal media, but remain silent when the twenty-nine-year-old democratic socialist whom DNC chair Tom Perez called the "future of the party" outright banned press from her townhall meetings?

■   ■   ■   ■

Talking point: The Republican tax reform will devastate the middle class! We Democrats want to repeal the GOP tax reform!

Contradiction: How can the Left claim to care about the middle class while they're campaigning to repeal the GOP tax reform law that gave a tax break to 90 percent of the American people?

Then-House Minority Leader Nancy Pelosi proclaimed the tax reform bill to be "probably one of the worst bills in the history of the United States of America. It robs from the future; it rewards the rich and corporations at the expense of tens of millions of working middle-class families in our country." Pelosi continued, "The debate on health care is like death. This is Armageddon."[34]

The tax reform bill is projected to give a tax cut to 90 percent of Americans.[35] The majority of the middle class can expect to see a paycheck increase. This is in addition to the bonuses and wage hikes that came as a result of the law. That's hardly Armageddon for the middle class.

Yet every single Democrat in the House of Representatives and the Senate voted against the bill. The Democrats now want to repeal it.

How can the Democrats claim to care about the middle class while they're campaigning to raise taxes on the middle class?

■   ■   ■   ■

Talking point: If we can save even one life, we should ban all guns to stop school shootings.

Contradiction: How can the Left claim to care about stopping school shootings when they ignored the radical Islamist compound in New Mexico where terrorists were training children...to commit school shootings?

In August of 2018, a radical Islamist was arrested on a compound in New Mexico for the murder of his three-year-old son. At the compound, law enforcement found eleven other children living in squalor. The sheriff described them as looking like refugees from a third world country. No fresh food. No fresh water. No hygiene. No clothes except for rags.[36]

This radical Islamist was training the children to commit school shootings.

In other words, Siraj Wahhaj was running an Islamist extremist terror training camp. He was actively training eleven children to commit terror attacks intended to kill Americans. Wahhaj told the children the time would come for their terror attacks, whether the targets be schools and teachers, law enforcement, or other institutions.[37]

The point is, motivated by his radical Islamist religious beliefs, Wahhaj was training eleven people to commit school shootings.

If the Left cares about school shootings as much as they say, how can they ignore a radical Islamist terror training camp on U.S. soil where children were being groomed to commit school shootings?

(By the way, Wahhaj is not just an average Muslim extremist. Wahhaj's father was an unindicted co-conspirator in the 1993 World Trade Center bombing and a character witness for the Blind Sheik, the mastermind of the bombing. Sounds like a bad guy, right? Women's March co-founder Linda Sarsour doesn't think so. Sarsour began her speech at the Islamic Society of North America conference in 2017 by thanking her "favorite person in the room…Imam Siraj Wahhaj, who has been a mentor, motivator, and encourager of mine.")[38]

■　■　■　■

And there we have it. For every Democratic position, there is a hypocritical and obvious contradiction.

For every example presented in this chapter, there are ninety-nine more my word count won't allow me to include.

As you can see, there is no constant moral principle underlying the platform of the radical Left. There is no commitment to liberty or limited government or dignity for all people or equal justice under the law (all of which underlie the conservative platform).

The radical Left simply seeks seek power and wealth at the expense of the people they swore an oath to serve. Their radical leftist agenda, outlined in Chapter 2, is the total destruction of the family, religious institutions, and the social bulwarks of our nation. Their goal: complete power and control. Their tactics: whittle away at the freedoms of the American people and consolidate power into the hands of the elite few.

In other words, the underlying principle of the radical Left is impos-ing their agenda at any cost. And we can expose that diabolical agenda by exposing the contradictions and falsehoods we see in every liberal argument.

This hypocrisy is on every page of the radical Left's playbook. The Democratic platform is rife with contradictions. In fact, I have never met a liberal argument that didn't come with a side dish of logical inconsis-tency, hypocrisy, or contradiction.

I challenge you to find a single liberal policy issue or talking point that doesn't blatantly contradict another.

I won't hold my breath.

In the meantime, in order to defeat the radical leftist ideology, we conservatives must flip the leftist arguments on their head and stomp on them. It's not difficult to do. Just find the contradiction and expose it. Every leftist argument will fall apart under this scrutiny, and *voilà!* we're halfway to relegating the radical leftist ideology to where it belongs: on the trash heap of history.

Chapter 11

The Media Bias Framework
(They All Use It)

I picture the trash heap of history as a garbage dump. Neatly arranged with old metal cans like the one Oscar the Grouch lives in, lined up next to each other, with dripping spray paint on the sides of the cans depicting in black letters the contents of each can.

Liberal contradictions, reads one can.

Revisionist history, says the next one.

Communism. That's an especially full one. Give it a kick for good measure as you pass.

Mainstream Media Bias Framework, reads another. Wait…at this fourth garbage can, we pause. The lid sits on the muddy ground beside it, the basin filled with murky water. Even the birds fly past that water. Too toxic for a bath.

And yet some on our own side act like this can is empty. Some people in the Republican Party will tell us you can't build a conservative movement on criticizing the mainstream media. These Republican skeptics will tell you, "Don't even look in that garbage can! Don't give the leftist mainstream media ratings by giving them attention!"

On the first point, these people are correct—you can't build principles around criticizing the media.

But on the second point our fellow travelers are wrong. This is why
the image of that trash can labeled Mainstream Media Bias Framework
sitting in the trash heap of history haunts our minds as we continue
our walk.

After all, this is how the Democratic Party disseminates and protects
their message—by means of the mainstream media shills who repeat
false narratives so often and so loudly that those warped snippets are the
only soundbites many Americans hear. How can we defeat the leftist
ideology if we don't expose the bias of the mainstream media and the
tactics they use to deliver that bias?

Short answer: we can't.

We conservatives must consistently and thoroughly expose the lying,
cheating, and corruption of the liberal media in order to defeat the radical
leftist ideology.

Grab your trash bag, and let's get to work!

■ ■ ■ ■

After all, every leftist media outlet uses the same pattern of bias. It's
like clockwork. Once you see the pattern, it's almost laughably easy to
stick your croquet mallet in the spokes of that wheel and overturn the
bicycle.

In this chapter, I'll walk you through the Media Bias Framework.
The pattern of *how* the MSM inserts their bias into the news is the exact
same every single time. It's sort of a framework (hence the name). The
elements the MSM uses to frame stories in order to push the liberal
agenda are the same every day, every story. Once you identify the elements in real time, debunking the bias and the biased narrative is easy.

We'll get to those elements in a moment.

But first we as conservatives need to ask, well what if we do debunk
the mainstream media? What if we succeed in exposing their bias? What

if the American people reject the partisan liberal dishonesty of the MSM shills? What next?

First, platform competition. Compete with dishonest platforms. Do you dislike Twitter shadow banning conservatives? Build an alternative. There is no Silicon Valley monopoly precluding conservative web developers from designing a new social network. Compete. Take back some of that market space.

That's what One America News Network is doing in the cable news sphere. Don't like the other mainstream cable news outlets? Great— here's an alternative. In less than six years, OANN has become a competitor in the cable news marketplace across the entire United States. My show, *Tipping Point with Liz Wheeler*, draws tens of millions of eyeballs every year.

Second, challenge the biased outlets; don't dismiss them. I'm aware I'm repeating myself. This chapter details *how* to successfully challenge the liberal networks. We'll get to those tactics in a moment. But before we do that, we must understand the importance of *why* we're doing what we're going. It's too easy to simply write off CNN or Jimmy Kimmel or the *Washington Post* and pretend they don't exist.

It's like the kid who covers his own eyes and says, "You can't see me!" Spoiler alert: we can see you.

The liberal networks exist. They do have impact. The mainstream media helps shape the worldview of the electorate. Therefore, it's vitally important to recognize that that only way to budge the radical leftist echo chamber is to shake it up.

■ ■ ■ ■

I once read a book about a group of girls at a boarding school. The book itself was nothing to write home about, but one scene sticks out in my mind, and I'll never forget it. It went approximately as follows.

The girls at the boarding school suspected that their literature teacher did not read the inordinately long essays she demanded they write, so one mischievous girl included this on page fourteen of a twenty-five-page dissertation: "I am sitting by my window at this moment, and a red cow is going down the street. I wonder if she is any relation to Mrs. Seccomb's cow?"[1] The girl then bet her schoolmates the teacher would not notice the errant (and insulting) sentence. She won the bet.

This became a running joke in our household growing up. Think somebody isn't listening to your story? Without changing your tone, slip in, "A red cow just walked down the street; I wonder what the cow is thinking?" and continue with your story. Did the other person notice? Great, they're listening. Did they nod and say "mhmm"? Time to find a new listener!

Now take this outside the fictional schoolroom. Imagine if a conglomeration of people (say, newscasters!) thought so little of your intelligence that they added, "I saw a red cow walking down the street today" into every broadcast and either A) expected you not to notice, or B) expected you to believe them.

Insulting, right?

This is what the mainstream media do. The radical leftists who populate the newsrooms and TV screens of liberal outlets pretend that their viewers (ostensibly you and I) are too stupid to notice when they trot out giant red cows in the middle of their stories. They then pretend the herd they invented is a figment of *your* imagination.

This is how they do it.

I call it the Media Bias Framework.

Unveil the beast.

■　■　■　■

These are the elements you're looking for in reports from liberal media outlets. The MSM uses this framework every single time, no matter what issue they're talking about. I'll tell you what the elements are, and then we'll apply the formula to a variety of news stories, and you can see for yourself. In other words, this is the recipe the MSM uses to cook up their biased version of whatever issues they're covering.

Element #1: Blame something you hate. Plant that idea in people's minds.

Element #2: Ignore the facts and—this is critical—while ignoring the facts, accuse anybody who speaks in facts instead of emotions of not *having* emotions. Accusing them of not caring.

Element #3: Tie the story to something larger that people already have established feelings about (for example, Watergate, the oppression of women, and so forth).

Element #4: Exploit people's emotions.

Element #5: Ridicule the other side and then accuse them of cruelty—even of killing.

Element #6: Lather, rinse, repeat until the warped snippets are the only points people remember when they think about the issue. It's like that principle we talked about in marketing—you have to show a consumer an advertisement something like seven times before they'll act on it and purchase the product. That's what the MSM does. Repeat a lie often enough, and suddenly people buy it because it seems like the truth.

So let's apply these elements to stories we've experienced in the past two years. Let's start with the Parkland school shooting—the shooting at Marjory Stoneman Douglas High School in Florida that killed fourteen students and three administrators. From the moment this news story broke, the MSM applied their bias framework. The agenda of the leftist media: gun control.

Element #1: Blame something you hate. What does the Left hate? Well, firearms. So, blame the gun then. It's the gun's fault. If you noticed, the MSM barely mentioned and barely even condemned the killer himself. The gun is far worse than the killer, according to the MSM.

Element #2: Ignore the facts. Studies have shown repeatedly that states in our country with the harshest gun control measures boast the most dangerous cities with the highest rates of gun violence,[2] while areas with higher legal gun ownership have lower violent crime rates.[3] There's a reason three out of five felons say they won't mess with an armed victim.[4] Only 2.5 percent of homicides in our country are committed with rifles, even fewer with AR-15s.[5] Ninety-eight percent of mass shootings in our nation since the 1950s have happened in gun-free zones.[6] Never mind that—ignore these facts. And accuse anybody who brings up the facts of not caring about dead kids:

How can you defend AR-15s after the school shooting in Parkland, Florida? Don't you care about kids at all? I wish you cared half as much about those murdered kids as you do about your own gun fetish. You'd rather be a vigilante with an AR-15 than keep our kids safe. That's heartless. Why do you need an assault rifle for self-defense when kids are dying at school?

(By the way, all of these things were said to me by leftists on air on my show in the week after Parkland...but you can tune into any network and see liberals saying exactly the same thing.)

Element #3: Tie it to something larger that people already have established feelings about. Nobody on either side of the aisle likes corrupt money in politics, do they? People don't like the fact that we feel like our politicians are bought and paid for by special interest groups, so...blame the NRA! It's the NRA's fault—the NRA bought off politicians.

Element #4: Exploit people's emotions. This element was literally verbalized by the former Broward County sheriff during that infamous CNN town hall. Sheriff Scott Israel didn't even try to hide it. He said, "You're not standing up for [the kids], until you say I want less weapons."[7] The MSM gives us that binary choice. Either you support the radical leftist agenda, or you don't care.

Element #5: Whenever possible, ridicule the other side, and even accuse them of murder. Case in point. The students at CNN's townhall actually yelled "Killer! and "Murderer!" at NRA spokeswoman Dana Loesch. The Left's favorite word is *complicit*. It's their way of blaming somebody who has nothing to do with the topic for whatever tragedy happened. Unless you are fighting for the political agenda radical leftists are pushing, you are complicit in whatever tragedy befalls us.

Element #6: Lather, rinse, repeat until the warped snippets are the only points people remember when they think about the issue. Repeat a lie often enough, and suddenly it seems like the truth.

Once you recognize these elements, I promise you'll see them everywhere. When you see them, when you identify them for the tactics they are, you can disrupt them and trip the MSM up at their own dishonest game.

It doesn't even have to be a tragedy. The MSM uses this bias framework for all their biased stories.

Look at the MSM coverage of North Korean dictator Kim Jong-un's sister at the 2018 Olympics in Pyeongchang. The media practically bowed to the North Korean dictator's sister, Kim Yo-jong, because she was caught giving Vice President Mike Pence the side eye during the Opening Ceremonies.[8] The MSM made Kim Jong-un's sister into some kind of pop culture idol meme. From the moment this was caught on camera, the MSM applied their bias framework.

Element #1: Blame something you hate. What does the Left hate? Well, Donald Trump. They hate the president. So, blame the president: *Other nations don't respect us. Look at how North Korea disdains the vice president because Donald Trump is such an embarrassment to the United States.* You'll notice, the MSM didn't mention that Kim Yo-jong is the sister of one of the most brutal dictators in the world. Donald Trump, according to the media, is far worse.

Element #2: Ignore the facts. Kim Jong-un's sister was proudly representing North Korea. North Korea brutalizes and starves their people.[9] North Korea forces parents to kill or banish their disabled babies[10] and forces school children to watch public executions.[11] North Korea tortures anybody who criticizes the regime.[12] The last time South Korea hosted the Olympic games, North Korea blew up a commercial airliner in midair months earlier and killed all the civilians on board.[13] Never mind that— ignore those facts. And this is critical: while ignoring the facts themselves, accuse anybody who speaks in facts instead of emotions of not *having* emotions: *How are you not genuinely worried about America? Do you* *not care that we are on the road to a dictatorship with Donald Trump as president? Other nations recognize it. Don't you feel that fear that Donald Trump will come for you next?*

Element #3: Tie it to something larger that people already have established feelings about. Well, people don't want to go to war again, do they? So blame Donald Trump's tweets about Little Rocket Man. *It's Trump's fault. Trump is about to ignite our world in a blaze of nuclear hell fire! If not for those tweets—my God, we might even be friends with North Korea. Who can blame Kim Jong-un's sister for rolling her eyes at the Trump administration?* Almost word for word the narrative is exactly the same, following this framework, from every liberal MSM network.

Element #4: Exploit people's emotions. *The more sanctions Donald Trump slaps on North Korea, the more North Korean kids die. Why do you want North Korean kids to die?* The MSM gives us that binary choice. Either you support the radical leftist agenda, or you don't care.

Element #5: Whenever possible, ridicule the other side and even accuse them of killing. In this case, it was ridicule. *Maybe Vice President Pence didn't speak to Kim Jong-un's sister because his wife wasn't at dinner with them. Get it? Because Pence is a misogynistic pig who won't dine alone with women other than his wife.*

Element #6: Lather, rinse, repeat until the warped snippets are the only points people remember when they think about the issue. Repeat a lie often enough and suddenly it seems like the truth.

You're getting the idea, right? No matter what kind of story it is—a tragedy like the Parkland shooting or celebrity gossip about Kim Jong-un's sister and Vice President Pence at the Olympics—you can apply this bias framework to anything: tax reform, Russian collusion, abortion, House Intelligence Committee memos, transgender bathrooms, the Democratic party's ties to radical hate preacher Louis Farrakhan, the photo the Congressional Black Caucus hid from the public of then–senator Barack Obama hugging Farrakhan, Obamacare, welfare reform, DACA, and the DREAMers. You name it—it follows this framework.

Now at the same time, the mainstream media talking heads will justify their bias by saying that the political division in our nation is unprecedented—we've never seen anything like this level of hate in our nation before. And of course they blame the division and the hate on President Trump. The rhetoric from Donald Trump, they claim, is unprecedented. The name calling. The tweets. Crooked Hillary. Crazy Bernie. Little Rocket Man. Cryin' Chuck. Pocahontas. (Pocahontas is my favorite, but if you don't think Little Rocket Man is funny...I don't know how to talk to you.)

But fighting among political figures is hardly unprecedented in our nation's history. In fact, the third vice president of our country (Aaron Burr) literally shot and killed the former secretary of the treasury (Alexander Hamilton).[14] Shot and killed. But the MSM today are shocked to their core when President Trump calls Elizabeth Warren Pocahontas.

Mudslinging, likewise, is not unprecedented. Let me give you some examples:

- A journalist working for Thomas Jefferson said that John Adams had a "hideous hermaphroditic character."[15]
- A newspaper supporting John Adams claimed that a Jefferson presidency would mean "Murder, robbery, rape, adultery and incest openly taught and practiced, the air will be rent with the cries of the distressed, the soil will be soaked with blood and the nation black with crimes."[16]
- Martha Washington, the very first first lady of the United States, called Thomas Jefferson "the most detestable of mankind."[17]
- John Quincy Adams was accused of playing pimp and arranging American prostitutes for the Russian Tsar. Why would he be accused of this, you ask? Great question. Opponents of John Quincy Adams asked how else Adams could have been so successful in his diplomatic post in Russia.

- John Quincy Adams beat Andrew Jackson in the Electoral College, but Jackson won the popular vote...and from then on Andrew Jackson's supporters always claimed John Quincy Adams was an illegitimate president. Sound familiar?[18]

You get the idea. Mudslinging is not unprecedented. Nasty politics is nasty, but it's not unprecedented. You know what is unprecedented? The media bias today is unprecedented. Never before in the history of our country have so-called journalists and newspapers and news networks been so committed to one particular political ideology and so willing to drop their journalistic integrity in order to systematically push that agenda.

Enter the Media Bias Framework again.

In August of 2018, the *New York Times*—once the preeminent source of highly respected and accurate reporting—hired a woman named Sarah Jeong as a technology writer and part of its editorial board.[19] The *Times* hired Ms. Jeong despite the fact that she has a long and sordid history of sending racist tweets.

When I say racist tweets, I mean *racist* tweets.

A few of Ms. Jeong's tweets:

> Oh man it's kind of sick how much joy I get out of being cruel to old white men.
>
> #CancelWhitePeople
>
> Are white people genetically predisposed to burn faster in the sun, thus logically being only fit to live underground like groveling goblins.
>
> [Profanity warning:] Dumbass fucking white people marking up the internet with their opinions like dogs pissing on fire hydrants.[20]

Lovely, right? There are dozens of other tweets such as these, but I won't subject you to more vitriolic drivel. You get the idea.

The *New York Times* was then flooded with messages of disgust and disbelief and entreaties from people like you and me to reverse their decision and fire this person who engages in such disgusting racist bile.

But the *Times* did not fire Ms. Jeong. In fact, they defended her. (Side note: You notice no leftist journalists asked during this whole scandal why the *Times* hired Jeong to begin with, since the newspaper claimed they knew about her racist tweets ahead of time? The question wasn't asked because the answer is damning. In short, the radical Left is not against all racism, as they claim. The radical Left embraces racism against white people. That's why.)

So, the radical Left deployed the Media Bias Framework to defend their inane hiring decision. As follows.

Element #1: Blame something you hate. What does the Left hate? Well—old, white men. So, blame old, white men. Remind people that old, white men once oppressed minority women like Sarah Jeong. If you noticed, the MSM was so busy recollecting the sordid racial history in our country—and condemning all white men for it, even white men who weren't alive during that era—that they didn't have time to condemn the racism coming from Sarah Jeong's fingertips. White privilege is far worse, according to the MSM, than racism against white people.

Element #2: Ignore the facts. As we discussed in Chapter 8, according to the FBI crime statistics from 2016, the fastest growing category of racial hate crimes in our country are crimes committed against white people for being white.[21] No matter. Ignore that. And this is critical: while ignoring the facts, accuse anybody who speaks in facts instead of emotion of not *having* emotion. Accuse them of not caring: *How can you attack this minority woman for an obviously satirical tweet she sent? Can't you take a joke? How dare you have an opinion on her identity as a minority woman, you horrible, old, white man? Do you not care that you and your kind once oppressed women just like Sarah? You heartless beast.*

Element #3: Tie the story to something larger that people already have established feelings about. Well, the Left is convinced President

Trump is waging an assault on the free press, right? (Spoiler alert: he's not.) So blame Trump supporters! *Trump hates the press and wants to kill the free press. Trump supporters are targeting Sarah Jeong because they want to silence her…they're just like Trump!*

Element #4: Exploit people's emotions. How about when *National Review*'s Kevin Williamson was fired from the *Atlantic*? Williamson was fired ostensibly because he made an inartful, hyperbolic comment about women and abortion. The leftist mob came after him, and people on the Right were rightly frustrated, angry, and just plain annoyed that Jeffrey Goldberg, the executive editor of the *Atlantic*, caved and fired Williamson three days later. So the leftist defenders of Sarah Jeong and the *Times* brought that that up: *Do you want to be like Goldberg? Do you want to fire people based on mistakes in their youth? Didn't you ever make any mistakes? Well then, embrace Sarah Jeong's right to stay at that position.* The MSM gives us that binary choice. Either you support the radical leftist agenda, or you don't care.

Element #5: Whenever possible, ridicule the other side and even accuse them of killing. In this case, it was both. The Left accused President Trump of killing the free press and putting journalists in physical danger (though there was no evidence of that). Meanwhile, they ridiculed white men who are supposedly threatened by their monopoly on power coming to an end.

Element #6: Lather, rinse, repeat until the warped snippets are the only points people remember when they think about the issue. Repeat a lie often enough, and suddenly people buy it because it seems like the truth.

This happens everywhere we look. The radical Left uses the mainstream media as a tool to defend or advance their pseudo-Marxist political agenda—even if it means manipulating people's emotions, withholding facts, distracting from important context, or telling outright lies.

Take the press coverage of radical hate preacher Louis Farrakhan, whom we discussed in Chapter 10. The man has joked that gay people should be beheaded.[22] He called Jewish people "Satanic Jews"[23] and blamed them for the September 11, 2001, terror attacks.[24] He says white people are going down.[25] He called Adolf Hitler a very great man.[26] You don't find many people with views more grotesque than Reverend Farrakhan. We've established that.

Fast forward to singer Aretha Franklin's funeral, where Farrakhan appeared on the stage in a position of honor. Farrakhan was seated with Reverend Al Sharpton, Reverend Jesse Jackson, and former president Bill Clinton. (The ties between the Democratic party and Farrakhan are a topic that could fill an entire chapter, if not another book.)

Suffice it to say, conservatives like me noticed and began to tweet about the position of honor given to an anti-Semite like Farrakhan. Within minutes of tweeting a photo of Farrakhan, Jackson, Sharpton, and Bill Clinton buddying it up on stage, MSBNC conveniently cropped Farrakhan—who sat on the end of the row of four men—out of the photos and showed just Sharpton, Jackson, and Clinton instead. As if it were just the three of them on the stage, and not Farrakhan.

Moments later, the mainstream media as a whole responded in kind by rolling out the Media Bias Framework.

Element #1: Blame something you hate. Plant that idea in people's minds. Well, what does the Left hate? The Left hates conservative media. So, attack that. *Right this way, folks—we have the right-wing media hacks politicizing the funeral of the greatest soul singer in American history. Why are you trying to make Aretha's funeral political? Why are you ruining the funeral of the great Aretha Franklin with your divisive rhetoric? Why can't you just stop for one minute and honor this woman?* Conservatives are far worse, according to the MSM, than an anti-Semitic, homophobic, sexist, Adolf Hitler–praising bigot.

Element #2: Ignore the facts. The facts are: Farrakhan is anti-Semitic, homophobic, sexist, and racist against white people. No matter. Ignore that. And this is critical—while ignoring the facts, accuse anybody who speaks in facts instead of emotion of not *having* emotion. Accuse them of not caring: *Don't you care about the black community? Reverend*

Farrakhan has done so much for the black community. So much good. (Like what? Teaching the black community that Adolf Hitler is a good person? Teaching young black men that Jews are evil and white men should be put down? But I digress.) *Why must terrible conservatives care more about their own political bickering than the impact Farrakhan has on black Americans?*

Element #3: Tie the story to something larger that people already have established feelings about. In this case, criminal justice reform. *That's why Aretha's family invited former president Bill Clinton, Reverend Al Sharpton, and Reverend Jesse Jackson to attend the funeral. All three are committed to civil rights and criminal justice reform. Bill Clinton was practically the first black president!* (Distract, distract, distract.) *Meanwhile, Republicans support police officers who kill black people for being black. Shameful.*

Element #4: Exploit people's emotions: *Aretha was a single mother. She gave birth to her first baby at age twelve. Her second at fourteen. If she did hobnob with a man who has a sordid past, are you really going to condemn her for that after the life she lived?* The MSM gives us that binary choice. Either you support the radical leftist agenda, or you don't care.

Element #5: Ridicule the other side and even accuse them of killing. In this case, it was ridicule. Aretha Franklin's funeral was the same day as Senator John McCain's funeral. *Did you notice?* The Left snickered: *President Trump wasn't invited to McCain's service. What a gut-wrenching blow to a dreadful orange president like Trump . . . not even invited to the funeral of the decade! Snicker, snicker.*

Element #6: Lather, rinse, repeat until the warped snippets are the only points people remember when they think about the issue. Repeat a lie often enough and suddenly people buy it because it seems like the truth.

So there you have it.

Since the radical Left has built the foundation of their party around the mainstream media shills who repeat false narratives so often, so loudly (even with tears like Jimmy Kimmel) until those warped snippets are the only soundbites many Americans hear, we conservatives must consistently and thoroughly expose the lying, cheating, and corruption of the progressive media in order to defeat the radical leftist ideology.

This is how to do it.

We must battle the mainstream media (rhetorically, not physically—we're not Antifa!) so that we can carve out a space to speak directly to the American people. Because, like it or not, truth is not enough by itself when the truth is drowned out by fifty liberal talking heads screaming lies on cable news.

This is the crux of the battle between the MSM and President Donald Trump. The battle is larger than a president versus a news network that criticizes him. It's a battle between the conservative ideology of limited government, individual liberty, free markets, and equal treatment under the law (a philosophy President Trump has spent his first two years in office fighting for) and the radical leftist ideology of big government, thought control, mind control, speech control, gun control, high taxes, identity politics, and socialism that comes from a party that uses the MSM as their PR firm and megaphone to drown out anybody who challenges their beliefs.

All we have to do to defeat the Media Bias Framework is recognize it for what it is and challenge the bias where we see it. We need tough politicians who will call out the bias in the media. We need politicians who won't back down when they are attacked by the Left for calling out this bias. We the people need to learn how to argue effectively. I repeat: you and I can't be afraid to argue with the Left. We must be capable of and willing to meet the Left's arguments and beat them at their own game.

Do we believe what we stand for as conservatives? (We established that in earlier chapters.) Do we believe what the Left peddles is demonstrably false? (Also established earlier in this book.) Then we have a responsibility to call BS on their arguments when we see the Left and the MSM using the Media Bias Framework to paint all issues as a binary choice between the radical leftist agenda or you being a terrible person.

Now that you know the elements of the Framework, you'll see it every time you turn on a leftist cable news channel or open up a newspaper. And once you see it, you can effectively destroy it.

It's time to defeat the dishonest liberal media. It's time to fight.

Conclusion

W e've now laid out a fighting strategy to defeat the radical leftist ideology in America. I said in the introduction to this book that this was a conservative alternative to Saul Alinsky's *Rules for Radicals*. A handbook for *how* to fight the radical Left. I hope that's what I have given you in the past 220 pages.

After reading this book, I hope you feel empowered to do battle. I hope you feel confident that you know what to do, instead of feeling helpless and wondering when somebody else will come save America.

In Part 1, we laid out 5 crucial Tipping Points facing our country: the Left's use of California as the "patient zero" state from where they disseminate their radical Leftist agenda across the entire country, the Left's effort to codify politically correct culture into law, and the Left's war on Christianity, on education, and on the family.

In Chapter 1, we started by exploring what the Left envisions for the future of America by looking at their pet project: California. We looked at the Left's actions, which reveal their true agenda with chilling clarity. We can see the Left actively working to dismantle the fundamental core of individual liberty in our nation and impose instead a politically correct, Marxist, big government, anti-freedom, socialist state. What emerged in the first chapter is a snapshot of a leftist America: a dystopian, oppressive state filled with mindless minions controlled by an all-powerful government.

In Chapter 2, we established that the purpose of liberals' strategic agenda is an effort to morph culture into law. To morph *extreme leftist politically correct* culture into the laws of our nation. To do this, the radical Left normalizes the insane political correctness we see on college campuses in an attempt to trick the frog in the pot of water so that Froggy doesn't notice when the Left turns up the heat and Froggy boils to death. In other words, so we the people don't notice (and object) to the moment when the Left transform their culture of identity politics and safe spaces into codified law. They are making every effort to bridge this gap between culture and codified law as we speak in order to force "We the People" to adhere to their ideology.

We then detailed in Chapter 3 how (and why) the Left attacks the bedrock values of our nation by undermining America's cultural cornerstones: religion, family, and education. They do this to render people dependent on government instead of God by replacing parents and spouses with bureaucrats. They render our next generation compliant by indoctrinating children with the warped, leftist agenda taught in public schools run by…you guessed it…the same government elitists positioning themselves to be obeyed instead of the Deity, and to replace the support of our families with government regulations and government assistance. Remember, the more dependent on government the people are, the more power the government holds over our lives. That is the ultimate goal of the radical Left. The first three chapters in this book detail how they work to achieve that goal.

Then in Part 2, we discussed how to tip the scales in favor of limited government and individual liberty.

In Chapter 4, we laid out 11 tactics for winning a debate against a radical leftist, starting with the premise: do not be afraid to debate liberals! The tactics themselves are as follows:

- Be aggressive (but polite)
- Let them talk until they run out of B.S.
- Laugh when the left is serious (but in a good-natured way)
- Ask micro-questions (to highlight their ignorance)
- Tackle their big point (which they try to protect with distractions)
- Know what you would say if you were a liberal
- Pick the point you don't want to answer and answer it preemptively
- Call out liberals for their silly talking points
- Flip the argument and call out the contradiction
- Mirror their tactics
- Always reframe the question

Armed with the knowledge of the Left's overall vision for America and the strategies and tactics they're employing to bring their ultimate agenda to fruition, plus with the rhetorical skills to verbally challenge the Left on their talking points, we moved forward to unpack why the Left believes what they believe.

In Chapter 5, we illustrated the radical shift in the ideology of the Left since the founding of our nation. In other words, we demonstrated how the modern Left doesn't believe in the same fundamental principles as we do anymore. The political gridlock between liberals and conservatives is no longer an argument that starts with a common goal and in which the disagreement is over how to achieve that common goal. Not anymore. Now the Left wants to redefine right, wrong, and justice. We no longer share common goals or common values with the Left. All we have to do is look at their actions to prove this.

This makes it dangerous to lose any battle to the Left.

In Chapter 6, we challenged ourselves: if we know what we believe, prove it! We tackled the talking points from the Left and some of the trickiest questions the Left poses to the Right. We unpacked exactly what we believe and *why* we believe it. Make no mistake—if we don't know why we believe what we believe, we will lose arguments with the radical Left. If we lose arguments, we will lose policy battles, and because the Left's goals are no longer in line with our constitutional values, when we lose battles, that will result ultimately in losing our nation as we know it.

Then in Chapter 7, we listed concrete steps for learning the philosophy that underpins our conservative principles and political platform—with a book list to educate ourselves so that we can *understand* what we believe rather than simply associating with our principles intuitively and resorting to repeating talking points in defense of those principles.

In Part 3, we detailed how the Left has built their House of Cards.

In Chapter 8, we debunked common liberal talking points that are unequivocally false. There is an epidemic of murders with assault rifles in our nation: false. Illegal immigrants commit fewer crimes than natural-born American citizens: false. We provide the numbers, the statistics, and the facts to expose the most commonly peddled (but false) leftist arguments.

Then in Chapter 9, we explored the revisionist history of the Left. The stories the Left tells the American people about our past that are simply...lies. We laid out the truth and showed that the Left's warped version of history is a lie. Most importantly, we tied together their false revisionist history and the current platform of the Democratic Party. Without the revisionist history to validate the Left's current policies, the Left's platform crumbles—when they can't point to the revisionist history as proof that their current politics are necessary or effective.

In Chapter 10, we demonstrated the quickest way to punch a hole in the leftist platform: for every liberal position, there is an equal and opposite contradiction. This is a useful (and easy) tactic to use to expose the fact that the radical Left has built their ideological foundation on sand. No consistency, no morality, just a conglomeration of policies that help advance their ultimate goal of government control.

Finally in Chapter 11, we took on the Mainstream Media Bias Framework: the tactics utilized by the MSM to insert bias into their reporting and stories. Once you know the tactics used by liberal media outlets to shape their stories in a way that tilts left and favors leftist politicians and leftist ideology, you can easily disrupt the dishonest reporting and expose the corruption of the media. We also cover *why* this is important. It's not just bickering with the media. The leadership of the Democratic Party uses the mainstream media as their PR firm—the media are the medium through which the Left disseminates their liberal message to the people. You know the phrase, "Don't bite the hand that feeds you"? This is the hand feeding liberal garbage to the liberal electorate. It's time to bite that hand.

That's it. That's the whole handbook. My hope for you after reading this book is that you feel empowered to take the fight to liberals. So many conservative books cause us to nod our heads in agreement or serve as encouragement to corroborate our views or feelings. My book is different. This book, I hope, provides you with concrete information *and* tactics so that you know how to do battle.

We can't rely on politicians to fight for what's right. We can't rely on the proverbial *somebody else* to defend life, liberty, and the pursuit of happiness.

That's up to you and me.

And this book, I hope, will give you the tools to do that.

As I say on my show, "Our nation is at a Tipping Point. If we don't turn America towards liberty, then we risk losing the freedom that makes America exceptional."

Let's not let that happen.

Acknowledgments

This book is something I've dreamed about since I was ten years old. As a small child, I would contemplate the colossal failure of communism and wonder why progressives cry "social justice!" while they divide our nation by race, gender, age, and religion. Just kidding. I *have* dreamed about writing a book since I was ten years old, but my scribbles then leaned more toward fairy tales written in longhand with a lead pencil on pre-collated pink printer paper and stories about child detectives (think Encyclopedia Brown, a girl version who looked like me).

The concept for this book was as far from my reality as a ten-year-old making up pen names for myself as it should have been—and I believe *because* of that, it's been possible for me now to write a manifesto of sorts on the incalculable value of our liberty, the duty we have to protect that liberty, and the tactics we can use to defeat those who threaten the very essence of what it means to be a free people.

The people in my life are the ones who made this book possible. They formed who I am—and they continue this ongoing, sometimes struggle of a formation.

Thank you to my husband, Dan, who suffered through a lot of take-out dinners during the writing of this book. I love you with my whole heart. Of all the things in the world (even this book!), I am proudest to be your wife. Oorah!

Thank you to my parents, Steve and Kathy, who raised me to love God, family, and country, and fed my nerdiness as a kid. Your love for your family is the most Christlike of anybody I know.

Thanks to my youngest sister, Anne. We may be thirteen years apart, but you're my best friend. You are thoughtful, smart, holy, and wise beyond your years. I thank God for you every day. I also appreciate the fact that your first question when I told you about this book was, "You're dedicating it to me, right?!"

Thank you to the best in-house sounding board in the world, who has been proofing and critiquing my work with a brutally honest eye since the days of Lady Encyclopedia Brown and her adventures: my sister Maria. I have never met anybody else who can say, "That sentence is dumb, delete it," with such reckless abandon and it doesn't hurt my feelings. I guess I never outgrew the stage where I crawled after you when we were babies and tried to copy everything you did. I adore you, you grammar torpedo.

Thanks to my in-laws, Tom and Jennifer, for sharing your son with me, accepting me into your family, supporting me, and telling me at every opportunity that you're proud of me. And thank you to Tom for the honest critique of each chapter and the insightful additions you suggested that appear throughout this book!

Thank you to OANN's founding family, the Herrings—Robert Sr., Charles, and Bobby—for the incredible opportunity and privilege to host *Tipping Point* on One America News Network. I've had the time of my life building this show. Thank you for building the channel and believing in me.

Thank you to my incredible team of producers at *Tipping Point*— Victoria, Alec, and Jonah. The show is truly a team effort, and it's a joy to work with each of you. Thank you, too, to April. As I write, we've aired almost one thousand episodes of the show. I'm incredibly proud to be a part of it.

Thank you to the studio and control room crew: Trey, Michael, girl Adrian, boy Adrian, Andrew, Drew, Gitau, Kenneth, Monica, and Vince, and the marvelous makeup crew, Mele, Karina, and Amy. Thank you, too, to Marco, Cecilia, Rafael, Michael, Lauren, and Tony. (And by "thanks" I mean thanks for putting up with me even though most of y'all don't agree with my politics.)

Thank you to Regnery Publishing for emailing me back when I pitched the idea for this book. Thank you to Harry Crocker, Tom Spence, and Elizabeth Kantor. Thank you to John Caruso for the spectacular cover design. Thank you to photographer Michael Franke for the cover portrait.

And thank you to all the people who love me for who I am: Amy and Brian, Matt, Alyen, Tim, David, Rose and Trey, Audrey and Andy, Kelly and Joel, Grace, Gram and Gramps, Uncle Kevin, and Mr. and Mrs. E.

Any errors or inadvertent inaccuracies in this book are entirely my own.

The Academy has begun to play the music (and it's getting loud) so I will close by saying, thank YOU for reading this book. It means the world to me that so many people watch my show every night, write to me, and encourage me. Thank you for buying my book. I truly hope you enjoyed it.

Notes

Chapter 1: Professor Unidentified Blob Is Coming to Get You

1. Eliza Graves-Browne, "What It Means to Be Trans Species," VICE, April 17, 2016, https://www.vice.com/en_us/article/yvwknv/what-does-it-mean-to-be-trans-species.
2. Sophie Saint Thomas, "What It Means If Someone Is Gender Fluid," Refinery29, April 19, 2017, https://www.refinery29.com/en-us/2017/04/150470/what-is-gender-fluid.
3. Eugene Volokh, "UC Teaching Faculty Members Not to Criticize Race-Based Affirmative Action, Call America 'Melting Pot,' and More," *Washington Post*, June 16, 2015, https://www.washingtonpost.com/news/volokh-conspiracy/wp/2015/06/16/uc-teaching-faculty-members-not-to-criticize-race-based-affirmative-action-call-america-melting-pot-and-more/?noredirect=on&utm_term=.95d05e6c30bc.
4. Qazi Rahman, "'Gay Genes': Science Is on the Right Track, We're Born This Way. Let's Deal with It," *Guardian*, July 24, 2015, https://www.theguardian.com/science/blog/2015/jul/24/gay-genes-science-is-on-the-right-track-were-born-this-way-lets-deal-with-it.
5. Brooke Singman, "New California Law Allows Jail Time for Using Wrong Gender Pronoun, Sponsor Denies That Would Happen," Fox News, October 9, 2017, https://www.foxnews.com/politics/new-california-law-allows-jail-time-for-using-wrong-gender-pronoun-sponsor-denies-that-would-happen.
6. "How to Change Your Gender (Adult)," California Courts, http://www.courts.ca.gov/25798.htm.
7. EnHaleCentral, "Obama: We are 5 days from FUNDAMENTALLY transforming America," YouTube, October 31, 2008, https://www.youtube.com/watch?v=_cqN4NIEtOY.
8. Kathleen Ronayne, "California Democrats Temporarily Lose Assembly Supermajority," *Mercury News*, December 11, 2017, https://www.mercurynews.com/2017/12/11/california-democrats-temporarily-lose-assembly-supermajority/.
9. "AB-775 Reproductive FACT Act," California Legislative Information, https://leginfo.legislature.ca.gov/faces/billNavClient.xhtml?bill_id=201520160AB775.

10. Madeline Farber, "Supreme Court Rules in Favor of Pro-Life Crisis Pregnancy Centers: A Breakdown of NIFLA v. Becerra," Fox News, June 26, 2018, https://www.foxnews.com/politics/supreme-court-rules-in-favor-of-pro-life-crisis-pregnancy-centers-a-breakdown-of-nifla-v-becerra.

11. Amy Howe, "Opinion Analysis: Divided Court Rules for Anti-Abortion Pregnancy Centers in Challenge to California Law," SCOTUSblog, June 26, 2018, https://www.scotusblog.com/2018/06/opinion-analysis-divided-court-rules-for-anti-abortion-pregnancy-centers-in-challenge-to-california-law/.

12. Xavier Becerra, "Attorney General Becerra Issues Statement on Supreme Court's Ruling in NIFLA v. Becerra," State of California Department of Justice, June 26, 2018, https://oag.ca.gov/news/press-releases/attorney-general-becerra-issues-statement-supreme-court%E2%80%99s-ruling-in%C2%A0nifla-v.

13. "SB-174 Citizens of the State," California Legislative Information, https://leginfo.legislature.ca.gov/faces/billTextClient.xhtml?bill_id=201720180SB174.

14. Taryn Luna, "Undocumented Immigrants Could Serve on California Boards under New Bill," *Sacramento Bee,* April 30, 2018, https://www.sacbee.com/latest-news/article210184089.html.

15. "AB-2926 Private Schools: Home Schools: Advisory Committee," California Legislative Information, http://leginfo.legislature.ca.gov/faces/billNavClient.xhtml?bill_id=201720180AB2926.

16. "AB-2756 Private Schools: Home Schools: Filing," California Legislative Information, http://leginfo.legislature.ca.gov/faces/billNavClient.xhtml?bill_id=201720180AB2756.

17. Joseph Hong, "In Turpin Aftermath, Two California Assembly Members Seek Tighter Homeschool Regulations," *Desert Sun*, April 9, 2018, https://www.desertsun.com/story/news/education/2018/04/09/turpin-aftermath-two-california-assembly-members-seek-tighter-homeschool-regulations/500373002/.

18. "Turpin Case," Wikipedia, https://en.wikipedia.org/w/index.php?title=Turpin_case&oldid=881810649.

19. Brian D. Ray, "Child Abuse of Public School, Private School, and Homeschool Students: Evidence, Philosophy, and Reason," National Home Education Research Institute, January 23, 2018, https://www.nheri.org/child-abuse-of-public-school-private-school-and-homeschool-students-evidence-philosophy-and-reason/.

20. California Department of Education, "Private Schools Frequently Asked Questions," https://www.cde.ca.gov/sp/ps/psfaq.asp#a15.

21. Chris Klicka, "The Myth of Teacher Qualifications," Homeschool Legal Defense Association, September 2007, https://hslda.org/content/docs/nche/000002/00000214.asp.

22. "AB-2756."

23. "Sacramento Report: Both Sides Dig in on Sanctuary Debate," Voice of San Diego, April 27, 2018, https://www.voiceofsandiego.org/topics/government/sacramento-report-both-sides-dig-in-on-sanctuary-debate/.

24. "Senate Republican Leader Bates' Effort to Prevent Early Release of Serious Felons and Sex Offenders Blocked by Senate Public Safety Committee," April 24, 2018, https://bates.cssrc.us/content/senate-republican-leader-bates-effort-prevent-early-release-serious-felons-and-sex-offenders.

25. "SB-974 Medi-Cal: Immigration Status: Adults," California Legislative Information, https://leginfo.legislature.ca.gov/faces/billTextClient.xhtml?bill_id=201720180SB974.

26. "Steps to Medi-Cal—How to Apply," California Department of Healthcare Services, https://www.dhcs.ca.gov/individuals/Pages/How.aspx.

27. Timothy P. Carney, "Men Buying Maternity Coverage: Insurance and Redistribution Are Different Things," American Enterprise Institute, May 23, 2017, http://www.aei.org/publication/men-buying-maternity-coverage-insurance-and-redistribution-are-different-things/.

28. "Preventive Care Benefits for Adults," Healthcare.gov, https://www.healthcare.gov/preventive-care-adults/.

29. Sammy Caiola, "The Doctor Isn't In: Medi-Cal Patients Struggle to Find Primary Care," Sacramento Bee, October 6, 2016, https://www.sacbee.com/news/local/health-and-medicine/article106271347.html.

30. Scott A. Hodge, "Tyranny of California's Nonpayers," Tax Foundation, June 6, 2006, https://taxfoundation.org/tyranny-californias-nonpayers/.

31. "Medi-Cal and Gender Reassignment Procedures," Transgender Law Center, https://transgenderlawcenter.org/wp-content/uploads/2012/07/Medical-Fact-Sheet.pdf.

32. Singman, "New California Law Allows Jail Time."

33. Amy Swearer, "California Bill Threatens Waiters with Jail for Providing Plastic Straws," January 29, 2018, https://www.dailysignal.com/2018/01/29/california-bill-threatens-waiters-jail-providing-plastic-straws/.

34. Josh Hafner, "Plastic Straws Illegal Unless Requested under California Bill—with Up to a $1,000 Fine Attached," USA Today, January 29, 2018, https://www.usatoday.com/story/money/nation-now/2018/01/29/plastic-straws-illegal-unless-requested-under-california-bill/1074610001/.

35. Taryn Luna, "Californians Say Farewell to the Plastic Bag," *Sacramento Bee*, November 10, 2016, https://www.sacbee.com/news/politics-government/capitol-alert/article113898813.html.

36. Ben Smithwick, "Is State's Plastic Bag Ban Causing Rise in Hepatitis Cases?" Pacific Research Institute, September 28, 2017, https://www.pacificresearch.org/is-states-plastic-bag-ban-causing-rise-in-hepatitis-cases/.

37. David Maccar, "How Gun Control Initiatives Fared on Election Day," Range 365, November 9, 2016, https://www.range365.com/how-gun-control-initiatives-fared-on-election-day.

38. Patrick McGreevy, "NRA, Olympic shooter sue California over its restrictions on ammunition sales," *Los Angeles Times,* April 26, 2018, https://www.latimes.com/politics/essential/la-pol-ca-essential-politics-updates-nra-olympic-shooter-sue-california-over-1524786702-htmlstory.html.

39. "Kim Rhode," Wikipedia, https://en.wikipedia.org/w/index.php?title=Kim_Rhode&oldid=868120109.

40. Eli Rosenberg, "Knowingly Exposing Others to HIV Is No Longer a Felony in California," *Washington Post*, October 10, 2017, https://www.washingtonpost.com/news/to-your-health/wp/2017/10/09/knowingly-infecting-others-with-hiv-is-no-longer-a-felony-in-california-advocates-say-it-targeted-sex-workers/?noredirect=on&utm_term=.f3ce948b02ed.

41. "Advertising Oleomargarine—Restrictions," Iowa Legislative Information, https://www.legis.iowa.gov/docs/ico/code/2013/191.5.pdf.

42. Rob Bluey, "Q&A: The Politically Incorrect Book That Debunks Climate Change Myths," The Daily Signal, June 3, 2018, https://www.dailysignal.com/2018/06/03/qa-the-politically-incorrect-book-that-debunks-climate-change-myths/.

43. Jessica Vrazilek, "Study: North Pole Once Was Tropical," CBS News, June 1, 2006, https://www.cbsnews.com/news/study-north-pole-once-was-tropical/.

44. Ivan Penn, "California Will Require Solar Power for New Homes," *New York Times,* May 9, 2018, https://www.nytimes.com/2018/05/09/business/energy-environment/california-solar-power.html.

45. Brooke Singman, "California Becomes First State to Mandate Solar Panels on New Homes," Fox News, May 9, 2018, https://www.foxnews.com/politics/california-becomes-first-state-to-mandate-solar-panels-on-new-homes.

46. Sebastien Malo, "California Becomes First U.S. State to Require Solar Panels on New Homes," Reuters, May 9, 2018, https://www.reuters.com/article/usa-solar-california/

california-becomes-first-u-s-state-to-require-solar-panels-on-new-homes-idUSL1N1SG0SP.

47. "West Sacramento Launching Controversial Program Watching Public's Social Media Posts," CBS 13 Sacramento, May 10, 2018, https://sacramento.cbslocal.com/2018/05/10/west-sacramento-tracking-social-media/.

48. Ibid.

49. Ibid.

50. Zachary A. Goldfarb, "IRS Admits Targeting Conservatives for Tax Scrutiny in 2012 Election," *Washington Post*, May 10, 2013, https://www.washingtonpost.com/business/economy/irs-admits-targeting-conservatives-for-tax-scrutiny-in-2012-election/2013/05/10/3b6a0ada-b987-11e2-92f3-f291801936b8_story.html?noredirect=on&utm_term=.e649851777b5.

51. "The Boycott of Jewish Businesses," United States Holocaust Memorial Museum, https://encyclopedia.ushmm.org/content/en/article/the-boycott-of-jewish-businesses.

52. Ian Schwartz, "Dem Rep. Himes: Nobody Wants to Take Away Guns, We Just Want to Be Like Australia, Canada & Great Britain," RealClearPolitics, February 19, 2018, https://www.realclearpolitics.com/video/2018/02/19/dem_rep_himes_nobody_wants_to_take_away_guns_we_just_want_to_be_like_australia_canada__great_britain.html.

53. Douglas Ernst, "Nancy Pelosi Scoffs at 'Crumb' Bonuses by U.S. Companies as a Result of Tax Cuts," *Washington Times*, January 11, 2018, https://www.washingtontimes.com/news/2018/jan/11/nancy-pelosi-scoffs-at-crumb-bonuses-by-us-compani/.

54. "Nancy Pelosi's Voting Records on Issue," Vote Smart Facts Matter, https://votesmart.org/candidate/key-votes/26732/nancy-pelosi/2/abortion#.XFuL_p9KgdV.

55. "A Look at Pelosi's Voting Record," *Washington Times*, November 2, 2006, https://www.washingtontimes.com/news/2006/nov/2/20061102-090358-9812r/.

56. Chris McGreal, "Nancy Pelosi: Is This the Most Powerful Woman in US History?" *Guardian*, March 26, 2010, https://www.theguardian.com/world/2010/mar/26/nancy-pelosi-politician-speaker.

57. Valerie Richardson, "California Attorney General behind Raid of Pro-Life activist Slammed for Planned Parenthood Advocacy," *Washington Times*, April 6, 2016, https://www.washingtontimes.com/news/2016/apr/6/kamala-harris-california-ag-behind-daleiden-raid-s/.

58. John Bresnahan, "Holder Held in Contempt," *Politico*, June 28, 2012, https://www.politico.com/story/2012/06/holder-held-in-contempt-of-congress-077988

59. Associated Press, "California Hires Former Attorney General Eric Holder to Combat Trump," KPBS, January 4, 2017, https://www.kpbs.org/news/2017/jan/04/california-hires-former-attorney-general-eric-hold/.

Chapter 2: Just Tell Us How to Beat Liberals Already

1. "Facebook Asks Users, 'Does This Post Contain Hate Speech?'" CBS Sacramento, May 1, 2018, https://sacramento.cbslocal.com/2018/05/01/facebook-asks-users-does-this-post-contain-hate-speech/.

2. Abby Ohlheiser, "Facebook Accidentally Asked Its Users Whether the Posts They Saw Contained Hate Speech," *Washington Post*, May 1, 2018, https://www.washingtonpost.com/news/the-intersect/wp/2018/05/01/facebook-accidentally-asked-its-users-if-the-posts-they-saw-contained-hate-speech/.

3. Josh Constine and Kate Conger, "Clinton Campaign and Dems get $20M from Facebook Co-Founder Dustin Moskovitz," TechCrunch, https://techcrunch.com/2016/09/08/a-friend-of-hillary/.

4. Lauretta Brown, "Zuckerberg Can't Define 'Hate Speech' in Senate Hearing Despite Pushing to Police It," Townhall, April 11, 2018, https://townhall.com/tipsheet/laurettabrown/2018/04/11/zuckerberg-cant-define-hate-speech-in-senate-hearing-despite-pushing-to-police-it-n2469747.

5. Eugene Volokh, "Supreme Court Unanimously Reaffirms: There Is No 'Hate Speech' Exception to the First Amendment," *Washington Post*, June 19, 2017, https://www.washingtonpost.com/news/volokh-conspiracy/wp/2017/06/19/supreme-court-unanimously-reaffirms-there-is-no-hate-speech-exception-to-the-first-amendment/.

6. Derrick Johnson, "Before the Next Videotaped Starbucks Disaster, Everyone Should Take Implicit Bias Training," *USA Today*, May 8, 2018, https://www.usatoday.com/story/opinion/2018/05/08/starbucks-naacp-implicit-bias-training-racism-column/587402002/.

7. Joshua A. Krisch, "Are Most Men Sexist? The Data Says Yes Even If They Say No," Fatherly, December 24, 2018, https://www.fatherly.com/health-science/are-men-sexist-data-male-feminism/.

8. "Project Implicit," Harvard, https://implicit.harvard.edu/implicit/takeatest.html.

9. Heather Mac Donald, "Are We All Unconscious Racists?" *City Journal*, Autumn 2017, https://www.city-journal.org/html/are-we-all-unconscious-racists-15487.html.

10. Johnson, "Before the Next Videotaped Starbucks Disaster."

11. "Planned Parenthood 2013-2014 Annual Report," Planned Parenthood Action Fund, December 29, 2014, https://issuu.com/actionfund/docs/annual_report_final_proof_12.16.14_

12. Willis L. Kumholz, "Yes, Planned Parenthood Targets and Hurts Poor Black Women," The Federalist, February 18, 2016, http://thefederalist.com/2016/02/18/yes-planned-parenthood-targets-and-hurts-poor-black-women/.

13. "Planned Parenthood Accepts Racially Motivated Donations," Live Action, https://www.liveaction.org/what-we-do/investigations/racially-motivated-donations/.

14. "Who was Margaret Sanger?" American Life League, https://www.stopp.org/pdfs/brochures/whowasmarsan.pdf.

15. Quoctrung Bui and Amanda Cox, "Surprising New Evidence Shows Bias in Police Use of Force but Not in Shootings," New York Times, July 11, 2016, https://www.nytimes.com/2016/07/12/upshot/surprising-new-evidence-shows-bias-in police-use-of-force-but-not-in-shootings.html.

16. Valerie Richardson, "No Racial Bias in Police Shootings, Study by Harvard Professor Shows," Washington Times, July 11, 2016, https://www.washingtontimes.com/news/2016/jul/11/no-racial-bias-police-shootings-study-harvard-prof/.

17. "China Assigns Every Citizen A 'Social Credit Score' to Identify Who Is and Isn't Trustworthy," CBS New York, April 24, 2018, https://newyork.cbslocal.com/2018/04/24/china-assigns-every-citizen-a-social-credit-score-to-identify-who-is-and-isnt-trustworthy/.

18. EnHaleCentral, "Obama: We are 5 days from FUNDAMENTALLY transforming America," YouTube, October 31, 2008, https://www.youtube.com/watch?v=_cqN4NIEtOY.

19. Amanda Prestigiacomo, "EXPOSED: Obama Advisors' Emails in Immediate Sandy Hook Aftermath Reveal Anti-Gun Agenda: 'Tap Peoples Emotions,'" The Daily Wire, May 28, 2018, https://www.dailywire.com/news/30993/exposed-emails-obama-staffers-minutes-following-amanda-prestigiacomo.

Chapter 3: Go for Their Achilles Heel

1. Michael Jones, "University Event Aims to Combat 'Christian Privilege,'" The College Fix, April 3, 2018, https://www.thecollegefix.com/university-event-aims-to-combat-christian-privilege/.

2. "AB-2943 Unlawful Business Practices: Sexual Orientation Change Efforts," California Legislative Information, https://leginfo.legislature.ca.gov/faces/billTextClient.xhtml?bill_id=201720180AB2943.

3.   Author interview of Chad Felix Greene, June 11, 2018.
4.   Casey Tolan, "As a Gay Teen, Evan Low Thought about Changing His Sexuality. Now He's Fighting Conversion Therapy in California," *Mercury News*, May 27, 2018, https://www.mercurynews.com/2018/05/27/evan-low-lgbt-conversion-therapy-california/.
5.   Ibid.
6.   Doug Mainwaring, "Christian Ministry Forced to Cancel LA Conference due to Bill Banning Biblical Views on Sexuality," Life Site News, May 2, 2018, https://www.lifesitenews.com/news/christian-ministry-forced-to-cancel-la-conference-due-to-bill-banning-bibli.
7.   Dan MacGuill, "Would a Proposed Law 'Ban the Bible' in California?" Snopes, April 20, 2018, https://www.snopes.com/fact-check/california-bible-ban/.
8.   Valerie Richardson, "New York Farm Owners Give Up Legal Fight after Being Fined $13,000 for Refusing to Host Gay Wedding," *Washington Times*, February 23, 2016, https://www.washingtontimes.com/news/2016/feb/23/robert-cynthia-giffords-give-legal-fight-over-same/.
9.   Hank Berrien, "Christian Couple Fined for Refusing Gay Marriage on Their Farm Comes Up with Perfect Solution," The Daily Wire, March 26, 2018, https://www.dailywire.com/news/28701/christian-couple-fined-refusing-gay-marriage-their-hank-berrien.
10. Liberty Ridge Farm, Weddings, https://libertyridgefarmny.com/weddings/.
11. "Jack Phillips," Alliance Defending Freedom, http://adflegal.org/detailspages/client-stories-details/jack-phillips.
12. Adam Edelman, "Baker Who Refused to Make Cake for Gay Wedding: 'I Don't Discriminate,'" NBC News, June 5, 2018, https://www.nbcnews.com/politics/politics-news/baker-who-refused-make-cake-gay-wedding-i-don-t-n880061.
13. *Masterpiece Cakeshop, Ltd. v. Colorado Civil Rights Commission*, 584 U.S. ___ (2018), https://supreme.justia.com/cases/federal/us/584/16-111/.
14. Ken McIntyre, "24 Questions for Jack Phillips, the Baker Who Gave Up Wedding Cakes for God," The Daily Signal, August 19, 2015, https://www.dailysignal.com/2015/08/19/24-questions-for-jack-phillips-the-baker-who-gave-up-wedding-cakes-for-god/.
15. Crystal Woodall, "It's a Deal, but Not for Christians: What's Missing from DC's Newly Approved Spending Bill," CBN News, March 23, 2018, http://www1.cbn.com/cbnnews/politics/2018/march/its-a-deal-but-not-for-christians-whats-missing-from-dcs-new-spending-bill.
16. John McCormack, "Little Sisters of the Poor Cheer Changes to Contraception Mandate," *Weekly Standard*, October 6, 2017, https://www.weeklystandard.com/john-mccormack/little-sisters-of-the-poor-cheer-changes-to-contraception-mandate.

17. Todd Starnes, "School Sends Sheriff to Order Child to Stop Sharing Bible Verses," Fox News, June 3, 2016, https://www.foxnews.com/opinion/school-sends-sheriff-to-order-child-to-stop-sharing-bible-verses.

18. Humberto Fontova, "Anti-NRA Student Walkout Features Che Guevara as Poster Child," Townhall, March 17, 2018, https://townhall.com/columnists/humbertofontova/2018/03/17/antinra-student-walkout-features-che-guevara-as-poster-child-n2461624.

19. "School Bans U.S. Flag T-Shirts on Cinco de Mayo," Snopes, https://www.snopes.com/fact-check/school-bans-u-s-flag-t-shirts-cinco-de-mayo/.

20. Joshua Gill, "Christian Parent Furious After School Instructs Children to Write Out Their Submission to Allah," The Daily Caller, May 17, 2018, https://dailycaller.com/2018/05/17/west-virginia-christian-parent-school-submissions-to-allah/.

21. Caleb Parke, "College Student Kicked Out of Class for Telling Professor There Are Only Two genders," Fox News, March 12, 2018, https://www.foxnews.com/us/college-student-kicked-out-of-class-for-telling-professor-there-are-only two-genders.

22. Nicole Russell, "Ohio Judge Strips Custody from Parents for Not Letting Daughter Take Trans Hormones," The Federalist, February 20, 2018, http://thefederalist.com/2018/02/20/ohio-judge-strips-custody-parents-not-letting-daughter-taking-trans-hormones/.

23. Ryan T. Anderson, "Sex Reassignment Doesn't Work. Here Is the Evidence," the Heritage Foundation, May 9, 2018, https://www.heritage.org/gender/commentary/sex-reassignment-doesnt-work-here-the-evidence.

24. "Dr. Ryan T. Anderson: '80-95% of Children with Gender Dysphoria Grow Out of It,'" YouTube, One America News Network, February 27, 2018, https://www.youtube.com/watch?v=eQq6QCviMq0.

25. "From John Adams to Massachusetts Militia, 11 October 1798," National Archives, https://founders.archives.gov/documents/Adams/99-02-02-3102.

26. Bias Response Team Report 2017, FIRE, https://www.thefire.org/first-amendment-library/special-collections/fire-guides/report-on-bias-reporting-systems-2017/#examples.

27. John Sexton, "Lawsuit Takes on University of Michigan's 'Bias Response Team,'" Hot Air, May 8, 2018, https://hotair.com/archives/2018/05/08/lawsuit-takes-university-michigans-bias-response-team/.

28. Andrew O'Reilly, "Gaza Preschoolers Seen Performing Mock Execution of Israeli Soldier," Fox News, June 3, 2018, https://www.foxnews.com/world/gaza-preschoolers-seen-performing-mock-execution-of-israeli-soldier.

29. Jennifer Walker, "Sex Ed. Video Played at Western Albemarle Causes Concern among Parents," NBC 29, April 18, 2018, http://www.nbc29.com/story/37988396/sex-ed-video-played-at-western-albemarle-causes-concern-among-parents.

30. Gill, "Christian Parent Furious."

31. "Shahada," Wikipedia, https://en.wikipedia.org/w/index.php?title=Shahada&oldid=881385089.

32. Spencer Brown, "'YAF Is Not a Suitable Platform': Bellarmine University Administrator Blocks YAF Chapter," Young America's Foundation, May 24, 2018, https://www.yaf.org/news/yaf-is-not-a-suitable-platform-bellarmine-university-administrator-blocks-yaf-chapter/.

33. Graham Allen, "Rapid-Fire with Phil Robertson! Phil's Take on Culture," *Rant Nation with Graham Allen*, April 23, 2018, https://www.facebook.com/OfficialPhilRobertson/posts/1776788272382343.

34. Brooke Sopelsa, "Gender 'X': New York City to Add Third Gender Option to Birth Certificates," NBC News, September 12, 2018, https://www.nbcnews.com/feature/nbc-out/gender-x-new-york-city-add-third-gender-option-birth-n909021.

35. Ibid.

36. "Rachel Dolezal," Wikipedia, https://en.wikipedia.org/w/index.php?title=Rachel_Dolezal&oldid=882324360.

37. Sarah Boesveld, "Becoming Disabled by Choice, Not Chance: 'Transabled' People Feel like Impostors in Their Fully Working Bodies," *National Post*, June 3, 2015, https://nationalpost.com/news/canada/becoming-disabled-by-choice-not-chance-transabled-people-feel-like-impostors-in-their-fully-working-bodies

38. Blake Neff, "North Carolina Woman Identifies as Blind, Pours Drain Cleaner in Her Eyes," The Daily Caller, October 1, 2015, https://dailycaller.com/2015/10/01/north-carolina-woman-identifies-as-blind-pours-drain-cleaner-in-her-eyes/.

39. Robert Rector, "Marriage: America's Greatest Weapon against Child Poverty," the Heritage Foundation, September 5, 2012, https://www.heritage.org/poverty-and-inequality/report/marriage-americas-greatest-weapon-against-child-poverty.

Chapter 4: 11 Tactics for Debating Liberals

1. Laurie Penny, "What the 'Transgender Tipping Point' Really Means," *New Republic*, June 27, 2014, https://newrepublic.com/article/118451/what-transgender-tipping-point-really-means.

2. "Aiding Abusers," Live Action, https://www.liveaction.org/wp-content/uploads/2018/05/Planned%20Parenthood%20Sexual%20Abuse%20Report%202018.pdf.

3. Sarah Terzo, "41 Quotes from Medical Textbooks Prove Human Life Begins at Conception," LifeNews, January 8, 2015, https://www.lifenews.com/2015/01/08/41-quotes-from-medical-textbooks-prove-human-life-begins-at-conception/.

4. Jack Dorsey, "Boost @ChickFilA," Twitter, June 9, 2018, https://twitter.com/jack/status/1005611653176496128.

5. David Carrig, "Twitter CEO Slammed for Chick-fil-A Tweet during Pride Month," *USA Today*, June 11, 2018, https://www.usatoday.com/story/tech/nation-now/2018/06/11/twitter-jack-dorsey-chick-fil-pride/691298002/.

6. Noah Michelson, "If You Really Love LGBTQ People, You Just Can't Keep Eating Chick-fil-A," The Huffington Post, June 12, 2018, https://www.huffingtonpost.com/entry/lgbtq-eating-chick-fil-a_us_5b1fb4cee4b09d7a3d770c81.

7. "Arizona Obamacare Plan to Jump By 116 Percent When Premiums Go Up Next Year," CBS New York, October 25, 2016, https://newyork.cbslocal.com/2016/10/25/arizona-obamacare-premiums/.

8. Michael Hiltzik, "The First Projections for Trumpcare 2019 Are In: Expect Rate increases of Up to 30%," *Los Angeles Times*, January 26, 2018, https://www.latimes.com/business/hiltzik/la-fi-hiltzik-trumpcare-2019-story.html.

9. "Key Facts about the Uninsured Population," Henry J. Kaiser Family Foundation, December 7, 2018, https://www.kff.org/uninsured/fact-sheet/key-facts-about-the-uninsured-population/

10. Betsey McCaughey, "Another 25 Million ObamaCare Victims," *New York Post*, January 14, 2014, https://nypost.com/2014/01/14/another-25-million-obamacare-victims/

11. Genevieve Wood, "Why Obamacare's '20 Million' Number Is Fake," The Daily Signal, January 13, 2017, https://www.dailysignal.com/2017/01/13/why-obamacares-20-million-number-is-fake/.

12. "Full Transcript: Democratic Presidential Debate," *New York Times*, October 14, 2015, https://www.nytimes.com/2015/10/14/us/politics/democratic-debate-transcript.html.

13. Hannah Strange, "Children Evacuated from Venezuela Hospital Hit by Tear Gas as Death Toll in Protests Rises to Nine," *Telegraph*, April 21, 2017, https://www.telegraph.co.uk/news/2017/04/21/children-evacuated-venezuela-hospital-hit-tear-gas-death-toll/.

14. "Youth Shot Dead during Protest against Venezuela President Maduro," *Hindustan Times*, April 7, 2017, https://www.hindustantimes.com/world-news/youth-shot-dead-during-protest-against-venezuela-president-maduro/story-MpXFX91UoIKt8fpEk7zosM.html.

15. John Otis, "Venezuela's Bread Wars: With Food Scarce, Government Accuses Bakers of Hoarding," NPR, April 7, 2017, https://www.npr.org/sections/thesalt/2017/04/07/522912791/venezuelas-bread-wars-with-food-scarce-government-accuses-bakers-of-hoarding.

16. Bret Stephens, "Yes, Venezuela Is a Socialist Catastrophe," *New York Times*, January 25, 2019, https://www.nytimes.com/2019/01/25/opinion/venezuela-maduro-socialism-government.html.

17. "Stoneman Douglas High School Shooting," Wikipedia, https://en.wikipedia.org/w/index.php?title=Stoneman_Douglas_High_School_shooting&oldid=882499362.

18. "Santa Fe High School Shooting," Wikipedia, https://en.wikipedia.org/w/index.php?title=Santa_Fe_High_School_shooting&oldid=881818357.

19. "Port Arthur Massacre (Australia)," Wikipedia, https://en.wikipedia.org/w/index.php?title=Port_Arthur_massacre_(Australia)&oldid=878926893.

20. "Miguel A. Faria Jr.," Guns and Violence," Women Against Gun Control, http://www.wagc.com/guns-and-violence-miguel-a-faria-jr-md/.

21. Kim Hjelmgaard, "London's Murder Rate Now Tops New York City's," *USA Today*, April 3, 2018, https://www.usatoday.com/story/news/world/2018/04/03/londons-murder-rate-higher-than-new-york-citys/480860002/.

22. John Lott, "Some Notes on Claims about Australia's Crime Rates," John Lott's website, August 13, 2012, https://johnrlott.blogspot.com/2012/08/some-notes-on-claims-about-australias.html.

23. Christopher Ingraham, "There Are More Guns than People in the United States, according to a New Study of Global Firearm Ownership," *Washington Post*, June 19, 2018, https://www.washingtonpost.com/news/wonk/wp/2018/06/19/there-are-more-guns-than-people-in-the-united-states-according-to-a-new-study-of-global-firearm-ownership/.

24. Lott, "Some Notes on Claims."

25. Erica York, "Lessons from the 2002 Bush Steel Tariffs," Tax Foundation, March 12, 2018, https://taxfoundation.org/lessons-2002-bush-steel-tariffs/.

26. Mark J. Perry, "2009 Tire Tariffs Cost US Consumers $926K per Job Saved and Led to the Loss of 3 Retail Jobs per Factory Job Saved," American Enterprise Institute, January 25, 2017, http://www.aei.org/publication/2009-tire-tariffs-cost-us-consumers-926k-per-job-saved-and-led-to-the-loss-of-3-retail-jobs-per-factory-job-saved/.

27. Dennis C. Blair and Keith Alexander, "China's Intellectual Property Theft Must Stop," *New York Times*, April 15, 2017, https://www.

nytimes.com/2017/08/15/opinion/china-us-intellectual-property-trump. html.

28. Mike Reed, "Democrats Then vs. Now on Border Wall Funding," GOP. com, August 24, 2017, https://gop.com/democrats-then-vs-now-on-border-wall-funding/.

29. Malia Zimmerman, "Elusive Crime Wave Data Shows Frightening Toll of Illegal Immigrant Criminals," Fox News, September 16, 2015, https://www.foxnews.com/us/elusive-crime-wave-data-shows-frightening-toll-of-illegal-immigrant-criminals.

30. "DOJ Report: Nearly Half of Fed Crimes Near Mexican Border," Judicial Watch, August 5, 2014, https://www.judicialwatch.org/blog/2014/08/doj-report-nearly-half-fed-crimes-near-mexican-border/.

31. Ibid.

32. Ron Martinelli, "The Truth about Crime, Illegal Immigrants and Sanctuary Cities," *The Hill*, April 19, 2017, https://thehill.com/blogs/pundits-blog/crime/329589-the-truth-about-crime-illegal-immigrants-and-sanctuary-cities.

33. Hans Von Spakovsky, "What the Media Won't Tell You About Illegal Immigration and Criminal Activity," the Heritage Foundation, March 13, 2017, https://www.heritage.org/immigration/commentary/what-the-media-wont-tell-you-about-illegal-immigration-and-criminal-activity.

34. Bob Bryan, "Nancy Pelosi Says Companies' Bonuses to Workers because of the Tax Bill are 'Crumbs,'" Business Insider, January 11, 2018, https://www.businessinsider.com/nancy-pelosi-tax-bill-bonuses-crumbs-2018-1.

35. Rebecca Lee, "Nancy Pelosi Net Worth: 5 Fast Facts You Need to Know," Heavy.com, May 15, 2018, https://heavy.com/money/2018/05/nancy-pelosi-net-worth/.

36. Molly Moorhead, "In Context: Sandra Fluke on Contraceptives and Women's Health," PolitiFact, March 6, 2012, https://www.politifact.com/truth-o-meter/article/2012/mar/06/context-sandra-fluke-contraceptives-and-womens-hea/.

37. Sean Parnell, "Birth Control & Self-Pay Patients," Self Pay Patient, July 1, 2014, http://selfpaypatient.com/2014/07/01/birth-control-self-pay-patients/.

38. Renu Zaretsky, "Tax Cuts in 2018: Will We Feel Them? Will It Matter?" Tax Policy Center, January 3, 2018, https://www.taxpolicycenter.org/taxvox/tax-cuts-2018-will-we-feel-them-will-it-matter.

39. Campus Reform, "Students Blast Supreme Court Ruling on Gay Wedding Cake," YouTube, June 12, 2018, https://www.youtube.com/watch?v=_iMaR5IEcnE.

40. Lawrence B. Finer, Lori F. Frohwirth, Lindsay A. Dauphinee, Susheela Singh, and Ann M. Moore, "Reasons U.S. Women Have Abortions: Quantitative and Qualitative Perspectives," Guttmacher Institute, https://www.guttmacher.org/sites/default/files/pdfs/pubs/psrh/full/3711005.pdf

41. Declaration of Independence, National Archives, https://www.archives.gov/founding-docs/declaration-transcript.

Chapter 5: Liberty Once Lost

1. "2016 United States Presidential Election," Wikipedia, https://en.wikipedia.org/w/index.php?title=2016_United_States_presidential_election&oldid=882453164.

2. Sari Horwitz and Maria Sacchetti, "Sessions Vows to Prosecute All Illegal Border Crossers and Separate Children from Their Parents," *Washington Post,* May 7, 2018, https://www.washingtonpost.com/world/national-security/sessions-says-justice-dept-will-prosecute-every-person-who-crosses-border-unlawfully/2018/05/07/e1312b7e-5216-11e8-9c91-7dab596e8252_story.html?utm_term=.e2c795b9103a.

3. "A Review of Various Actions by the Federal Bureau of Investigation and Department of Justice in Advance of the 2016 Election," Office of the Inspector General U.S. Department of Justice, June 2018, https://www.justice.gov/file/1071991/download.

4. Tim Hains, "Maxine Waters: 'God Is On Our Side,' If You See a Member of Trump Cabinet, 'Push Back'" RealClearPolitics, June 25, 2018, https://www.realclearpolitics.com/video/2018/06/25/maxine_waters_god_is_on_our_side.html.

Chapter 6: If You Know What You Believe, Prove It

1. Keith L. Moore, *The Developing Human: Clinically Oriented Embryology,* 7th edition (Philadelphia: Saunders, 2003), 16, 2.

2. *Clark Edward and Corliss Patten's Human Embryology,* McGraw-Hill Inc., 30, qtd. in Sarah Terzo, "41 Quotes from Medical Textbooks Prove Human Life Begins at Conception," Life News, January 8, 2015, https://www.lifenews.com/2015/01/08/41-quotes-from-medical-textbooks-prove-human-life-begins-at-conception/.

3. Ibid.

4. "HARVARD STUDY: GUN CONTROL IS COUNTERPRODUCTIVE," American Civil Rights Union, https://www.theacru.org/2007/05/08/harvard_study_gun_control_is_counterproductive/.

5. John R. Lott Jr., "WHAT A BALANCING TEST WILL SHOW FOR RIGHT-TO-CARRY LAWS," Crime Research, https://crimeresearch. org/wp-content/uploads/2014/04/Univ-of-Maryland-Law-Review-Lott-Concealed-Carry.pdf.

6. Aaron Bandler, "Report: Concealed Carry Permit Holders Are the Most Law-Abiding People in the Country," The Daily Wire, August 10, 2016, https://www.dailywire.com/news/8255/ report-concealed-carry-permit-holders-are-most-law-aaron-bandler.

7. Gary Kleck and Marc Gertz, "Armed Resistance to Crime: The Prevalence and Nature of Self-Defense with a Gun," *Journal of Criminal Law and Criminology* 86: 1 (autumn 1995): 150–87, https:// scholarlycommons.law.northwestern.edu/cgi/viewcontent.cgi?referer= &httpsredir=1&article=6853&context=jclc.

8. "A Little Gun History," Snopes, https://www.snopes.com/fact-check/ little-gun-history/.

9. Christina Wille, "How Many Weapons Are There in Cambodia?" Small Arms Survey, June 2006, http://www.smallarmssurvey.org/fileadmin/ docs/F-Working-papers/SAS-WP4-Cambodia.pdf.

10. "A Little Gun History."

11. Clayton E. Cramer, "The Racist Roots of Gun Control," Firearms & Liberty, http://www.firearmsandliberty.com/cramer.racism.html.

12. The Bill of Rights, National Archives, https://www.archives.gov/ founding-docs/bill-of-rights-transcript.

13. "Vietnam War U.S. Military Fatal Casualty Statistics," National Archives, https://www.archives.gov/research/military/vietnam-war/ casualty-statistics.

14. "Planned Parenthood 2016–2017 Annual Report," Planned Parenthood, https://www.plannedparenthood.org/uploads/filer_public/ d4/50/d450c016-a6a9-4455-bf7f-711067db5ff7/20171229_ar16-17_p01_ lowres.pdf.

15. "Planned Parenthood Pamphlet from 1952 Admits: Abortion 'Kills the Life of a Baby'" Live Action, May 17, 2017, https://www.liveaction.org/ news/planned-parenthood-in-1952-abortion-kills-the-life-of-a-baby/.

16. "Forced Abortion in America," Elliot Institute, August 2012, http://www. theunchoice.com/pdf/FactSheets/ForcedAbortions.pdf.

17. Mika Gissler, Elina Hemminki, and Jouko Lonnqvist, "Suicides after pregnancy in Finland, 1987–94: Register Linkage Study," British Medical Journal, December 7, 1996, https://www.bmj.com/ content/313/7070/1431.

18. "Women's Right to Know: Abortion Risks," Louisiana Department of Health, http://ldh.la.gov/index.cfm/page/1063.
19. John Adams, "John Adams to Abigail Adams, 7 July 1775," National Archives, https://founders.archives.gov/documents/Adams/04-01-02-0160.
20. Jason Richwine and Robert Rector, "The Fiscal Cost of Unlawful Immigrants and Amnesty to the U.S. Taxpayer," the Heritage Foundation, May 6, 2013, https://www.heritage.org/immigration/report/the-fiscal-cost-unlawful-immigrants-and-amnesty-the-us-taxpayer.
21. "Southwest Border Migration FY 2019," U.S. Customs and Border Protection, February 8, 2019, https://www.cbp.gov/newsroom/stats/sw-border-migration.
22. "Efforts by DHS to Estimate Southwest Border Security between Ports of Entry," Office of Immigration Statistics, Department of Homeland Security, September 2017, https://www.dhs.gov/sites/default/files/publications/17_0914_estimates-of-border-security.pdf.
23. Malia Zimmerman, "Elusive Crime Wave Data Shows Frightening Toll of Illegal Immigrant Criminals," Fox News, September 16, 2015, https://www.foxnews.com/us/elusive-crime-wave-data-shows-frightening-toll-of-illegal-immigrant-criminals.
24. Jessica M. Vaughan, "Fact Sheet: MS-13 Arrests by ICE: 2005–2014," Center for Immigration Studies, November 3, 2016, https://cis.org/Fact-Sheet/Fact-Sheet-MS13-Arrests-ICE-20052014.
25. Zameena Mejia, "These Are the Top 10 Happiest Countries in the World," CNBC, March 16, 2018, https://www.cnbc.com/2018/03/16/these-are-the-top-10-happiest-countries-in-the-world.html.
26. "Income Inequality in Sweden," Wikipedia, https://en.wikipedia.org/w/index.php?title=Income_inequality_in_Sweden&oldid=876103910.
27. "What Is the Current Poverty Rate in the United States?," Center for Poverty Research, https://poverty.ucdavis.edu/faq/what-current-poverty-rate-united-states.
28. "Jimmy Carter Reaffirms His Commitment to Human Rights," History.com, https://www.history.com/this-day-in-history/jimmy-carter-reaffirms-his-commitment-to-human-rights.
29. David Satter, "100 Years of Communism—and 100 Million Dead," *Wall Street Journal*, November 6, 2017, https://www.wsj.com/articles/100-years-of-communismand-100-million-dead-1510011810.
30. Peter S. Goodman, "Finland Has Second Thoughts About Giving Free Money to Jobless People," *New York Times*, April 24, 2018, https://www.nytimes.com/2018/04/24/business/finland-universal-basic-income.html.

31. "Sweden's Turn from Socialism," *Washington Times*, June 6, 2007, https://www.washingtontimes.com/news/2007/jun/16/20070616-080932-5740r/.

32. Hannah Dreier, "A Child's Scraped Knee a Life or Death Matter in Venezuela," Associated Press, October 4, 2016, https://apnews.com/42cfecb776ac4541b55a1aec944908ac.

33. Clifford Krauss, Nicholas Casey, and Bill Vlasic, "Amid Venezuela Protests, G.M. Plant Is Seized, and Company Exits," *New York Times*, April 20, 2017, https://www.nytimes.com/2017/04/20/business/venezuela-general-motors-business-protests.html.

34. Jay Nordlinger, "The Myth of Cuban Health Care," *National Review*, July 11, 2007, https://www.nationalreview.com/2007/07/myth-cuban-health-care/.

35. "Free Healthcare?" The Real Cuba, http://www.therealcuba.com/?page_id=77.

36. "Castro 'Admitted to Spanish hospital,'" *Daily Mail*, January 2, 2007, https://www.dailymail.co.uk/news/article-426119/Castro-admitted-Spanish-hospital.html.

37. Dan Bigman, "John Stossel: Tax the Rich? The Rich Don't Have Enough. Really," *Forbes*, April 3, 2012, https://www.forbes.com/sites/danbigman/2012/04/03/john-stossel-tax-the-rich-the-rich-dont-have-enough-really/#6b3e24026e7d.

38. Philip Klein, "Amazing Chart Shows Thanks to Capitalism, Global Poverty Is at Its Lowest Rate in History," *Washington Examiner*, March 30, 2015, https://www.washingtonexaminer.com/amazing-chart-shows-thanks-to-capitalism-global-poverty-is-at-its-lowest-rate-in-history.

39. James Pethokoukis, "700 Million Humans Have Moved Out of Deep Poverty in the 21st Century. Thank Capitalism," American Enterprise Institute, July 14, 2015, http://www.aei.org/publication/700-million-humans-have-moved-out-of-deep-poverty-in-the-21st-century-thank-capitalism/.

40. Gabrielle Okun, "WATCH: ANTI-TRUMP PROTESTERS ATTACK TRANSGENDER WHO WORE MAGA HAT IN HOLLYWOOD," The Daily Caller, November 13, 2017, https://dailycaller.com/2017/11/13/woman-wears-trump-hat-around-hollywood-and-the-reactions-were-even-worse-than-she-expected/.

41. Philip Bump, "The President Was Never Intended to Be the Most Powerful Part of Government," *Washington Post*, February 13, 2017, https://www.washingtonpost.com/news/politics/wp/2017/02/13/the-president-was-never-intended-to-be-the-most-powerful-part-of-government/?noredirect=on&utm_term=.8e935e9ea67a.

42. James Madison, "The Federalist No. 10: The Utility of the Union as a Safeguard Against Domestic Faction and Insurrection (continued)," *Daily Advertiser*, November 22, 1787, https://www.constitution.org/fed/federa10.htm.
43. John Adams, From John Adams to John Taylor, 17 December 1814," National Archives, https://founders.archives.gov/documents/Adams/99-02-02-6371.
44. "Madison Debates June 4, 1787," The Avalon Project, Yale Law School, http://avalon.law.yale.edu/18th_century/debates_604.asp.
45. Lukas Mikelionis, "Democrats' Illegal Immigration Tune Has Changed over Years Despite Incoming Caravan," Fox News, October 24, 2018, https://www.foxnews.com/politics/democrats-illegal-immigration-tune-has-changed-over-years-despite-incoming-caravan.
46. Anna Giaritelli, "Keith Ellison Sports 'I Don't Believe in Borders' T-shirt," *Washington Examiner*, May 7, 2018, https://www.washingtonexaminer.com/news/keith-ellison-sports-i-dont-believe-in-borders-t-shirt.
47. "Senator Calls to Eliminate ICE," CNN, June 29, 2018, https://www.cnn.com/videos/politics/2018/06/29/sen-kirsten-gillibrand-abolish-ice-cpt-vpx.cnn.

Chapter 7: Read and Improve Your Mind, My Son

1. Harry S. Truman, "Truman Quotes," Truman State University, https://www.truman.edu/about/history/our-namesake/truman-quotes/.
2. Sara C., "When You Say 'I Would Never Date A Trans Person,' It's Transphobic. Here's Why," Medium, August 19, 2017, https://medium.com/@QSE/when-you-say-i-would-never-date-a-trans-person-its-transphobic-here-s-why-aa6fdcf59aca.
3. Christine Rousselle, "VIDEO: Anti-Trump Protestors Destroy Starbucks, Bank of America, Bus Stop," Townhall, January 20, 2017, https://townhall.com/tipsheet/christinerousselle/2017/01/20/watch-antitrump-protestors-smash-windows-at-dc-businesses-n2274483.
4. Michael Gordon, Mark Washburn, and Fred Clasen-Kelly, "Inside the 48 Hours That Shook Charlotte: As Rocks Flew, Riot Cops Fled for Safety," *Charlotte Observer*, October 28, 2016, https://www.charlotteobserver.com/news/local/crime/article111056262.html.
5. Jack Crowe, "Two Minnesota Republican Candidates Assaulted," *National Review*, October 17, 2018, https://www.nationalreview.com/news/two-minnesota-republican-candidates-assaulted/.
6. Ben Tobin, "San Antonio Police Probe Alleged Assault of Teen Wearing a Make America Great Again Hat," *USA Today*, July 5, 2018, https://www.usatoday.com/story/money/2018/07/05/san-antonio-police-investigate-alleged-assault-teen-wearing-maga-hat/761370002/.

7. Marc Lamont Hill, "I actually don't advocate throwing drinks...." Twitter, July 5, 2018, https://twitter.com/marclamonthill/status/1014904101988167685.

8. Tristan Smith, "California University Works to Reduce Number of White People on Campus," The College Fix, July 10, 2018, https://www.thecollegefix.com/california-university-combats-issue-of-too-many-white-people-on-campus/.

9. "Office of University Diversity and Inclusion Diversity Action Initiatives," Cal Poly, Jun 7, 2018, https://content-calpoly-edu.s3.amazonaws.com/diversity/1/images/Diversity%20Action%20Initiatives%20Final%206-7-18_%232.pdf.

10. "Part Three: Life in Christ," Catechism of the Catholic Church, the Vatican, http://www.vatican.va/archive/ccc_css/archive/catechism/p3s2c2a6.htm.

11. "21 Books You Don't Have to Read," GQ, April 19, 2018, https://www.gq.com/story/21-books-you-dont-have-to-read.

12. Proverbs 18:2 (ESV), https://biblehub.com/proverbs/18-2.htm.

13. John 3:16, https://biblehub.com/john/3-16.htm.

14. Mark 13:13 (New American Standard 1977), https://biblehub.com/mark/13-13.htm.

15. Ephesians 6:11 (New American Standard Bible), https://biblehub.com/ephesians/6-11.htm.

16. Matthew 7:27 (New American Standard Bible), https://biblehub.com/context/matthew/7-27.htm.

17. Matthew 7:25 (New American Standard Bible), https://biblehub.com/matthew/7-25.htm.

18. Jeffrey M. Jones, "In U.S., Record-Low 47% Extremely Proud to Be Americans," Gallup, July 2, 2018, https://news.gallup.com/poll/236420/record-low-extremely-proud-americans.aspx.

19. Alexandra Sifferlin, "Here's How Happy Americans Are Right Now," Time, July 26, 2017, http://time.com/4871720/how-happy-are-americans/.

20. David Rutz, "MSNBC's Katy Tur: Is It 'Appropriate' to Take Originalist View of Constitution Since Americans Are More Progressive Now?" Free Beacon, July 11, 2018, https://freebeacon.com/politics/katy-tur-appropriate-originalist-view-constitution-americans-progressive/.

21. Aaron Blake and Frances Stead Sellers, "Hillary Clinton, Saul Alinsky and Lucifer, explained," Washington Post, July 20, 2016, https://www.washingtonpost.com/news/the-fix/wp/2016/07/20/hillary-clinton-saul-alinsky-and-lucifer-explained/.

22. Michael Kruse, "The First Time Hillary Clinton Was President," *Politico*, August 26, 2016, https://www.politico.com/magazine/story/2016/08/hillary-clinton-2016-wellesley-president-214188.

23. Peter Slevin, "Former '60s Radical Is Now Considered Mainstream in Chicago, Washington Post, April 18, 2018, http://www.washingtonpost.com/wp-dyn/content/article/2008/04/17/AR2008041703910.html.

24. Matt Patterson, "Study Saul Alinsky to understand Barack Obama," *Washington Examiner*, February 6, 2012, https://www.washingtonexaminer.com/study-saul-alinsky-to-understand-barack-obama.

25. Catalina Camia, "Hillary Clinton hasn't driven a car since 1996," *USA Today*, January 27, 2014, https://www.usatoday.com/story/money/cars/2014/01/27/hillary-clinton-car-auto-drive-nada/4942881/.

26. Frank Camp, "WikiLeaked Speech: Hillary 'Kind of Far Removed' From the Struggles of the Middle Class," The Daily Wire, October 10, 2016, https://www.dailywire.com/news/9840/wikileaked-speech-hillary-kind-far-removed-frank-camp.

27. Spig Wead, "Waterboarding: A SERE-ing Experience for Tens of Thousands of US Military Personnel," Human Events, November 5, 2007, http://humanevents.com/2007/11/05/waterboarding-a-sereing-experience-for-tens-of-thousands-of-us-military-personnel/.

28. Nicole Russell, "Ohio Judge Strips Custody from Parents For Not Letting Daughter Take Trans Hormones," The Federalist, February 20, 2018, http://thefederalist.com/2018/02/20/ohio-judge-strips-custody-parents-not-letting-daughter-taking-trans-hormones/.

Chapter 8: Facts Liberals Ignore

1. "2016 Crime in the United States: Murder Victims by Weapon," FBI, https://ucr.fbi.gov/crime-in-the-u.s/2016/crime-in-the-u.s.-2016/tables/expanded-homicide-data-table-4.xls.

2. Jesse T. Richman, Gulshan A. Chattha, David C. Earnest, "A Valid Analysis of a Small Subsample: The Case of Non-Citizen Registration and Voting," working paper, January 28, 2018, https://fs.wp.odu.edu/jrichman/wp-content/uploads/sites/760/2015/11/AnsolabehererResponse1-28-17.pdf.

3. Dan Bigman, "John Stossel: Tax the Rich? The Rich Don't Have Enough. Really," *Forbes*, April 3, 2012, https://www.forbes.com/sites/danbigman/2012/04/03/john-stossel-tax-the-rich-the-rich-dont-have-enough-really/#6b3e24026e7d.

4. Ben Popken, "Dick's Sporting Goods Will Stop Selling Assault-Style Rifles, Walmart Raising Age for Gun Sales," NBC News, February 28,

2018, https://www.nbcnews.com/business/business-news/dick-s-sporting-goods-will-stop-selling-assault-style-rifles-n851881.

5. Nina Golgowski, "Houston Woman Found Guilty of Killing Boyfriend with Stiletto Heel," April 9, 2014, *New York Daily News*, https://www.nydailynews.com/news/national/tx-woman-found-guilty-killing-boyfriend-stiletto-heel-article-1.1749860.

6. "2016 Crime in the United States: Murder Victims by Weapon," FBI, https://ucr.fbi.gov/crime-in-the-u.s/2016/crime-in-the-u.s.-2016/tables/expanded-homicide-data-table-4.xls.

7. Matt Vespa, "Surprise, Surprise: March for Our Lives Once Again Shows Why the Left Can't Be Trusted on Gun Control," Townhall, March 25, 2018, https://townhall.com/tipsheet/mattvespa/2018/03/25/surprise-surprise-march-for-our-lives-once-again-shows-why-the-left-cant-be-trusted-on-gun-control-n2464461.

8. Gary Kleck and Marc Gertz, "Armed Resistance to Crime: The Prevalence and Nature of Self-Defense with a Gun," The Journal of Criminal Law and Criminology (1973–), 86:1 (autumn 1995): 150–87, https://concealedguns.procon.org/sourcefiles/Kleckarmed.pdf.

9. Aaron Bandler, "Report: Concealed Carry Permit Holders Are the Most Law-Abiding People in the Country," The Daily Wire, August 10, 2016, https://www.dailywire.com/news/8255/report-concealed-carry-permit-holders-are-most-law-aaron-bandler.

10. Dave Boyer, "Schools Safer Today than in 1990s, Study on Shootings Says," *Washington Times*, February 27, 2018, https://www.washingtontimes.com/news/2018/feb/27/schools-safer-today-1990s-study-shootings-says/.

11. John R. Lott Jr., "WHAT A BALANCING TEST WILL SHOW FOR RIGHT-TO-CARRY LAWS," Crime Research, https://crimeresearch.org/wp-content/uploads/2014/04/Univ-of-Maryland-Law-Review-Lott-Concealed-Carry.pdf.

12. John R. Lott Jr. "More Guns, Less Violent Crime," *Wall Street Journal*, August 28, 1996, https://www.wsj.com/articles/SB841185795318576500.

13. Lateef Mungin, "College Women Told to Urinate or Vomit to Deter a Rapist," CNN, February 20, 2013, https://www.cnn.com/2013/02/20/justice/colorado-rape-prevention-guidelines/index.html.

14. John R. Lott Jr., "Opposing View: Guns in Schools Can Save Lives," *USA Today*, December 25, 2012, https://www.usatoday.com/story/opinion/2012/12/25/gun-free-zone-john-lott/1791085/.

15. Jordan McPerson, Manny Navarro, and Linda Robertson, "Stoneman Douglas Football Coach 'Died a Hero' Protecting Students during

Shooting," *Miami Herald*, February 15, 2018, https://www.miamiherald.com/news/local/community/broward/article200248784.html.

16. Belinda Grant Geary, "Australians Now Own MORE Guns Than They Did before the 1996 Port Arthur Massacre—As It's Revealed We Imported a Record Number of Firearms Last Year," *Daily Mail*, April 27, 2016, https://www.dailymail.co.uk/news/article-3562714/Australians-guns-did-1996-Port-Arthur-massacre-revealed-country-imported-record-number-firearms-year.html.

17. Mark Antonio Wright, "Australia's 1996 Gun Confiscation Didn't Work—and it Wouldn't Work in America," *National Review*, October 2, 2015, https://www.nationalreview.com/2015/10/australia-gun-control-obama-america/.

18. Ibid.

19. Stephen Gutowski, "The Australia Gun Ban Conceit," The Federalist, September 3, 2015, http://thefederalist.com/2015/09/03/the-australian-gun-ban-conceit/.

20. Ibid.

21. Lukas Mikelionis, "Non-Citizens, Illegal Immigrants Now May Register to Vote in San Francisco School Board Elections," Fox News, July 19, 2018, https://www.foxnews.com/politics/non-citizens-illegal-immigrants-now-may-register-to-vote-in-san-francisco-school-board-elections.

22. Jesse T. Richman, Gulshan A. Chattha, and David C. Earnest, "Do Non-Citizens Vote in U.S. elections?" Electoral Studies 36 (December 2014): 149–57, https://www.sciencedirect.com/science/article/pii/S0261379414000973.

23. Jesse T. Richman, Gulshan A. Chattha, David C. Earnest, "A Valid Analysis of a Small Subsample: The Case of Non-Citizen Registration and Voting," January 28, 2018, https://fs.wp.odu.edu/jrichman/wp-content/uploads/sites/760/2015/11/AnsolabehererResponse1-28-17.pdf.

24. Spencer Raley, "How Many Illegal Aliens are in the US?" FAIR, October 23, 2017, http://fairus.org/issue/illegal-immigration/how-many-illegal-immigrants-are-in-us.

25. Pam Fessler, "Study: 1.8 Million Dead People Still Registered to Vote," NPR, February 14, 2012, https://www.npr.org/2012/02/14/146827471/study-1-8-million-dead-people-still-registered-to-vote.

26. "39 MILLION: IRLI Investigation Reveals Massive Identity Fraud by Illegal Aliens," Immigration Reform Law Institute, September 11, 2007, https://www.irli.org/single-post/2018/09/11/39-MILLION-IRLI-Investigation-Reveals-Massive-Identity-Fraud-by-Illegal-Aliens.

27. Stephen Goss, Alice Wade, J. Patrick Skirvin, Michael Morris, K. Mark Bye, and Danielle Huston, "EFFECTS OF UNAUTHORIZED

IMMIGRATION ON THE ACTUARIAL STATUS OF THE SOCIAL
SECURITY TRUST FUNDS," Social Security Administration, April
2013, https://www.ssa.gov/oact/NOTES/pdf_notes/note151.pdf.

28. Patricia Zengerle, "Young, Hispanics, Poor Hit Most by US Voter ID
Laws: Study," Reuters, September 26, 2012, https://www.reuters.com/
article/us-usa-campaign-voterid-idUSBRE88P1CW20120926.

29. Judson Berger, "States Dispute Criticism of New Voter Laws, Move to
Offer Photo ID Free of Charge," Fox News, July 20, 2011, https://www.
foxnews.com/politics/states-dispute-criticism-of-new-voter-laws-move-to-
offer-photo-id-free-of-charge.

30. Evan D. Montgomery, "The Missouri Photo-ID Requirement for Voting:
Ensuring Both Access and Integrity," Missouri Law Review, Spring 2007,
https://scholarship.law.missouri.edu/cgi/viewcontent.
cgi?article=3731&context=mlr.

31. Maggie Astor, "Seven Ways Alabama Has Made It Harder to Vote,"
New York Times, June 23, 2018, https://www.nytimes.com/2018/06/23/
us/politics/voting-rights-alabama.html.

32. Vann R. Newkirk II, "African American Voters Made Doug Jones a U.S.
Senator in Alabama," *The Atlantic*, December 12, 2017, https://www.
theatlantic.com/politics/archive/2017/12/despite-the-obstacles-black-
voters-make-a-statement-in-alabama/548237/.

33. Justin McCarthy, "Four in Five Americans Support Voter ID Laws, Early
Voting," Gallup, August 22, 2016, https://news.gallup.com/poll/194741/
four-five-americans-support-voter-laws-early-voting.aspx.

34. Emma Hinchliffe, "College Majors Dominated by Women Lead to
Lower-Paying jobs, Glassdoor Found," Mashable, April 19, 2017, https://
mashable.com/2017/04/19/
college-major-gender-pay-gap-glassdoor/#IRQ9muLRoSqE.

35. Mark J. Perry, "Highest-Paying College Majors, Gender Composition of
Students Earning Degrees in Those Fields and the Gender Pay Gap,"
American Enterprise Institute, October 19, 2016, http://www.aei.org/
publication/highest-paying-college-majors-gender-composition-of-
students-earning-degrees-in-those-fields-and-the-gender-pay-gap/.

36. "Time Spent Working by Full-and Part-Time Status, Gender, and
Location in 2014," Bureau of Labor Statistics, July 2, 2015, https://www.
bls.gov/opub/ted/2015/time-spent-working-by-full-and-part-time-status-
gender-and-location-in-2014.htm.

37. Ibid.

38. Patricia Garcia, "These 10 Careers Pay Women More Than Men,"
Vogue, April 20, 2017, https://www.vogue.com/article/careers-pay-women-
more-than-men.

39. Belinda Luscombe, "Workplace Salaries: At Last, Women on Top," *Time*, September 1, 2010, http://content.time.com/time/business/article/0,8599,2015274,00.html.

40. Ali Meyer, "Majority of Households Paying Obamacare Penalty Are Low and Middle-Income," Free Beacon, October 9, 2017, https://freebeacon.com/issues/majority-households-paying-obamacare-penalty-low-middle-income/.

41. "Key Facts about the Uninsured Population," Kaiser Family Foundation, December 7, 2018, https://www.kff.org/uninsured/fact-sheet/key-facts-about-the-uninsured-population/.

42. Betsy McCaughey, "Another 25 million ObamaCare Victims," *New York Post*, January 14, 2014, https://nypost.com/2014/01/14/another-25-million-obamacare-victims/.

43. Richard Adams, "Joe Biden: 'This Is a Big Fucking Deal,'" *Guardian*, March 23, 2010, https://www.theguardian.com/world/richard-adams-blog/2010/mar/23/joe-biden-obama-big-fucking-deal-overheard.

44. Bjørn Lomborg, "Bjørn Lomborg: Climate-Change Misdirection," *Wall Street Journal*, January 23, 2013, https://www.wsj.com/articles/SB10001424127887323485704578258172660564886.

45. Larry Bell, "In Their Own Words: Climate Alarmists Debunk Their 'Science,'" *Forbes*, February 5, 2013, https://www.forbes.com/sites/larrybell/2013/02/05/in-their-own-words-climate-alarmists-debunk-their-science/#13b3f14068a3.

46. Mark J. Perry, "An Inconvenient Fact: The Frequency of Violent Tornadoes like the Ones in the Midwest Has Been Declining, Not Increasing," American Enterprise Institute, November 19, 2013, http://www.aei.org/publication/an-inconvenient-fact-the-frequency-of-violent-tornadoes-like-the-ones-in-the-midwest-has-been-declining-not-increasing/.

47. "US Tornado Count Plummeting to Record Low Levels Three Consecutive Years," Real Science, October 1, 2014, https://stevengoddard.wordpress.com/2014/10/01/us-tornado-count-plummeting-to-record-low-levels-three-consecutive-years/.

48. Barbara Hollingsworth, "NOAA: U.S. Completes Record 11 Straight Years without Major Hurricane Strike," CNS News, October 24, 2016, https://www.cnsnews.com/news/article/barbara-hollingsworth/noaa-us-completes-record-breaking-11-years-without-major.

49. Roger Pielke Jr. "A Short Threa….," Twitter, October 7, 2018, https://twitter.com/RogerPielkeJr/status/1049114370884521984.

50. Amanda Prestigiacomo, "FAKE NEWS: 'Nat Geo' Photographer Admits Viral Photo of Polar Bear 'Dying from Climate Change' Is False," The Daily Wire, July 30, 2018, https://www.dailywire.com/news/33782/fake-news-nat-geo-admits-viral-photo-polar-bear-amanda-prestigiacomo.

51. Anthony Watts, "The UN 'Disappears' 50 Million Climate Refugees, Then Botches the Disappearing Attempt," Watts Up With That?, April 15, 2011, https://wattsupwiththat.com/2011/04/15/the-un-disappears-50-million-climate-refugees-then-botches-the-disappearing-attempt/.

52. Peter James Spielman, "U.N. Predicts Disaster If Global Warming Not Checked," Associated Press, June 29, 1989, https://www.apnews.com/bd45c372caf118ec99964ea547880cd0.

53. Damian Carrington, "IPCC Officials Admit Mistake over Melting Himalayan Glaciers," *Guardian*, January 20, 2010, https://www.theguardian.com/environment/2010/jan/20/ipcc-himalayan-glaciers-mistake.

54. Julie Cart, "42,000 Homes in California Will Be under water due to Rising Seas, Researchers Project," *Desert Sun*, May 2, 2017, https://www.desertsun.com/story/news/environment/2017/05/02/california-submerging-rising-seas-claiming-its-famed-coast-faster-than-scientists-imagined/307228001/.

55. Brett Samuels, "Economist Larry Summers: 10,000 People Will Die Annually from GOP Tax Bill," *The Hill*, December 4, 2017, https://thehill.com/policy/healthcare/363152-larry-summers-10000-people-will-die-annually-from-gop-tax-bill.

56. "'People Will Die': At Davos Forum, Kerry Blasts 'Lying' Trump for Pulling Out of Paris Accord," Fox News Insider, January 23, 2019, https://insider.foxnews.com/2019/01/23/john-kerry-blasts-donald-trump-paris-climate-accord-says-us-burdened-climate-change.

57. Benjamin Sledge, "The Repeal of Net Neutrality Will Cripple Mental Health," Medium, December 6, 2017, https://medium.com/@benjaminsledge/the-repeal-of-net-neutrality-will-cripple-mental-health-f0af144d7423.

58. Mike LaChance, "Yale Law School Students and Alums: 'People Will Die' If Kavanaugh Is Confirmed," Legal Insurrection, July 12, 2018, https://legalinsurrection.com/2018/07/yale-law-school-students-and-alums-people-will-die-if-kavanaugh-is-confirmed/.

59. Peter Cappelli, "It's Not OK That Your Employees Can't Afford to Eat," *Harvard Business Review*, December 16, 2013, https://hbr.org/2013/12/scrooge-is-alive-and-well.

60. Tim Worstall, "Surprise, San Diego's Minimum Wage Rise Appears to Be Killing Restaurant Jobs," *Forbes*, April 12, 2017, https://www.forbes.com/sites/timworstall/2017/04/12/surprise-san-diegos-minimum-wage-rise-appears-to-be-killing-restaurant-jobs/#5a0e25fd4177.

61. Ekaterina Jardim, Mark C. Long, Robert Plotnick, Emma van Inwegen, Jacob Vigdor, AND Hilary Wething, "MINIMUM WAGE

INCREASES, WAGES, AND LOW-WAGE EMPLOYMENT: EVIDENCE FROM SEATTLE," NATIONAL BUREAU OF ECONOMIC RESEARCH, June 2017, https://evans.uw.edu/sites/default/files/NBER%20Working%20Paper.pdf.

62. Andrew Burger, "Study: Minnesota's Minimum Wage Hikes Lead to Job Losses for Younger Workers," Minnesota Watchdog, August 2, 2018, https://www.watchdog.org/minnesota/study-minnesota-s-minimum-wage-hikes-lead-to-job-losses/article_3a5a8e62-9663-11e8-90c1-6b14ddf63eb2.html.

63. "Facts & Data on Small Business and Entrepreneurship," Small Business & Entrepreneurship Council, https://sbecouncil.org/about-us/facts-and-data/.

64. "Characteristics of Minimum Wage Workers, 2016," United State Department of Labor, Bureau of Labor Statistics, April 2017, https://www.bls.gov/opub/reports/minimum-wage/2016/home.htm.

65. David Neumark, "Reducing Poverty via Minimum Wages, Alternatives," FRBSF Economic Letter, December 28, 2015, https://www.frbsf.org/economic-research/publications/economic-letter/2015/december/reducing-poverty-via-minimum-wages-tax-credit/.

66. Ibid.

67. Dan Bigman, "John Stossel: Tax the Rich? The Rich Don't Have Enough. Really," Forbes, April 3, 2012, https://www.forbes.com/sites/danbigman/2012/04/03/john-stossel-tax-the-rich-the-rich-dont-have-enough-really/#6b3e24026e7d.

68. Michael Durkheimer, "What You Don't Know About The Top One Percent," Forbes, March 1, 2018, https://www.forbes.com/sites/michaeldurkheimer/2018/03/01/0-001-percent-one-percent/#673273cb2cf2.

69. Charles Blahous, "The Costs of a National Single-Payer Healthcare System," Mercatus Center, July 30, 2018, https://www.mercatus.org/publications/federal-fiscal-policy/costs-national-single-payer-healthcare-system.

70. Brian Reidl, "America Might Be Ready for Democratic Socialism. It's Not Ready for the Bill," Vox, August 7, 2018, https://www.vox.com/the-big-idea/2018/8/7/17658574/democratic-socialism-cost-medicare-college-sanders-deficits-taxes.

71. David Morgan, "Poll Finds Some U.S. Muslim Support for Suicide Attacks," Reuters, May 22, 2007, https://www.reuters.com/article/us-usa-muslims-poll-id USN2244293620070522.

72. Daniel Pipes, "More Survey Research from a British Islamist Hell," Middle East Forum, July 26, 2005, http://www.danielpipes.org/blog/2005/07/more-survey-research-from-a-british-islamist.

73. Laura Mowat, "'Astonishing' Two in Three British Muslims Would NOT Give Police Terror Tip-Offs," *Express*, April 11, 2016, https://www.express.co.uk/news/uk/659913/two-in-three-British-Muslims-would-NOT-give-police-terror-tip-offs.

74. Pipes, "More Survey Research."

75. Patrick Hennessy and Melissa Kite, "Poll Reveals 40pc of Muslims Want Sharia Law in UK," *Telegraph*, February 19, 2006, https://www.telegraph.co.uk/news/uknews/1510866/Poll-reveals-40pc-of-Muslims-want-sharia-law-in-UK.html.

76. "BBC RADIO 4 TODAY MUSLIM POLL," BBC Radio 4 Today, February 25, 2015, https://www.comresglobal.com/polls/bbc-radio-4-today-muslim-poll/.

77. David Morgan, "Poll: 26% of Young U.S. Muslims OK Bombs," CBS News, May 22, 2007, https://www.cbsnews.com/news/poll-26-of-young-us-muslims-ok-bombs/.

78. Nationwide Online Survey among 600 Muslim-Americans," the Center for Security Policy, June 2015, http://www.centerforsecuritypolicy.org/wp-content/uploads/2015/06/150612-CSP-Polling-Company-Nationwide-Online-Survey-of-Muslims-Topline-Poll-Data.pdf.

79. Michelle Malkin, "Never Forget: Muslim Hate Crime Hoaxes," *Toronto Sun*, September 16, 2017, https://torontosun.com/2017/09/16/never-forget-muslim-hate-crime-hoaxes/wcm/1d081b75-d0c1-4d32-aff1-79afe61ef330.

80. Christopher Mele, "Muslim Woman Made Up Hate Crime on Subway, Police Say," *New York Times*, December 14, 2016, https://www.nytimes.com/2016/12/14/nyregion/manhattan-yasmin-seweid-false-hate-crime.html.

81. Malkin, "Never Forget."

82. "Police: Lafayette Student Lied about Being Robbed of Wallet, Hijab by Trump Supporters—Will Face Charges," WGNO ABC, November 10, 2016, https://wgno.com/2016/11/10/police-lafayette-student-lied-about-being-robbed-of-wallet-hijab-by-trump-supporters/.

83. Justin Caruso, "FBI: ANTI-WHITE HATE CRIMES ARE THE FASTEST GROWING RACIAL HATE CRIMES IN AMERICA," The Daily Caller, November 13, 2017, https://dailycaller.com/2017/11/13/fbi-anti-white-hate-crimes-are-the-fastest-growing-racial-hate-crimes-in-america/.

84. "Incidents, Offenses, Victims, and Known Offenders," U.S. Department of Justice Federal Bureau of Investigation, https://ucr.fbi.gov/hate-crime/2016/tables/table-1.

Chapter 9: A Comprehensive List of Liberal Lies—and How to Call Them Out

1. "George Santayana," Wikiquote, https://en.wikiquote.org/w/index. php?title=George_Santayana&oldid=2514536.
2. Kenneth Rapoza, "Socialist Venezuela Falling Apart As President Maduro Shockingly Blames Party," *Forbes,* August 1, 2018, https://www. forbes.com/sites/kenrapoza/2018/08/01/socialist-venezuela-falling-l apart-president-maduro-shockingly-blames-party/#46d43bf52a01.
3. Clifford Krauss, Nicholas Casey, and Bill Vlasic, "Amid Venezuela Protests, G.M. Plant Is Seized, and Company Exits," *New York Times,* August 20, 2017, https://www.nytimes.com/2017/04/20/business/ venezuela-general-motors-business-protests.html.
4. "The Origins of the Republican Party," USHistory.org, http://www. ushistory.org/gop/origins.htm.
5. "Abraham Lincoln," Wikipedia, https://en.wikipedia.org/w/index. php?title= Abraham_Lincoln&oldid=884110619.
6. "List of African-American United States Representatives," Wikipedia,
7. https://en.wikipedia.org/w/index.php?title=List_of_African-American_ United_States_Representatives&oldid=884015816.
8. "Arthur Wergs Mitchell," Wikipedia, https://en.wikipedia.org/w/index. php?title=Arthur_Wergs_Mitchell&oldid=876321103.
9. Wikipedia contributors, "Hiram Rhodes Revels," *Wikipedia, The Free Encyclopedia,* https://en.wikipedia.org/w/index. php?title=Hiram_Rhodes_Revels&oldid=884020429.
10. Wikipedia contributors, "Carol Moseley Braun," *Wikipedia, The Free Encyclopedia,* https://en.wikipedia.org/w/index. php?title=Carol_Moseley_Braun&oldid=881877403.
11. "Grant, Reconstruction and the KKK," PBS, https://www.pbs.org/wgbh/ americanexperience/features/grant-kkk/.
12. PragerU, "Why Did the Democratic South Become Republican?" YouTube, July 24, 2017, https://www.youtube.com/ watch?v=UiprVX4os2Y&t=8s.
13. "Civil Rights Act of 1964," Wikipedia, https://en.wikipedia.org/w/index. php?title=Civil_Rights_Act_of_1964&oldid=883307667.
14. Jennifer Calfas, "Here Are the Cities That Celebrate Indigenous Peoples' Day Instead of Columbus Day," *Time,* October 8, 2017, http://time. com/4968067/indigenous-peoples-day-columbus-day-cities/.

15. "The Story of … Smallpox—and other Deadly Eurasian Germs," PBS, https://www.pbs.org/gunsgermssteel/variables/smallpox.html.
16. Robert Krachik, "Columbus Day: What Really Killed So Many Natives Post-Contact?," The Daily Wire, October 8, 2017, https://www.dailywire.com/news/22040/columbus-day-what-really-killed-so-many-natives-robert-kraychik.
17. Michael J. Knowles, "Historical Record Shows Christopher Columbus Actually Was a Great Man," the Daily Wire, October 5, 2017, https://www.dailywire.com/news/21968/historical-record-shows-christopher-columbus-michael-j-knowles.
18. Ibid.
19. Giles Tremlett, "Lost Document Reveals Columbus as Tyrant of the Caribbean," *Guardian*, August 7, 2006, https://www.theguardian.com/world/2006/aug/07/books.spain.
20. Knowles, "Historical Record."
21. Andres Resendez, "NATIVE AMERICANS WERE KEPT AS SLAVES, TOO," *Newsweek*, April 30, 2016, https://www.newsweek.com/native-americans-were-kept-slaves-too-454023.
22. "Romanus Pontifex," Wikipedia, https://en.wikipedia.org/w/index.php?title=Romanus_Pontifex&oldid=875628088.
23. Stephen P. Halbrook, "How the Nazis Used Gun Control," *National Review*, December 2, 2013, https://www.nationalreview.com/2013/12/how-nazis-used-gun-control-stephen-p-halbrook/.
24. Christina Wille, "How Many Weapons Are There in Cambodia?" Small Arms Survey, June 2006, http://www.smallarmssurvey.org/fileadmin/docs/F-Working-papers/SAS-WP4-Cambodia.pdf.
25. "A Little Gun History," Snopes, https://www.snopes.com/fact-check/little-gun-history/.
26. Clayton E. Cramer, "The Racist Roots of Gun Control," Firearms & Liberty, http://www.firearmsandliberty.com/cramer.racism.html.
27. David Kopel and Joseph Greenlee, "The Racist Origin of Gun Control Laws," *The Hill*, August 22, 2017, https://thehill.com/blogs/pundits-blog/civil-rights/347324-the-racist-origin-of-gun-control-laws.
28. "2009 Graff Diamonds Robbery," Wikipedia, https://en.wikipedia.org/w/index.php?title=2009_Graff_Diamonds_robbery&oldid=874870493.
29. Jon Clements, "Graff Jewellery Heist Robber Jokes 'Even Mum Wouldn't Recognise Me' in Latex Disguise," *Mirror*, August 14, 2009, https://www.mirror.co.uk/news/uk-news/graff-jewellery-heist-robber-jokes-412497.
30. Douglas Ernst, "Late-Night Comic Deploys LGBT Stereotypes to Mock Christian Baker: 'His Whole Life is Gay,'" *Washington Times*, August 17,

2018, https://www.washingtontimes.com/news/2018/aug/17/jimmy-kimmel-uses-lgbt-stereotypes-to-mock-colorad/.

31. The Bill of Rights, National Archives, https://www.archives.gov/founding-docs/bill-of-rights-transcript.

32. Mark David Hall, "Did America Have a Christian Founding?" the Heritage Foundation, July 7, 2011, https://www.heritage.org/political-process/report/did-america-have-christian-founding.

33. "Washington's Farewell Address 1796," The Avalon Project, Yale Law School, http://avalon.law.yale.edu/18th_century/washing.asp.

34. The Constitution: Amendments 11-27, National Archives, https://www.archives.gov/founding-docs/amendments-11-27.

35. "Abortion Defenders Explain Why Roe v. Wade Was a Terrible Legal Decision," National Right to Life News, January 22, 2016, https://www.nationalrighttolifenews.org/news/2016/01/abortion-defender.

36. Ibid.

37. Ramesh Ponnuru, "Yes, It's Constitutional for Congress to Pass Abortion Laws," *National Review*, January 23, 2015, https://www.nationalreview.com/2015/01/yes-its-constitutional-congress-pass-abortion-laws-ramesh-ponnuru/.

Chapter 10: For Every Liberal Position, There Is an Equal and Opposite Contradiction

1. Planned Parenthood of Indiana & Kentucky, Twitter, March 1, 2018, https://twitter.com/ppindkentucky/status/969384341636861952?lang=en.

2. Frank Camp, "WATCH: Panelist on MSNBC Suggests Trump Wants to Round People Up and 'Murder' Them," The Daily Wire, August 18, 2018, https://www.dailywire.com/news/34699/watch-panelist-msnbc-suggests-trump-wants-round-frank-camp.

3. Eric Branch, "49ers' Kaepernick wore socks depicting police as pigs," *SFGate*, September 1, 2016, https://www.sfgate.com/49ers/article/49ers-Kaepernick-wore-socks-depicting-police-9197707.php.

4. Peter Hasson, "BLACK CAUCUS MEMBERS REFUSE TO DENOUNCE HATE GROUP LEADER LOUIS FARRAKHAN," The Daily Caller, February 7, 2018, https://dailycaller.com/2018/02/07/black-caucus-members-refuse-to-denounce-farrakhan/.

5. "Farrakhan Again Describes Hitler as a 'Very Great Man,'" *New York Times*, July 17, 1984, https://www.nytimes.com/1984/07/17/us/farrakhan-again-describes-hitler-as-a-very-great-man.html.

6. Katelyn Caralle, "Louis Farrakhan: 'Jews Are My Enemy,' 'White Folks Are Going Down,'" *Washington Examiner*, February 28, 2018, https://www.washingtonexaminer.com/louis-farrakhan-jews-are-my-enemy-white-folks-are-going-down.

7. Jessica Chasmer, "Louis Farrakhan: 'Israelis and Zionist Jews' Played Key Roles in 9/11 Attacks," *Washington Times*, March 5, 2015, https://www.washingtontimes.com/news/2015/mar/5/louis-farrakhan-israelis-and-zionist-jews-played-k/.

8. Jeremy Sharon, "FARRAKHAN COMPARES JEWS TO TERMITES, SAYS JEWS ARE 'STUPID,'" *Jerusalem Post*, October 17, 2018, https://www.jpost.com/Diaspora/Farrakhan-compares-Jews-to-termites-says-Jews-are-stupid-569627.

9. Nicole Darrah, "Schumer Slammed for Citing Skin Color in Vote against White Judicial Nominee," Fox News, March 2, 2018, https://www.foxnews.com/politics/schumer-slammed-for-citing-skin-color-in-vote-against-white-judicial-nominee.

10. Sergio Quintana, "Coffee Shop in Oakland Refuses to Serve Police Officers," NBC Bay Area, March 8, 2018, https://www.nbcbayarea.com/news/local/Coffee-Shop-in-Oakland-Refuses-to-Serve-Police-Officers-476352703.html.

11. Steven Ertelt, "60,069,971 Abortions in America Since Roe v. Wade in 1973," Life News, January 18, 2018, https://www.lifenews.com/2018/01/18/60069971-abortions-in-america-since-roe-v-wade-in-1973/.

12. Gary Kleck and Marc Gertz, "Armed Resistance to Crime: The Prevalence and Nature of Self-Defense with a Gun," Journal of Criminal Law and Criminology (1973–) 86: 1 (autumn 1995), 150–87, https://www.jstor.org/stable/1144004?seq=1#page_scan_tab_contents.

13. "Killing of Mollie Tibbetts," Wikipedia, https://en.wikipedia.org/w/index.php?title=Killing_of_Mollie_Tibbetts&oldid=884141909.

14. "Shooting of Kate Steinle," Wikpedia, https://en.wikipedia.org/w/index.php?title=Shooting_of_Kate_Steinle&oldid=884011358.

15. David Rutz, "Town Hall Crowd Jeers NRA Spokeswoman's Story of Rape Survivor Who Wished She Was Armed," Free Beacon, February 21, 2018, https://freebeacon.com/issues/town-hall-crowd-jeers-nra-spokeswomans-story-rape-survivor-armed/.

16. Jesse T. Richman, Gulshan A. Chattha, and David C. Earnest, "A Valid Analysis of a Small Subsample: The Case of Non-Citizen Registration and Voting," (working paper), January 28, 2018, https://fs.wp.odu.edu/jrichman/wp-content/uploads/sites/760/2015/11/AnsolabehererResponse1-28-17.pdf.

17. Kate Gibson, "McDonald's Workers March on New Chicago HQ for $15 an Hour Wages," CBS News, May 21, 2018, https://www.cbsnews.com/news/mcdonalds-workers-march-on-new-chicago-hq-for-15-an-hour-wages/.

18. Adam Levy, "These Companies Gave Bonuses or Raises After Tax Reform," The Motley Fool, May 24, 2018, https://www.fool.com/slideshow/these-companies-gave-bonuses-or-raises-after-tax-reform/.

19. Ylan Mui, "Kamala Harris and Other Prominent Democrats Want to Repeal Trump's Tax Cuts and Replace Them with Cash payouts for the Poor and Working Class," CNBC, October 19, 2018, https://www.cnbc.com/2018/10/19/kamala-harris-democrats-push-to-repeal-and-replace-trump-tax-cuts.html.

20. Zeeshan Aleen, "Bernie Sanders Wants to Tax the Rich at 90%. Here's Why That's Not So Crazy," Mic, May 29, 2015, https://mic.com/articles/119630/bernie-sanders-wants-to-tax-the-rich-at-90-here-s-why-that-s-not-so-crazy#.eVG8FUPH2.

21. Bernie Sanders, "How many yachts do billionaires need....", Twitter, April 20, 2017, https://twitter.com/berniesanders/status/855240333650788353?lang=en.

22. Daniel Chaitin, "Bernie Sanders Slams Billionaires, Gets Reminded He Owns 3 Houses," Washington Examiner, April 20, 2017, https://www.washingtonexaminer.com/bernie-sanders-slams-billionaires-gets-reminded-he-owns-3-houses.

23. Teen Vogue, "Can't #endpoverty without Ending Capitalism!," Twitter, October 17, 2018, https://twitter.com/TeenVogue/status/1052641654367313921.

24. Frank Newport, "Democrats More Positive About Socialism Than Capitalism," Gallup, August 13, 2018, https://news.gallup.com/poll/240725/democrats-positive-socialism-capitalism.aspx.

25. "Socialist 'It' Candidate Ocasio-Cortez Rips 'Unregulated' Uber, Then Spends $4,000 on.... Uber," Investors Business Daily, August 28, 2018, https://www.investors.com/politics/editorials/socialist-candidate-ocasio-cortez-uber/.

26. Kelsey Harkness, "Michael Wolff Is the Misogynist the Left Loves," The Daily Signal, January 26, 2018, https://www.dailysignal.com/2018/01/26/michael-wolff-is-the-misogynist-the-left-loves/.

27. Emily Zanotti, "And the Most Popular Politician In America I...." The Daily Wire, April 26, 2018, https://www.dailywire.com/news/29924/and-most-popular-politician-america-emily-zanotti.

28. "Female Genital Mutilation in the United States," Wikipedia, https://en.wikipedia.org/w/index.php?title=Female_genital_mutilation_in_the_United_States&oldid=883895135.

29. Abbey Schubert, "24 States Have No laws against Female Genital Mutilation. Here's Why That needs to Change," Mic, July 14, 2017, https://mic.com/articles/182161/24-states-have-no-laws-against-female-genital-mutilation-heres-why-that-needs-to-change.

30. Lorie Johnson, "Maine Democrats Refuse to Pass Law Forbidding 'Barbaric Practice' on Little Girls," CBN News, April 29, 2018, http://www1.cbn.com/cbnnews/us/2018/april/maine-democrats-refuse-to-pass-law-forbidding-barbaric-practice-on-little-girls.

31. "Journalists Are Not the Enemy," *Boston Globe*, August 15, 2018, https://www.bostonglobe.com/opinion/editorials/2018/08/15/editorial/Kt0NFFonrxqBI6NqqennvL/story.html.

32. Alexandria Ocasio-Cortez, "To Be Honest, the Event Was Very Successful....", Twitter, August 19, 2018, https://twitter.com/AOC/status/1031208600377679
872.

33. Alexandria Ocasio-Cortez, "Catching Up on How This Became a Thing....", Twitter, August 19, 2018, https://twitter.com/AOC/status/1031206377048494
080.

34. Mike Lillis, "Pelosi Denounces GOP Tax Reform as 'Armageddon,'" *The Hill*, December 4, 2017, https://thehill.com/homenews/house/363238-pelosi-denounces-gop-tax-reform-as-armageddon.

35. Dan Clark, "Are Americans Already Benefiting from the New Tax Law?" PolitiFact, March 9, 2018, https://www.politifact.com/new-york/statements/
2018/mar/09/chris-collins/are-americans-already-benefiting-new-tax-law/.

36. Mark Osborne, Morgan Winsor, and Anna Maria Gibson, "11 Children Rescued from Filthy Compound Looked like 'Third-World Country Refugees,'" ABC News, August 5, 2018, https://abcnews.go.com/US/11-children-rescued-filthy-compound-looked-world-country/
story?id=57040114.

37. Janon Fisher," Children on New Mexico Compound Were Forced to Wash Body of Dead Boy as Punishment, Prosecutors Say," *New York Daily News*, August 27, 2018, https://www.nydailynews.com/news/crime/ny-news-abdul-ghani-imam-siraj-wahhaj-new-mexico-abdul-ghani-20180827-story.html.

38. Alex Van Ness, "Linda Sarsour And Her "Mentor,"" Center for Security Policy, July 6, 2017, https://www.centerforsecuritypolicy.org/2017/07/06/linda-sarsour-and-her-mentor/.

Chapter 11: The Media Bias Framework (They All Use It)

1. Susan Coolidge, *What Katy Did at School*, (Boston: Roberts Brothers, 1985), 200.

2. Kristine Frazao, "Some States with Strictest Gun Laws Also Have Most Dangerous Cities," WJLA, February 27, 2018, https://wjla.com/news/nation-world/some-states-with-strictest-gun-laws-also-have-most-dangerous-cities.

3. John R. Lott Jr., "WHAT A BALANCING TEST WILL SHOW FOR RIGHT-TO-CARRY LAWS," Crime Research, https://crimeresearch. org/wp-content/uploads/2014/04/Univ-of-Maryland-Law-Review-Lott-Concealed-Carry.pdf.

4. James D. Wright AND Peter H. Rossi, "Armed Criminal in America—A Survey of Incarcerated Felons," National Criminal Justice Reference Service, 1985, https://www.ncjrs.gov/App/Publications/abstract. aspx?ID=97099.

5. "2016: Crime in the United States," U.S. Department of Justice Federal Bureau of Investigation, https://ucr.fbi.gov/crime-in-the-u.s/2016/crime-in-the-u.s.-2016/tables/expanded-homicide-data-table-4.xls.

6. John R. Lott Jr., "Opposing View: Guns in Schools Can Save Lives," *USA Today*, December 25, 2012, https://www.usatoday.com/story/ opinion/2012/ 12/25/gun-free-zone-john-lott/1791085/.

7. "Transcript: Stoneman Students' Questions to Lawmakers and the NRA at the CNN Town Hall," CNN, February 22, 2018, https://www.cnn. com/2018/02/22/politics/cnn-town-hall-full-video-transcript/index.html.

8. Ryan Saavedra, "Kim Jong Un's Sister Gives Pence Some Serious Side-Eye," The Daily Wire, February 9, 2018, https://www.dailywire.com/ news/26979/ kim-jong-uns-sister-gives-pence-some-serious-side-ryan-saavedra.

9. Rebecca Perring, "North Korea Drought: 18 MILLION Could Starve to Death as Kim Diverts Funds to Build Nukes," *Express,* November 8, 2017, https://www.express.co.uk/news/world/877007/North-Korea-news-drought-Kim-Jong-un-nuclear-war-weapons-North-Korea-latest.

10. Thomas Hunt, "North Korean Parents 'Kill Disabled Children at Birth,'a Sickening New Report Reveals," *Express,* July 20, 2017, https://www. express.co.uk/news/world/830797/north-korea-kim-jong-un-disabled-killing-donald-trump-usa-Pyongyang-human-rights.

11. Rebecca Pinnington, "Brutal Life of North Korea Children: Propaganda in Schools and Forced to Watch Executions," *Express*, November 4, 2017, https://www.express.co.uk/news/world/875134/North-Korea-child-labour-abuse-Kim-Jong-un-Human-Rights-Watch.

12. Justin McCurry, "North Korea's Appetite for Executions Remains Undiminished," *Guardian,* December 13, 2013, https://www. theguardian.com/world/2013/dec/13/ north-korea-executions-torture-kim-jong-un.

13. Sebastien Roblin, "North Korea Blew Up an Airliner the Last Time the Olympics Came to Korea," *The National Interest,* January 23, 2018, https://nationalinterest.org/blog/the-buzz/ north-korea-blew-airliner-the-last-time-the-olympics-came-24188.

14. "Aaron Burr Biography," Biography.com, https://www.biography.com/people/aaron-burr-9232241.
15. Kerwin Swint, "Founding Fathers' Dirty Campaign," CNN, August 22, 2008,
    http://www.cnn.com/2008/LIVING/wayoflife/08/22/mf.campaign.slurs.slogans/.
16. "Ten Memorable Inaugural Addresses," RealClearPolitics, January 16, 2013, https://www.realclearpolitics.com/lists/memorable_inaugural_addresses/jeffersons_first.html.
17. Swint, "Founding Fathers' Dirty Campaign."
18. Freeman Stevenson, "Top Scandals and Controversies of Each United States President," *Deseret News,* May 20, 2013, https://www.deseretnews.com/top/1512/6/John-Quincy-Adams-Top-scandals-and-controversies-of-each-United-States-president.html.
19. Jaclyn Peiser, "Times Stands by Editorial Board Member After Outcry over Old Tweets," *New York Times*, August 2, 2018, https://www.nytimes.com/2018/08/02/business/media/sarah-jeong-new-york-times.html.
20. Amber Athey, "NYTIMES' NEWEST HIRE SENT TONS OF ANTI-WHITE RACIST TWEETS," The Daily Caller, August 2, 2018, https://dailycaller.com/2018/08/02/new-york-times-sarah-jeong-racist/.
21. Justin Caruso, "FBI: ANTI-WHITE HATE CRIMES ARE THE FASTEST GROWING RACIAL HATE CRIMES IN AMERICA," The Daily Caller, November 13, 2017, https://dailycaller.com/2017/11/13/fbi-anti-white-hate-crimes-are-the-fastest-growing-racial-hate-crimes-in-america/.
22. Louis Farrakhan, "The Time & What Must Be Done," May 20, 1990, quoted at QRD, http://www.qrd.org/qrd/misc/text/farrakhan-homophobia.
23. Richard B. Muhammad, "Will the Real Anti-Semite Please Stand Up?" The Final Call, May 14, 2013, http://www.finalcall.com/artman/publish/National_News_2/article_9848.shtml.
24. Jessica Chasmer, "Louis Farrakhan: 'Israelis and Zionist Jews' Played Key Roles in 9/11 aAtacks," *Washington Times,* March 5, 2015, https://www.washingtontimes.com/news/2015/mar/5/louis-farrakhan-israelis-and-zionist-jews-played-k/.
25. Stop Hate Crimes, "Louis Farrakhan: White People Deserve to Die," YouTube, August 16, 2015, https://www.youtube.com/watch?v=LZschZMW3oU.
26. "Farrakhan Again Describes Hitler as a 'Very Great Man,'" *New York Times,* July 17, 1984, https://www.nytimes.com/1984/07/17/us/farrakhan-again-describes-hitler-as-a-very-great-man.html.

Index